RELIGIOUS EXPERIENCE, JUSTIFICATION, AND HISTORY

Recently, many philosophers of religion have sought to defend the rationality of religious belief by shifting the burden of proof onto the critic of religious belief. Some have appealed to extraordinary religious experience in making their case. *Religious Experience, Justification, and History* restores neglected explanatory and historical considerations to the debate. Through a study of William James, it contests the accounts of religious experience offered in recent works. Through reflection on the history of philosophy, it also unravels the philosophical use of the term "justification." Matthew Bagger argues that the commitment to supernatural explanations implicit in the religious experiences employed to justify religious belief contradicts the modern ideal of human flourishing. For contrast, and to demonstrate the indispensability of history, he includes a study of Teresa of Avila's mystical theology. The controversial supernatural explanations implicit in extraordinary religious experience place the burden of proof on the believer.

MATTHEW C. BAGGER is Assistant Professor in the Religion Department at Columbia University, and he was awarded his Ph.D. from the same university. Matthew Bagger has published articles in *Religious Studies* and the *Journal of the History of Philosophy*.

RELIGIOUS EXPERIENCE, JUSTIFICATION, AND HISTORY

MATTHEW C. BAGGER

CAMBRIDGE
UNIVERSITY PRESS

PUBLISHED BY THE PRESS SYNDICATE OF THE UNIVERSITY OF CAMBRIDGE
The Pitt Building, Trumpington Street, Cambridge, United Kingdom

CAMBRIDGE UNIVERSITY PRESS
The Edinburgh Building, Cambridge, CB2 2RU, UK http://www.cup.cam.ac.uk
40 West 20th Street, New York, NY 10011–4211, USA http://www.cup.org
10 Stamford Road, Oakleigh, Melbourne 3166, Australia

© Matthew C. Bagger 1999

First published 1999

Printed in the United Kingdom at the University Press, Cambridge

Typeset in Baskerville 11/12.5 pt [CE]

A catalogue record for this book is available from the British Library

Library of Congress Cataloguing in Publication data
Bagger, Matthew C.
Religious experience, justification, and history / Matthew C. Bagger.
p. cm.
Includes bibliographical references and index.
ISBN 0 521 62255 7 (hardback)
1. Experience (Religion) 2. Religion – Philosophy. 1. Title.
BL53.B24   1999
291.4′2 – dc21   98–33302   CIP

ISBN 0 521 62255 7 hardback

To Amy

Contents

Acknowledgments

Earlier versions of chapters 4 and 5 appeared in *Religious Studies* 27 (1991) and 29 (1993), respectively. Several paragraphs of chapter 6 appeared in *Union Seminary Quarterly Review* 47 (1993).
In writing this book I have had the good fortune to field questions and receive advice from many extraordinary individuals. The opportunity to express publicly if only some measure of my appreciation is a welcome occasion. Charles Stinson has proved an invaluable and seemingly inexhaustible resource. Robert Audi, Amy Hollywood, and Bill Throop read multiple chapters and all posed challenging, fruitful questions. Charles Larmore, Nancy Frankenberry, and Steven Katz read the manuscript in its entirety and their influence has resulted in a much improved book. Matthew Kapstein, who also read the entire manuscript, was unstinting with his time and helped me puzzle through complexities I had not foreseen. Ross Wilken and B. J. Williams offered many valuable suggestions and helped compile the index. Finally, I owe Wayne Proudfoot special tribute. Over the last several years Wayne has generously given his time and shared his expertise. In an era of growing demand on a university professor's time, he remains an uncompromising scholar, effective teacher, constructive colleague, wise mentor, and, I've been privileged to discover, good friend.

Abbreviations

IC   Teresa of Avila, *Interior Castle*, E. Allison Peers, tr. and ed. (New York: Image Books, 1961).

L   Teresa of Avila, *The Life of Teresa of Jesus*, E. Allison Peers, tr. and ed. (New York: Image Books, 1960).

PG   William Alston, *Perceiving God* (Ithaca: Cornell University Press, 1991).

PP   William James, *The Principles of Psychology*, 2 vols. (New York: Dover Publications, Inc., 1950).

WP   Teresa of Avila, *The Way of Perfection*, E. Allison Peers, tr. and ed. (New York: Image Books, 1964).

CHAPTER I

Introduction: spectral evidences

> The whole business is become hereupon so *snarled*, and the determination of the Question one way or another, so *dismal*, that our Honourable Judges have a Room for *Jehoshaphat's* Exclamation, *We know not what to do!* They have used, as Judges heretofore have done, the *Spectral Evidences*, to introduce their further Enquiries into the *Lives* of the persons accused; and they have thereupon, by the wonderful Providence of God, been so strengthened with *other evidences*, that some of the *Witch Gang* have been fairly Executed.
>
> Cotton Mather, *The Wonders of the Invisible World* (1692)[1]

Ever since Schleiermacher exalted feeling when addressing religion's "cultured despisers," apologists have periodically exploited religious experience. With all the more traditional avenues of theism's defense generally in disrepute, modern theologians and religious philosophers have repeatedly sought to justify religious belief rationally by reference to the individual's experience. Charles Darwin in 1876 remarked on the prevalence of this strategy. "At the present day the most usual argument for the existence of an intelligent God is drawn from the deep inward conviction and feelings which are experienced by most persons."[2] This argument left Darwin rightfully unpersuaded. Experience has recently once again, however, become the focus of those aiming to vindicate the rationality of religious belief. This time the apologists hail from the ranks of

---

[1] *Cotton Mather on Witchcraft* (New York: Dorset Press, 1991), p. 70.
[2] *The Autobiography of Charles Darwin*, Nora Barlow, ed. (New York: W.W. Norton & Co., 1969), p. 90.

analytic philosophy.[3] Increasingly, we find philosophers defending the justification of theistic beliefs based on extraordinary experiences (so-called "perceptions of God"). In this study I concentrate on this latter-day revival and ultimately deny that religious experiences rationally justify religious beliefs.

Both of the central concepts in this discussion, experience and justification, reward careful scrutiny. The philosophers sympathetic to an experiential justification of theism subscribe to congenial analyses of experience and justification. They stake out a position on each which, when taken together, license beliefs based on extraordinary religious experience. My inquiries into a proper understanding of experience and justification bring to the fore two features suppressed or ignored in this prevailing philosophical approach to religious experience: explanation and historical context.

First, I emphasize the ubiquity of explanation in both experience and justification. Experience is, and justification should be, informed by commitments about what constitutes the best explanation of the phenomena in question. Experience exhibits explanatory logic; we experience what we (usually unreflectively) suppose the best explanation of the experiential situation. Similarly, in justifying our beliefs about some domain, we should refer to our best overall explanatory account relevant to that domain. In a philosophical account of justification, to isolate it from explanation artificially segregates our epistemic resources. The apologetic character of much previous philosophical literature on religious experience accounts for its tendency to marginalize explanation; properly attending to the explanatory element in these issues opens the door to unsympathetic explanations.

---

[3] To name a few: William Alston, *Perceiving God* (Ithaca: Cornell University Press, 1991); Richard Swinburne, *The Existence of God* (Oxford: Oxford University Press, 1979), ch. 13; Caroline Franks Davis, *The Evidential Force of Religious Experience* (Oxford: Clarendon Press, 1989); Gary Gutting, *Religious Belief and Religious Skepticism* (Notre Dame: University of Notre Dame Press, 1982), ch. 5; Keith Yandell, *The Epistemology of Religious Experience* (Cambridge: Cambridge University Press, 1993); and Jerome Gellman, *Experience of God and the Rationality of Theistic Belief* (Ithaca: Cornell University Press, 1997).

Second (in part, because of the contextually conditioned nature of "good" explanations), I stress the paramount importance of historical and cultural context for philosophical inquiry about religious experience. The analytic style of the previous literature helps account for its tendency to pay little attention to historical, linguistic, and cultural context. Analytic philosophy generally neglects context. Indeed, it calls to mind Nietzsche's ironical observation, "As is the hallowed custom with philosophers, the thinking of all of them is *by nature* unhistorical."[4] When applied to religious experience, an analytic approach usually includes a few excerpts from different cultures or historical periods which serve merely to exemplify a "type" of experience. Such passages spin their wheels; rarely do the philosophers engage the texts in any deep way. A disciplinary parochialism within the humanities results whereby philosophers regularly laud philosophical works about religious experience which scholars of religion dismiss as inaccurate and anachronistic. Sampling the reviews of Nelson Pike's recent *Mystic Union*, ironically a book intended to surmount these weaknesses, reveals a case in point.[5] McGinn, the historian of Christian spirituality, objects that "Pike's account of Christian mysticism is at least as seriously limited and erroneous as those he criticizes" and claims that "it would be difficult to find a more recent expression of so outdated and narrow a view."[6] By contrast, Wainwright, a philosopher, declares *Mystic Union* "the best book of its kind to have appeared since ... the early part of the century. It is superior ... in its analytic acumen and philosophical sophistication."[7] The same disciplinary insularity which results in potted history and shallow textual interpretation on the philosophers' part conversely leads many scholars of religion to discount the questions addressed by the philosophers. To remedy this situation (for, as the epigraph evinces, I believe the philosophical questions potentially have tremendous

---

[4] *On the Genealogy of Morals*, Walter Kaufmann and R. J. Hollingdale, trs. (New York: Vintage Books, 1969), p. 25. Italics original.
[5] Ithaca: Cornell University Press, 1992. I discuss the shortcomings of Pike's hermeneutic in chapter 6.
[6] Bernard McGinn, *The Journal of Religion*, 74 (1994), p. 99.
[7] William Wainwright, *Faith and Philosophy*, 11 (1994), p. 495.

practical importance), I bring to the philosophical discussion of
religious experience the full weight of an historicism and a
careful study of one prominent Christian mystic: Saint Teresa
of Avila. In Emerson's words, "Man is explicable by nothing
less than all his history."

Few terms have as many incompatible uses as "historicism."
I employ it to call attention to an unexceptional relativism
which allows for communication and rational commensuration
between historical contexts but fully recognizes the extent of the
difference and discontinuity between them. "Historicism" as I
define it reminds us that *serious attention to history is integral to
textual or philosophical understanding.* This dark saying requires
some explication. First, I do not mean to say that serious
attention to history is necessary for *any* textual or philosophical
inquiry. The relative importance of history will depend on our
interests. I rest with the minimal claim that historical study
provides insight not necessarily available otherwise. Second, my
historicism does not necessarily hold that history is integral to
solving philosophical problems. One familiar stance today maintains that serious attention to history sometimes enables us to
dissolve or dismiss philosophical problems. In my chapter on
justification, I rely on historical understanding in this way to
evade a whole range of standard issues in the analysis of
justification that I link to a long-obsolete obsession with skepticism. The overall argument of this book, however, uses historical understanding to answer straightforwardly, rather than
evade, the philosophical question about the experiential justification of religious beliefs. Third, the history referred to in
"historicism" can be either philosophical history or cultural
and social history. I rely on both in my arguments. Fourth, by
the admittedly uninstructive phrase "serious attention to
history" I mean that historicism should try (as much as possible)
to view the historical data in light of the concerns of the subjects
of history, rather than viewing the data in light of contemporary
preoccupations. The understanding of a text or philosophical
problem which historical research can offer derives from this
insight into the relatively alien.

In chapters 2 and 3 I present my case for the centrality of

explanation and historicism to experience and justification respectively. Chapter 2, "The explanation in experience and the explanation of experience," compares the fuller account of experience William James offers in his *Principles of Psychology* with remarks he makes in *The Varieties of Religious Experience*. In arguing that the *Varieties* does not present as accurate nor as subtle a picture as the *Principles*, I adopt a view of experience wherein expectation and cognition play a crucial role. Expanding on some passages in James, I describe experience as including implicit explanatory commitments, commitments about the best explanation of the experience's cause. We experience what we suppose the best explanation of an event or series of events impinging on us. Obviously, the best available explanation will largely depend on context.

I must qualify my description of experience as including an inference to the best explanation. I do not mean that all experience includes conscious consideration of evidence leading to an adopted conclusion. Nor do I mean that experience relies on deductive argument. Rather, I do mean that experience includes tacit commitments as to how best to interpret a stimulus. These commitments rarely reach the light of day. The logic of experience comes most completely to light when we realize we have erred in a perception and can then view our mistaken presumptions. Historical allies of mine have occasionally referred to the explanatory character of experience as "unconscious inference." James astutely notes that this phrase sounds so preposterous because the process usually functions through habit. We must remember, moreover, to disambiguate phenomenological immediacy from epistemic immediacy. Much of our experience, unlike memory or cogitation, exhibits phenomenological immediacy or givenness. We usually do not *feel* ourselves bringing our background beliefs and commitments to bear on our experience. This fact does not mean, however, that experience is immediate in any sense that excludes the considerable influence of our epistemic background on it. The hypothesis of epistemic immediacy does not, in fact, comprise the best explanation of the cognitive mechanism of experience.

Explanation I construe as description relevant to a set of circumstances. I have in mind no conception of explanation as satisfying formal criteria. I understand explanation as a pragmatic notion, subordinating its structure to the uses mandated by the thinker's interests, and allowing the standards for an acceptable explanation to vary with a community of inquirers' interests. Roughly, an explanation answers a "why-question." For something to count as an explanation, the why-question need not be explicit, consciously recognized nor especially profound. In this sense, every experience answers a tacit why-question about sensory stimuli.

In chapter 3, "Justification by reasons alone," I explore the intuitions motivating the philosophical use of the term "justification," the seeming focal point for those debating the rationality of religious belief. A copious literature has grown around the explication of the concept. Naturally, a philosopher's intuition about justification depends on the epistemology of which it forms a part. I argue here that the early modern worry about skepticism continues to guide the discussion. Abjuring those concerns allows the philosophical use of "justification" to resemble more closely its non-philosophical uses. A justified belief is one for which someone has offered explanatory reasons, reasons that contribute to the best overall explanatory account of the relevant phenomena. Evidential goodness, on this view, presupposes explanatory goodness. I characterize a justified belief as one for which the reasons offered exemplify the good in the way of belief. Clearly, this conception of justification involves judgment. We must judge the goodness of reasons. Furthermore, judgments of goodness presuppose values. This conception of justification presupposes social standards for acceptability, reflecting shared epistemic values. I view our epistemic values as one species, alongside others like ethical values, constituting our conception of human flourishing. If one claims an experience justifies a belief, I argue, one must make its implicit explanation explicit and submit it to debate based on shared values.

In the next two chapters, which do not directly contribute to my positive argument, I undertake limited engagements against two recent philosophical works in the philosophy of religious experience. In chapter 4, "Perennialism revisited," I contend with Robert Forman's defense of a type of experience entirely unaffected by the subject's prior background beliefs. Forman challenges Steven Katz and promotes the possibility of a trans-cultural experience of pure consciousness, a waking, non-intentional consciousness.[8] He maintains that mystics in many traditions have perfected techniques for achieving experience unclouded by cognitive activity. Naturally, these different mystics enjoy the qualitatively identical experience because their differing background beliefs and expectations do not operate in this pure consciousness.

Forman's work ostensibly has little to do with religion *per se* because contentless consciousness cannot have an intrinsic religious importance; religious importance could only enter with a religious interpretation of this pure consciousness. The great interest his work generates stems in part, I think, from the central role the possibility of unmediated experience plays in the justification of religious beliefs. Forman himself notes that for some scholars "a transcultural perennial philosophy ... supported an argument for the existence of a (variously defined) divinity on the basis of experience."[9] Unmediated experience occupies such a place of prominence in discussions of religious experience because if other background beliefs or cognitions enter into the experience, then the justification conferred on the experiential beliefs depends at least in part on the background beliefs. When exploring the rationality of religious beliefs generally, the apologist cannot then, without vicious circularity, use the experiential evidence to justify the beliefs. Unmediated experience amounts to a protective strategy, whereby the scholar can "bracket" significant considerations to render the religious claims more convincing.[10]

In chapter 5, "The miracle of minimal foundationalism," I

---

[8] Robert K. C. Forman (ed.), *The Problem of Pure Consciousness* (New York: Oxford University Press, 1990).

[9] Ibid., p. 4.

[10] In this book I frequently use the term "protective strategy" borrowed from Wayne Proudfoot's book *Religious Experience* (Berkeley: University of California Press, 1985). I mean to employ it in a manner analogous to the specific sense outlined in his work.

address the work of William Alston (among others) who has provided the most nuanced and thoughtful version of an epistemological argument justifying religious beliefs based on direct perceptions of God. Alston's position works as a foil not only for my theory of justification, but also for my project as a whole. On his theory, the human epistemic makeup relies on a multitude of socially established doxastic practices, or belief-forming mechanisms. We cannot justify our doxastic practices, he sensibly maintains, in a non-circular manner. We cannot, for example, support our beliefs formed on the basis of sense perception without further recourse to sense perception. These doxastic practices nevertheless constitute the basic sources of *prima facie* justified beliefs (subject to defeat). Because none of our generally reliable belief-forming mechanisms has a more secure justification than any other, we cannot use the standards of one practice to indict another. Alston portrays the non-sensory perception of God as one of our basic, but unjustifiable, doxastic practices. To employ the criteria appropriate to sensory perception in order to judge religious perception un-satisfactory amounts to an unfair privileging of the character-istics of one practice over another. Doxastic practices thereby counter a whole range of standard objections to the argument from religious experience.

If, for example, we seek to debunk religious perception because it doesn't evince the sort of universal distribution enjoyed by sensory perception, we illicitly use the traits of one practice to judge another. Alston here parries those like Darwin who, farther into the passage I quoted above, rejects an analogy between religious experience and sense perception.

It may be truly said that I am like a man who has become colour-blind, and the universal belief by men of the existence of redness makes my present loss of perception of not the least value as evidence. This argument would be a valid one if all men of all races had the same inward conviction of the existence of one God; but we know that this is very far from being the case. Therefore I cannot see that such

He describes those who reject the explanatory reduction of religion as attempting "to preclude critical inquiry from outside the religious life" (p. xvi).

inward convictions and feelings are of any weight as evidence of what really exists.[11]

Darwin argues that the parochial character of religious experience vitiates any analogy with sense perception. Alston's doxastic practice approach attempts to preserve the analogy while disarming the significant disanalogies. As a result he licenses the isolation of our different sources of belief from one another. Obviously, he employs his epistemology as a protective strategy.

Although seemingly discrete issues, the possibility, raised by Forman, of pure consciousness shares both content and strategy with the attempt by Alston and others to justify religious beliefs by recourse to religious experience. They both arbitrarily narrow the scope of the experiences they consider in order to render their contentions more plausible. Forman distinguishes hallucinations, visions, and auditions from what Roland Fischer calls "trophotropic" states marked by low levels of cognitive and physiological activity. He limits his discussion to only these non-sensory, introvertive experiences. Alston, for his part, limits his aim to justifying beliefs based on non-sensory perceptions or awarenesses of God acting in some relation to the mystic. He excludes the types of experiences that Forman considers and also excludes the sensory sorts of experiences which Forman likewise shuns. By focusing on such specific agendas, they give the impression of greater unanimity between the mystical traditions than a broader sampling would suggest.

Additionally, Forman and Alston, despite the epistemological niceties of their theories, finally resort to intuition as a court of last appeal. They grant the fact that someone undergoes an extraordinary experience far too much weight in assessing the experience. This failing results from neglecting adequately to distinguish the event which causes an experience from the first-person experience of the event. Forman, for instance, in labeling contentless consciousness a "Pure Consciousness *Event*" (italics added), rather than a "Pure Consciousness *Experience*," lends the experience of putative pure consciousness greater authority. The insistence on unmediated experience

[11] Darwin, *Autobiography*, p. 91.

forms another case in point. Both Forman and Alston argue from the phenomenological immediacy of an experience, that it feels unmediated, to its actual epistemic immediacy, that it provides a source of evidential grounds at least relatively independent of background beliefs. In speaking of similar confusions, William James coined the phrase "the psychologist's fallacy." It occurs when psychologists impute their knowledge of a phenomenon to the mental state of the subjects. They introduce their explanations into the others' descriptions. These methods, shared by Forman and Alston, contribute to the carapace which privileges the claims of the mystics and fends off explanation from outside the religious life.

The protective intentions prevalent in the philosophy of mysticism finally shine most clearly in the repeated injunction to treat the mystics' claims as "innocent until proven guilty." This maxim follows from the epistemologies many contemporary philosophers promote, but plays to apologetic aims as well. The judicial conceit, gaining plausibility, no doubt, from its resonance with Plato's canonical *Apology*, enjoys a durable and prominent history in the philosophy of religion, first appearing no later than Thomas Sherlock's 1729 *The Tryal of the Witnesses of the Resurrection of Jesus*. By setting his dialogue as a court proceeding, Sherlock effectively shifts the onus of proof onto the religious skeptic. With religious believers literally on trial, it seems natural for the skeptic to bear the burden of proof; the believer need only provide a defense. The counsel for the defense argues, "And this I take to be the known Method of proceeding in such Cases; no Man is obliged to produce his Title to his Possession; it is sufficient if he maintains it when it is called in question."[12] Beliefs remain innocent until proven guilty. Sherlock cleverly extends juridical conventions beyond their accepted range of application and imports them into the philosophy of religion. This apologetic tactic has proved successful and is increasingly common. In the coming chapters I will subject to scrutiny the epistemological credentials for this

---

[12] London, p. 7.

incursion and (to speak in terms of the metaphor) restore the burden of proof to the theist.

In contrast to Forman and Alston, I would like to portray experience as something that includes inference (of a sort) from previous beliefs and commitments, something which we need not take at face value and which we can critique in light of our wider cultural values. Justification includes judgment informed by values and debate in light of values. I contest accounts of justification which obviate the giving of reasons. We would not, then, want to grant controversial beliefs based on religious experience *prima facie* justification as does Alston. Nor would we necessarily want to accept either the mystic's claims to content-less consciousness or the philosopher's claims to unmediated experience because such a claim itself represents an explanation which we might not accept as the best explanation of the event. I contend we can best profit from an account of religious experience and its evidential potential that attends to, rather than obscures, the values informing it. One important consequence of this view suggests that different cultures and historical epochs can take different stances regarding the justification of certain beliefs. Jeffrey Stout argues in defense of this position that "the rationality of a given person's beliefs or actions is relative to the reasons or reasoning available to that person. And the availability of reasons and reasoning varies with historical and social context."[13] A belief justified in an earlier age may no longer be justified today because of the very different epistemic commitments we hold in light of our evolving values.

As I made clear, I view explanation as the paramount factor in both the production of experience and the justification of beliefs. In addition, however, I also view explanation as fundamental to the epistemic character of an era. The sorts of explanations and the assessments of explanations uncontroversially accepted in an era reveal much about the epistemic values of the culture. In the last chapter, "Modernity and its discontents," I attempt to elucidate the epistemic values of two

---

[13] Jeffrey Stout, *The Flight from Authority* (Notre Dame: University of Notre Dame Press, 1981), p. 168.

different eras, the late medieval and the contemporary, by reference to the explanatory commitments they evince. I attempt to defend the conclusion that although religious experiences might well have justified religious beliefs at other points in Western history (had anyone conceived of employing them that way), in our contemporary context with our ultimate values and explanatory commitments, they can no longer do so. I must of necessity preserve a certain degree of vagueness in describing cultural values and commitments because we cannot boil a rich, embodied culture down to hard, skeletal criteria of rationality. I must also insist that I do not deny that both the medieval and the modern mystical perceiver belong to communities that validate for them their beliefs and provide them with interpretations of their experience. Both sets of experiences exhibit a grammar and make sense within a context and community. I contend that, given the present condition of Western culture, the explanations of experience licensed and encouraged in some sub-communities within the modern West nonetheless fail to exemplify the culture's larger commitments and values. The implicit religious explanation of religious experience no longer represents the best explanation of the event experienced religiously.

A religious perception of the sort singled out by Alston includes a commitment to a supernatural cause as the best explanation. The first section of the last chapter illustrates how even Alston's theory surreptitiously trades in supernatural explanations. The next section summarizes the results of the previous chapter where I carefully map out the mystical path as Teresa of Avila describes it. (In chapter 6, I depict her social setting and try to recount her thought and experiences comprehensively without distorting them through selective attention.) To read Teresa as justifying her beliefs through her experiences anachronistically misinterprets her testimony (if anything she justified her experiences through her beliefs). The point here, however, is to highlight the supernatural explanations she employs and to indicate that supernatural explanations were acceptable and informative for her and her contemporaries.

The final section argues that supernatural explanations no

longer represent good explanations. Claiming that self-assertion represents the defining feature of the modern world-view, I try here to demonstrate why supernatural explanations are both empty and unacceptable to us. Self-assertion denotes the tendency to judge our thought in accord with our own plans and by standards we ourselves set rather than by trying to satisfy God's plan. I argue that in a culture with this commitment to self-assertion, and the understanding of the supernatural/ natural bifurcation implicit in natural laws, we can never assert that, in principle, an event resists naturalistic explanation. A perfectly substantiated, anomalous event, rather than providing evidence for the supernatural, merely calls into question our understanding of particular natural laws. In the modern era, this position fairly accurately represents the educated response to novelty. Rather than invoke the supernatural, we can always adjust our knowledge of the natural in extreme cases. In the modern age in actual inquiry, we never reach the point where we throw up our hands and appeal to divine intervention to explain a localized event like an extraordinary experience.

This claim represents something more than a simple sociological observation; it carries normative weight. The advent of this form of self-assertion, furthermore, appears irreversible. While supernatural explanations might conceivably become culturally prevalent once more, there could be no foreseeable warrant for invoking them. We could have no good reason for asserting that an event, in principle, resists naturalistic explanation. The changes in our beliefs and values necessary to render supernatural explanations rationally acceptable again are so radical as to make such a circumstance unimaginable. To borrow Charles Taylor's idiom, self-assertion has become, through a "ratchet effect," a permanent feature of developed human potential.[14] Accordingly, I believe that although Teresa may have been justified in the beliefs she gained through her religious experiences, in our historical context, the implicit supernatural explanation of an experience can never be judged justified in the social sense I explicate as the best explanation.

[14] "Comparison, History, Truth," in *Myth and Philosophy*, Frank E. Reynolds and David Trac, eds. (Albany: SUNY Press, 1990), p. 52.

My approach to experience and justification centers on explanation and ultimately my position on mystical perception turns on my rejection of supernatural explanations. Essentially, I believe the whole issue concerning the justificatory value of extraordinary religious experience reduces to the equally live debate about the acceptability of supernatural explanations. A recent textbook in the philosophy of religion has come to this same conclusion:

> If religious experience is shaped by each person's concepts and beliefs, how can we determine which account – the natural or the super-natural – provides the best explanation . . . ? Let us suppose that Jane, as a strict naturalist, does not believe in God. Will not the imposition of Jane's own belief systems or her explanation of Joe's experience merely juxtapose belief structures, so that ultimately one cannot decide which explanation – naturalistic or supernaturalistic – is correct? This becomes clear when Proudfoot assigns the analyst the task of trying to ferret out why people who have had religious experiences understand them as they do and contends that "what we want is a historical or cultural explanation." This assignment begs the question concerning which belief system provides the appropriate framework for explaining the events, for why should one assume that a historical or cultural explanation is more to the point than a supernatural or theistic one?[15]

The authors want to know why, if we have competing explanations of an event, the naturalistic explanation takes precedence. They ask this question rhetorically. Similarly, Philip Clayton, in *Explanation from Physics to Theology*, limits the topic of his book and stops short of answering "the question of how rational it is to appeal to religious explanations in the modern world."[16] I intend to answer both these questions.

Edward Schoen in his 1985 book, *Religious Explanations*, lays down the gauntlet which I pick up in the last chapter. He defends the legitimacy of supernatural explanations of spatio-temporal events, but also allows that modernity somehow raises suspicions about supernatural explanations. "The simple possibility of formulating such explanations along rigidly scientific

15 Michael Peterson, William Hasker, Bruce Reichenbach, David Basinger, *Reason and Religious Belief* (New York: Oxford University Press, 1991), p. 22.
16 New Haven: Yale University Press, 1989, p. 132.

lines would lose much, if not all, of its interest," he concedes, "were it discovered that there is not even the remotest chance that they could prove acceptable to modern, educated people."[17] Supernatural explanations modeled on scientific explanations carry no weight, he observes, if the whole notion of a supernatural explanation of a spatio-temporal event proves unsatisfactory to the modern. Whereas he formulates this insight in terms of "people," I prefer to think in terms of cultural values because, sadly, "modern, educated people" all too often cling to patterns of thought and action incompatible with their basic values. With that caveat, the central focus of my work straightforwardly denies the acceptability of supernatural explanations.

Despite the occasional references to natural law and science both here and in the final chapter which might suggest otherwise, I intend my use of "natural" to entail (1) no commitments to a physicalistic ontology; (2) no valorization of the specific methods, vocabularies, presuppositions, or conclusions peculiar to natural science; (3) no view about the reducibility of the mental to the physical; (4) no position on the ontological status of logic or mathematics, and (5) no denial of the possibility of moral knowledge. Beliefs, values, and logical truths, for example, count as natural and folk psychological explanations, therefore, are natural explanations. The concept of the natural, in the sense I use it, has virtually no content except as the definitional correlative to the supernatural, taken here as a transcendent order of reality (and causation) distinct from the mundane order presupposed alike by the natural scientist and the rest of us in our quotidian affairs. My "naturalism" is perhaps best viewed as a variant of what we might refer to as the great New York school of naturalism, represented by such figures as Woodbridge, Dewey, Hook, and Cohen. Sydney Hook, in particular, took great pains to distinguish naturalism from materialism and positivism on the one hand and supernaturalism on the other. He defined naturalism as the view that "the furniture of heaven and earth, the way things are and the

[17] Durham: Duke University Press, p. 82.

way they behave, are best described by the scientific disciplines when the latter are conceived as continuous with, although sometimes critical of, common-sense experience."[18] Like Hook, I believe that ordinary problem-solving procedures sufficiently characterize naturalism and also serve to undermine the rationality of belief in the supernatural.

The conceptual distinction between the natural and the supernatural has a history, of course, but it is something which we in large part share with Teresa (even if perhaps it is somewhat sharper for us). The notion dates to pre-Christian Greece and Rome and the concept that theologians sometimes designate the "finite supernatural" enjoys a rich medieval heritage.[19] The finite supernatural concerns supernatural beings, qualities, or effects within the finite, created, natural universe. I will argue in the final chapter that although we share these conceptual distinctions with Teresa, our values put us in a position where we cannot make any good epistemic use of the finite supernatural. The supernatural has become explanatorily otiose, a category which has no legitimate application as an explanation of particular events within the mundane order. Its recent reappearance indicates (to echo Hook) a renewed failure of nerve.

I do not, however, consider my position a polemic directed against religious belief. In fact I have little to say about religious belief *per se* or its rationality. Rather, I intend to argue specifically against seeking evidential support for religious belief through the perception of God. In other words, although I have reservations about the supernatural in general, my argument concerns only the finite supernatural. Despite my conclusions and reluctance to address the larger issues of rationality and religious belief, I nonetheless see my work as broadly pertinent for believers. To remain strong and viable religious beliefs must not violate the norms and values we hold concerning epistemic goodness or flourishing. When our religious beliefs contravene

[18] *The Quest For Being* (New York: Delta, 1963), Introduction.
[19] Charles Stinson provides a brief but comprehensive history of the term "supernatural" in "The Finite Supernatural: Theological Perspectives," *Religious Studies* 9 (1973), pp. 325–337.

our ideal of human flourishing, they can only do so *malgré eux*. To retain a vibrant and healthy belief, the believer should self-critically reflect on the springs of his belief and subject them to scrutiny. Arguments for faith shouldn't fly in the face of our epistemic values, lest the faith become marginalized and idiosyncratic by way of consequence. Ironically, Schleiermacher, the theological figure who lurks in the background of the contemporary interest in religious experience, for these very reasons strongly opposed supernatural explanations of events occurring within the causal nexus. He concluded that when assigning causes to discrete phenomena, "we should abandon the idea of the absolutely supernatural . . . "[20] Recognizing the logic and impetus of modernity, he sought to establish an "eternal covenant" between religion and science whereby "we can . . . allow science the freedom to take into its crucible all facts of interest to us . . . "[21] Otherwise, he felt religion risked becoming isolated from and irrelevant to the animating center of cultural life.

Essentially, I maintain that we shouldn't seek to protect one subset of our beliefs and values from others. Clearly, my advocacy of self-critical scrutiny of the commitments informing our beliefs stems from my values, but self-critical reflection arguably represents one of the central values of modernity, one we would find ourselves at pains to repudiate. In one of his few felicitous phrases, Peirce nicely captures this component of the ethics of belief. "Integrity of belief," he declares, is "more wholesome than any particular belief."[22] This demand for reflective self-criticism, furthermore, can also derive from more traditional, religious scruples about purity and devotion. A central theme in Augustinean strands of Christianity, for instance, is the obligation to scrutinize reflectively the bases and role of one's belief, assessing the honesty, centrality and character of one's religious commitment. Not only do Nietzsche and

---

[20] Friedrich D. E. Schleiermacher, *The Christian Faith*, H. R. Mackintosh and J. S. Stewart, eds. (Edinburgh: T. & T. Clark, 1928), p. 183.

[21] Friedrich D. E. Schleiermacher, *On the "Glaubenslehre,"* James Duke and Francis Fiorenza, trs. (Atlanta: Scholars Press, 1981), pp. 64–65.

[22] "The Fixation of Belief," *Charles S. Peirce: Selected Writings*, Philip Wiener, ed. (New York: Dover Publications, 1966), p. 111.

Freud, but Augustine, Teresa and Kierkegaard also maintain that religious belief can be culpably self-deceptive. The latter three, therefore, all enjoin self-knowledge as essential to the Christian life. Kierkegaard's elusive term "transparency" gains its content from these concerns about purity. A religious ethics of belief can arrive at the same conclusion as mine: that one shouldn't seek to preserve one's faith at the cost of inconsistencies and protective strategies.[23]

One common and understandable charge I hear levied at me when I profess these views questions my right to judge the beliefs and experiences of others. I seem to offend "postmodern," pluralist sensibilities. How dare I presume to legislate the character of epistemic goodness for others who embrace different beliefs, values, and ideals? I don't completely deny this depiction; I only shun the tone of indignation. Alasdair MacIntyre captured the logic of my stance when in a now famous essay he asserted, "Thus the sceptic is committed to saying that he understands the Christian's use of concepts in a way that the Christian himself does not, and presumably *vice versa*."[24] As I made quite clear when discussing my intuitions about justification, I do wish to find rational ways, invoking our values, to criticize others' beliefs and for others to criticize my beliefs. Without this social element doesn't justification lose its point? If justification obtains solely relative to individuals, then as a notion it doesn't hold much interest.[25]

The claim that we cannot condemn values we do not share, while seemingly a popular stance today, needs further attention.

---

[23] David Wisdo conducts a suggestive inquiry into an ethics of religious belief that does not rely on evidentialist assumptions in *The Life of Irony and the Ethics of Belief* (Albany: SUNY Press, 1993).

[24] Alasdair MacIntyre, "Is Understanding Religion Compatible with Believing?," *Rationality*, Bryan Wilson, ed. (Oxford: Basil Blackwell, 1970), p. 76. On MacIntyre's view the skeptic claims to know how certain religious concepts, deracinated from the context to which they integrally belonged, have lost their purchase on us.

[25] I make this general point about justification in chapter 3, but the notion that justification is relative to individuals has a distinguished lineage in philosophy of religion. William James's conclusion about the evidential value of mysticism in the mysticism chapter of the *Varieties* gives such an answer and most everyone who has pondered James's conclusions goes away dissatisfied. Plantinga's apologetics result in something like this as well: the religious experience justifies the mystic's beliefs while it need not carry any authority for those who did not undergo the experience.

In fact, I would argue, under many circumstances we do summarily reject values with which we disagree, *but only* when we feel something of importance is at stake. Most of us, I trust, would condemn many of the values informing the religious community once inhabiting Jonestown, Guyana. Our scruples about pluralism don't restrain us much when we consider the consequences of divergent values serious enough. In the case of religious beliefs based on religious perception, we tolerate diversity because of the generally innocuous character of the issues involved. Nothing truly important to us rides on the respective positions espoused in this question. This fact is entirely contingent, however. Cotton Mather reminds us of a context in which a socially established practice of belief formation based on a sort of religious experience had profound civic importance. Moreover, because of the high stakes involved, even he, the ideological bulwark for the witch trials, insists that "spectral evidences" deliver no presumption in favor of the beliefs based on them.[26] Judges should not treat these beliefs as innocent until proven guilty (indeed, to presume the beliefs innocent would be tantamount to presuming the defendants guilty). They must seek evidence of a wholly different nature (i.e. from other practices of belief formation) to corroborate them in the best overall account of the case. The witch trials present an example wherein urgent consequences attend religious perception. They suggest that the indulgence toward religious perception lately recommended remains but a provisional luxury.

Let me draw out the analogy with ethical values further. Remember that ethical and epistemic values both constitute species of the good. Many in our culture embrace values that render the abortion of an unborn human fetus objectionable. Others embrace values that lead them to place greater weight on the well-being of the mother and the quality of the child's life once born. Both groups find social support within communities which share these values. Yet rather than manifesting outrage that one group would legislate about the values of the other

---

[26] Mather, *Witchcraft*, p. 23.

(though we do hear this complaint), at least a portion of the din raised by the issue represents (quasi-) reasoned argument from shared principles, beliefs, or values to convince the other group of the correctness of their values and beliefs. This underlying and often overlooked agreement serves to make the disagreement intelligible. All partisans to the debate find unjustified homicide abhorrent and support coercive laws preventing it. The pro-life faction believes abortion to be unjustified homicide and therefore supports coercive laws preventing it. Members of the various pro-choice factions, however, either do not believe abortion to be homicide because the fetus is not a person, or they believe it to be justified in some cases. They object, therefore, to coercive laws preventing abortion. But at the bottom of it all, there does lie a right answer (both sides believe at least this much, or they wouldn't evince such wholehearted commitment). Judging from the values we share, there subsists a fact of the matter. We haven't reached the point where we have any satisfying view of this answer and we can't guarantee that we will ever reach agreement about it, but the debate continues.

Likewise, I don't expect my colleagues, invoking a misplaced toleration, to recoil in dismay or censure me for contesting the beliefs of some believers. Stifling inquiry in this repressive manner functions as a powerful and effective protective strategy. Rather, if they disagree, I expect them to argue in defense of their values and explanatory commitments. Let the positions engage from the standpoint of shared values and see what emerges. In the long run reticence serves no purpose other than insulating ourselves against the possibility of cognitive dissonance, a possibility I believe we should willingly risk in pursuit of human flourishing.

CHAPTER 2

The explanation in experience and the explanation of experience

Among the topics dominating the modern philosophical agenda the nature of experience has figured as prominently as any. Questions regarding the status of knowledge claims based on different sorts of experience have occupied philosophy since at least the early seventeenth century. Modern philosophers have continually looked to perceptual experience or the experience of self-consciousness to ground knowledge claims. Roughly, empiricists wish to ground knowledge in the deliverances of perceptual experience and some so-called rationalists and idealists seek to ground knowledge in the experience of self-consciousness and/or the experience of conviction.[1] Increasingly, historians of philosophy recognize the poverty of schematic empiricist/rationalist or empiricist/idealist dichotomies, but we can safely assert that different philosophers and traditions within the course of modern philosophy have sought to ground knowledge by placing varying emphasis on these types of experience. Logical empiricism, for instance, attempted to correlate bits of perceptual experience to propositions. This

---

[1] Descartes, we sometimes forget, sought to evoke in his reader an experience of conviction generated by the experience of self-consciousness. He models his *Meditations* on the sort of religious meditations designed to evoke religious experience through purgation. In *The Search for Truth* Descartes (reiterating the same view expressed throughout his corpus) claims that after we sedulously clear away the preconceived opinions we imbibed in childhood, "What convinces us of them [the simple natures and common notions from which we build certain knowledge] is simply our own experience or awareness – that awareness or internal testimony which everyone experiences within himself when he ponders on such matters" (*The Philosophical Writings of Descartes*, II, John Cottingham, Robert Stoothoff, and Dugald Murdoch, trs. [Cambridge: Cambridge University Press, 1984], p. 418). The *cogito*, of course, provides the paradigmatic occasion for this experiential certainty based on Augustinean intellectual intuition.

project runs into trouble, however, when one accounts for the influence of beliefs and language on experience. If our beliefs, language, and expectations influence our experiences, then a vicious circularity ensues if we use those experiences to ground our beliefs.[2]

The same dynamic operates in the philosophy of religious experience. The modern interest in religious experiences derives largely from an ambition to ground religious beliefs autonomously in the experience of the believer. Mirroring the moves made in epistemology, religious thinkers have variously compared the grounding religious experience to either the experience of self-consciousness or perceptual experience. Although he denied that religion essentially concerns belief, both tactics ostensibly commence with Schleiermacher.[3] In the 1799 edition of *On Religion*, he posits a sense, akin to the five perceptual senses and in conjunction with them, which passively receives religious intuitions, "immediate experiences of the existence and action of the universe."[4] Later, in *The Christian Faith*, this sense evolves into a presupposed religious self-consciousness inhering more or less perfectly in our variable sensuous consciousness. Many of the later epigonic proponents of religious experience lack his subtlety and sophistication, but all must maintain the "immediacy" of religious experience. As we shall see, this claim still represents the core of the controversies about religious experience. Although precise claims differ, the general intuition behind "immediate experience" holds that religious experience comprises some form of experience unin-

---

[2] Interestingly, the demise of such philosophical programs as logical empiricism has contributed to the recent interest in religious experience. When Quine and others attacked the viability of logical empiricism, the hegemony of ordinary experience retreated enough for religious philosophers to employ religious experience as a foundation for religious belief. I discuss these projects more fully in chapters 5 and 7.

[3] Schleiermacher proves an interesting and equivocal case on this point, however. In *The Christian Faith* (H. R. Mackintosh and J. S. Stewart, eds. (Edinburgh: T. & T. Clark, 1928), he insists that he has no intention of providing evidence or a rational basis for faith. "We entirely renounce all attempt to prove the *truth* or *necessity* of Christianity ... " (p. 60, italics added). He does, nonetheless, consider the religious self-consciousness "an essential element of human nature" (p. 26) and believes Christianity represents its highest flowering (p. 696).

[4] Friedrich D. E. Schleiermacher, *On Religion*, Richard Crouter, tr. (Cambridge: Cambridge University Press, 1988), p. 105.

fluenced by prior beliefs, language, or ideas. If we admit that language or prior ideas mediate religious experience, then it loses the grounding role sought for it. Most theorists of religious experience have employed it to substantiate religious beliefs. If those beliefs have a hand in the constitution of the experience, then one engages in vicious circularity when using the experiences to substantiate the beliefs. Schleiermacher himself realized this fact keenly, and assiduously argued against his critics that ideas of God do not instigate the religious self-consciousness. He insists on the priority of feeling: "I must repeat that what I understand as pious feeling is not derived from a representation, but is the original expression of an immediate existential relationship."[5] Indeed Schleiermacher became exasperated over this issue and declared, "Each person must examine and decide the issue for himself. Further reiteration would be only a repetition."[6] The ensuing century and a half have witnessed considerable repetition.

In this chapter I propose to return to the source responsible for much of the repetition, William James, and highlight how his renowned conclusions about mysticism in *The Varieties of Religious Experience* depart from his more considered views expressed elsewhere about experience generally and religious experience specifically. James's remarks on mysticism serve as the inspiration for those who assimilate religious experience to perceptual experience. From my evaluative comments, it should become manifest that I agree with Schleiermacher's critics and promote an understanding of religious experience whereby experiences entail an explanatory claim about their cause. To explicate fully the notion that experiences include an explanatory commitment I must broach another topic of considerable philosophical controversy. The analysis of "explanation" has exercised the philosophy of science for at least the last forty years. Augmenting some of James's comments, I will recommend a pragmatic analysis of explanation: explanations consist in contextually relevant descriptive answers.

---

[5] Friedrich D. E. Schleiermacher, *On the "Glaubenslehre,"* James Duke and Francis Fiorenza, trs. (Atlanta: Scholars Press, 1981), p. 40. See also p. 38.
[6] Ibid., p. 39.

JAMES'S TWO VIEWS OF EXPERIENCE

Much of James's most astute work on perception and experience appears in his early *Principles of Psychology.* This study stands as a phenomenological masterpiece. James views psychology as a discipline primarily relying on first-person reports about consciousness. *"Introspective Observation,"* he insists, *"is what we have to rely on first and foremost and always"* (*PP,* 1, p. 185).[7] True to this principle he evinces an outstanding acuity in rendering intelligible the subtle deliverances of consciousness.

Introspection, he quickly admits however, offers no infallible evidence. Even in intending to report occurrent feelings, James notes, we make the report after the reported feeling has passed. We cannot observe and report simultaneously. The experience of reporting differs significantly from the original experience. We never have direct access to our own experience, either for observation or knowledge claims. To reflect on or observe our experience initiates a new experience. We describe the original experience from its remembered feel. Therein lies the possibility of error. To substantiate this point, James adduces empirical examples demonstrating the fallibility of introspection. He allows that we may correctly recount strong, distinct feelings, but claims that we often misjudge rapid, weak, or indistinct feelings. Finally, James declines to offer further argument because, he says, "the rest of this volume will be little more than a collection of illustrations of the difficulty of discovering by direct introspection exactly what our feelings and their relations are ... " (*PP,* 1, p. 191). He specifies that this difficulty *"is simply that of all observation of whatever kind,"* that we can misdescribe what we apprehend (*PP,* 1, p. 191).

The solution, he avers, rests in the self-correction that occurs in reconciling all our various beliefs about a topic, the process of finding the best explanation. Essentially, James denies any special powers for introspection (or for that matter, any type of observation). Even common sense beliefs about our current mental state have the status of hypotheses for James. These

---

[7] All italics original unless otherwise noted.

hypotheses must stand before the tribunal of the rest of our experience. In this sense, even introspective observation comprises a species of explanation. As we shall see, for James (and many later philosophers) all our cognitions represent explanations of one form or another.

Throughout his career James emphasized the conceptual contribution in all forms of experience. In the early *Principles* he maintains that our entire intellectual life comes to bear on each moment of experience. "Experience is remolding us at every moment, and our mental reaction on every given thing is really a resultant of our whole world up to that date" (*PP*, 1, p. 234). He arrives at this conclusion because he considers how every experience alters our mental state to some degree. Our mind reacts to every passing experience and changes in response. For this reason he repeatedly makes a claim that I will refer to in subsequent chapters. We never, he insists, have the same experience twice. We often experience the same object twice, but an experience of the object never completely overlaps with previous experiences of that object (*PP*, 1, pp. 230–231, 480). Our mental environment which contributes to the experience insures that we never relive an experience. Even mundane experiences such as, to use James's example, seeing my armchair on consecutive days never have a true qualitative identity.

Even at the end of his life and after the *Varieties*, James held reasonably close to the picture of consciousness and experience he painted in the *Principles*.[8] He writes, "My present field of consciousness is a center surrounded by a fringe that shades insensibly into a subconscious more."[9] The fringe in consciousness and the subconscious deliver much of the felt quality of experience. This description of consciousness, far more realistic than that of the traditional empiricists, has become James's

[8] He does, however, try to distance himself from the position he takes in the *Principles* regarding the stream of consciousness. In both the *Essays in Radical Empiricism* and *A Pluralistic Universe* it seems like he believes that the streamlike character of consciousness itself represents a conceptual construction imposed on "pure experience." In *A Pluralistic Universe* (New York: Longmans, Green, and Co., 1909), for example, he writes of the necessity of treating "our conscious 'selves' as 'streams' " (p. 248).

[9] James, *A Pluralistic Universe*, p. 288.

hallmark. It also makes clear how prior experience can influence present experience.

> In the pulse of inner life immediately present now in each of us is a little past, a little future, a little awareness of our own body, of each other's persons, of those sublimities we are trying to talk about, of the earth's geography and the direction of history, of truth and error, of good and bad, and of who knows how much more? Feeling, however dimly and subconsciously, all these things, your pulse of inner life is continuous with them, belongs to them and they to it.[10]

James explains that throughout all our experiences we harbor vague and fluctuating, though perhaps subconscious, awareness of manifold previous experiences, beliefs, and attitudes. This evolving and shifting conscious field which we bring to experience accounts for the fact we never have the same experience twice.

Naturally, therefore, James believes that perception, *"the consciousness of particular material things present to sense,"* fuses thought and sensation (*PP*, II, p. 76). He proposes "the general law of perception" that *"whilst part of what we perceive comes through our senses from the object before us, another part* (and it may be the larger part) *always comes . . . out of our own head"* (*PP*, II, p. 103). He ranges sensation and perception on a continuum. "Pure" sensation remains an unattainable ideal (not ideal in any normative sense) at one end of the spectrum and complex perceptions lie at the other. The experiences we commonly refer to as sensations arouse few associations and fall to one side of the continuum. *Bona fide* perceptions, on the other, *"arouse voluminous associative or reproductive processes"* (*PP*, II, p. 3). Throughout this analysis James takes care to avoid the associationist and spiritualist mythology of treating sensations as an integral, perduring and isolable part of perception, fused to its associates. To the contrary he argues that sensory input and its associations remain "indecomposable" (*PP*, II, p. 2n) as "one state of mind" (*PP*, II, p. 80). Both empiricists and Kantians wish to strongly separate sensations and perceptions; James brings them into proximity on a spectrum. C. S. Peirce's model for the entry of a sensory stimulus into consciousness illustrates the

---

[10] Ibid., pp. 286–287.

fruitlessness James detects in attempting to distinguish a putative pure sensation from its cognitive associations.

Peirce's final question in "Questions Concerning Certain Faculties Claimed For Man" renders James's view less counterintuitive.[11] One might wonder how, if we rule out pure sensation, sensory information enters consciousness at all. Peirce demonstrates that this worry is of a piece with the ancient paradox about motion. He asks whether we must suppose an intuition, a first cognition undetermined (that is, unmediated) by a previous cognition. Does the chain of determined cognitions terminate in a pure sensation? How does a new object of cognition enter consciousness, if not through intuition? Peirce begins this section by noting that the supposition of a primary or intuitive cognition makes a bad hypothesis. He shows that any explanation of a cognition must refer to facts gathered from cognitions in consciousness. Explanations pointing outside consciousness introduce an unknowable element to the explanation.

For something entirely out of consciousness which may be supposed to determine it [a cognition] can, as such, only be known and only adduced in the determinate cognition in question. So that to suppose that a cognition is determined solely by something absolutely external is to suppose its determinations incapable of explanation.[12]

Explanations aim to make phenomena more intelligible. Peirce claims that supposing intuitions determined only by something uncognized represents an explanation that renders the issues unintelligible. He therefore declares that explanation untenable. Furthermore, Peirce rejects primary intuitions because they would immediately transcend into new cognitions leaving no time for their apprehension. Cognitions, he also claims, presuppose relations, which naturally means previous determinations. To account for the obvious fact that new objects appear in our cognitions, Peirce resorts to a geometrical

---

[11] Charles S. Peirce, "Questions Concerning Certain Faculties Claimed For Man," *Charles S. Peirce: Selected Writings*, Philip Wiener, ed. (New York: Dover Publications, Inc., 1960) pp. 18–38. My emphasis on the importance of this article and my reading of it owe much to Proudfoot's discussion of Peirce in *Religious Experience* (Berkeley: University of California Press, 1985), pp. 60–69.

[12] Peirce, "Questions Concerning Certain Faculties," p. 36.

demonstration resembling Zeno's paradoxes. He imagines a triangle positioned apex downward representing an object. He pictures the surface level of a body of water as our consciousness. Peirce then asks us to imagine the triangle descending into the water. Before the apex meets the water, we have no consciousness of the object. After contact, however, Peirce suggests that no matter the marginal depth to which the apex has submerged, we cannot pick out a definitive first contact between triangle and water. There always remains an infinitely smaller distance between apex and surface. After giving this example Peirce insists that he doesn't intend to stake his position on a logical paradox, but merely wants to show that the entry of an object into consciousness "arises by a *process* of beginning, as any other subsequent change comes to pass."[13] We can locate no identifiable point where cognition enters into sense experience. Peirce's triangle could be only relatively free of the water and still cognitively register. Similarly, "pure sensation" for James refers only to an abstraction.

James wants to make clear a distinction and avoid any equivocation between phenomenological and epistemological immediacy when he claims we perceive a "fact as an *immediately present outward reality*" (*PP,* II, p. 2). That an experience *feels* immediate to someone does not necessarily mean that beliefs or concepts did not in some fashion influence the experience. We must distinguish between the phenomenological immediacy of an experience and its alleged epistemological immediacy. Wayne Proudfoot explores how Schleiermacher among others traded on this ambiguity and in chapters 4 and 5 I examine Forman's and Alston's similar mistake.[14] The phenomenological immediacy to which James calls attention does not negate, however, the role that associations and our conscious field play in the felt experience. In more than one place in the *Principles,* James notes that only infants could experience sensations because only they lack the "fringe" or memories and stores of associations which imbue our experience. Interestingly, James never strayed far from this early conception of sensory and

---

[13] Ibid., p. 38.
[14] Proudfoot, *Religious Experience,* ch. 1 ("Expression").

perceptual experience. Late in his life he describes his cryptic term "pure experience" in a manner which clearly manifests affinity with his early account of perception and sensation.

"Pure experience" is the name which I gave to the immediate flux of life which furnishes the material to our later reflection with its conceptual categories. Only new-born babes, or men in semi-coma from sleep, drugs, illness, or blows, may be assumed to have an experience pure in the literal sense of a *that* which is not yet any definite *what*, tho ready to be all sorts of whats; full both of oneness and of manyness, but in respects that don't appear; changing throughout, yet so confusedly that its phases interpenetrate and no points, either of distinction or of identity, can be caught. Pure experience in this state is but another name for feeling or sensation. But the flux of it no sooner comes than it tends to fill itself with emphases, and these salient parts become identified and fixed and abstracted; so that experience now flows as if shot through with adjectives and nouns and prepositions and conjunctions. Its purity is only a relative term, meaning the proportional amount of unverbalized sensation which it still embodies.[15]

Despite the difficulties engendered by James's apparent intention to substitute a theory of pure experience for traditional ontology, he still considers sensation an asymptote on the same line with other experience. Sensation or pure experience refers to an abstract, uncognized, passive reception of stimuli. In reality, however, the mind actively contributes to this reception and experience, as we know it, results.

Incidentally, one aspect of James's quoted description of this active contribution belies a common notion. Critics have often taken James to task for not reflecting the revolution in philosophy occurring around him. At the turn of the century, philosophers began fully to recognize the importance of language for philosophy. The traditional emphasis on ideas quickly succumbed to philosophies focusing on words, propositions, and linguistic structures. I find it interesting that in this passage, written shortly after the turn of the century, James observes that the "salient" portions of the flux of sensation appear "shot through with adjectives and nouns and prepositions and conjunctions." Despite his critics, it seems that James

[15] James, *A Pluralistic Universe*, p. 348.

to some extent realizes the close relation between experience and language. This view of the relationship between learning a language and perceptual knowledge reappears forcefully in the work of Wilfrid Sellars, an American philosopher influenced by Wittgenstein. I will have occasion to say more about Sellars in chapter 5, but here I wish to showcase some of James's insights in a more contemporary idiom.

Sellars, in a classic article, "Empiricism and the Philosophy of Mind," attacked what he called the "Myth of the Given."[16] He begins by drawing the distinction we have continually noted between phenomenological and epistemological immediacy. The Myth of the Given pertains to the forms of epistemological immediacy. He aims, similarly to Peirce and James, to undermine the traditional empiricist account of knowledge, that generalized knowledge presupposes observational knowledge and not *vice versa*. Sellars demonstrates conversely that observational knowledge presupposes a general knowledge of facts and concepts. He carefully illustrates how making simple observation statements requires a broader, basic knowledge of the proper application of terms in specific circumstances. For instance, he declares,

The point I wish to stress at this time, however, is that the concept of *looking green*, the ability to recognize that something *looks green*, presupposes the concept of *being green*, and that the latter concept involves the ability to tell what colours objects have by looking at them – which, in turn, involves knowing in what circumstances to place an object if one wishes to ascertain its colour by looking at it.[17]

Repeatedly, he makes the claim that to know or apply any concept requires the ability to employ many others besides. Anthony O'Hear has observed in this regard (although in his discussion he emphasizes language far less than Sellars) that to notice patterns in the flux of experience we would need more than the concept of similarity. We would need in advance specific concepts delineating the type of similarity, because "any

---

[16] Wilfrid Sellars, "Empiricism and the Philosophy of Mind," *Science, Perception and Reality* (London: Routledge & Kegan Paul, 1963), pp. 127–196.
[17] Ibid., p. 146.

two objects or sensations have an indefinite number of ways of being seen as both similar to and different from each other."[18]

The command of language, in turn, conditions our grasp of concepts. The epistemic functions of knowing cannot occur until we employ a language. Prior to the advent of language, sensations have no factual import. With the conceptual apparatus of language, we can perceive facts. Sellars calls this doctrine "psychological nominalism," that "*all* awareness of *sorts, resemblances, facts* etc., in short all awareness of abstract entities – indeed, all awareness even of particulars – is a linguistic affair."[19] The awareness a language confers is a sapient awareness (as opposed to mere sentience), an awareness which enables us to entertain beliefs and make inferences involving them. Psychological nominalism, in essence, means that we can know a fact because we have a concept, not that we have a concept because we know a fact. The very act of identifying a fact in the flux of experience, as James, Sellars, and O'Hear all insist, requires that it gain an emphasis from the concepts and knowledge we already possess. Any perceptual knowledge logically and crucially relies on our previous knowledge which in turn presupposes language. For these reasons, Sellars takes the position that James promotes and that has proven very influential with Rorty and others of late. He mitigates the claims to privileged access made for inner mental episodes.[20] If our ability to procure observational knowledge or identify aspects of our experience crucially depends on the concepts of a shared language, experience loses the solipsistic tinge it has acquired since Descartes. Introspective reporting, he asserts, represents a learned language whose terms maintain their intersubjective uses. Although we must grant a privileged access to the subject, the introspective reports remain fallible

---

[18] Anthony O'Hear, *Experience, Explanation and Faith* (London: Routledge & Kegan Paul, 1984), pp. 29–30.

[19] Sellars, "Empiricism," p. 160. See lecture IV of John McDowell's *Mind and World* (Cambridge: Harvard University Press, 1994) for the best discussion of the obvious question psychological nominalism raises: what about the perceptual sensitivity of animals?

[20] Sellars, "Empiricism," p. 195.

and accessible to criticism, in principle, from others who share a language.

James in the lengthy quotation above describes how sensory input immediately acquires emphases in our experience. It excites associations and is colored by memories and prior experiences which have left traces in the fringe of our conscious field and our subconscious. In the *Principles* James carefully elucidates the role played by selection and emphasis in perception. We actually ignore most of the sensory field and allow a few impressions to represent whole objects. The mind supplies that to which we do not in fact attend. James claims that the sensations to which we do attend usually point to absent sensations (*PP*, I, p. 286). From his experimental data, James concludes that, "Attention ... out of all the sensations yielded, picks out certain ones as worthy of its notice and suppresses all the rest" (*PP*, I, p. 285).[21] Attention, then, forms the basis of perception and James repeatedly, throughout the *Principles*, links attention to our interests.[22] What we perceive and how we perceive it depends on our interests, and Sellars would add, our language and its concepts.

James demonstrates the importance of prior experience and interest for perception in his chapter "Attention." Here he addresses precisely what attention in perception entails. He discusses two factors. The first concerns the adjustment of the sensory organs. The second, the one which pertains to our discussion, shows a more incisive study of consciousness. James claims that attention in perception amounts to a rehearsal of the expected perception before one perceives it, a "prepar-

---

[21] Nelson Goodman succinctly summarizes this fact about perception. "Our capacity for overlooking is virtually unlimited, and what we do take in usually consists of significant fragments and clues that need massive supplementation" (*Ways of World-making* [Indianapolis: Hackett, 1978]).

[22] James accords interest a paramount role in perception and therefore in the character of an individual's world. Such a view could abet the radical relativisms afield today. Despite the tremendous leeway James allows for diverse versions in the pluriverse, however, he nonetheless ultimately rests in the sane belief that, in fact, individuals share much common ground. "The human race as a whole largely agrees as to what it shall notice and name, and what not" (*PP*, II, p. 289). My discussion of relativism near the end of chapter 3 is informed by Davidson's argument to the effect that if some humans didn't largely agree with us about what to notice and name, we would have no reason to consider them persons.

ation" of "an imaginary duplicate of the object in the mind, which shall stand ready to receive the outward impression as if in a matrix" (*PP*, I, p. 439). James supports this claim with experimental evidence borrowed from Wundt and with his own phenomenological observation. He includes two figure draw- ings, which we might label gestalt images, and observes that we make the figure change its representation for us by changing our expectation. He calls this mental image or expectation a "preperception" and indicates that our expectations and inter- ests about what we will perceive in the course of our daily life determines to a large degree what we will perceive and how we will perceive it. One perception, through its associations in our store of past experience, brings the expectation of other related perceptions (*PP*, I, p. 555). He notes how rarely we notice details of objects until someone points them out to us. We generally perceive those things which we have learned to perceive. "In short, *the only things which we commonly see are those which we preperceive*, and the only things which we preperceive are those which have been labeled for us, and the labels stamped into our mind. If we lost our stock of labels we should be intellectually lost in the midst of the world" (*PP*, I, p. 444). Although lacking the twentieth-century sophistication in talking of language, James once again links the cognitive activity involved in per- ception to language and concepts. Perception includes accent- uation and emphasis guided by attention which derives from our interests, but works through linguistic concepts.

Because of the importance of preperception, James argues that we never perceive perceptual ambiguity *per se*. We only recognize ambiguity when we ourselves learn another possible interpretation. James labels the fact that our perception in itself never displays the ambiguity "figured consciousness."

In these ambiguous cases it is interesting to note that perception is rarely abortive; *some* perception takes place. The two discrepant sets of associates do not neutralize each other or mix and make a blur. What we more commonly get is first one object in its completeness, and then the other in its completeness. In other words, *all brain-processes are such as give rise to what we may call* FIGURED *consciousness*. (*PP*, II, p. 82)

James explains that habit contributes to our perception in these situations. We do not perceive a composite or blur because we have no familiarity with such objects. We cannot preperceive a mixture of the interpretations but only alternate between two probable possibilities. Again James wishes to emphasize that although perception includes elements of sensation and elements of cognitive influence, we cannot attempt to cull the one from the other. "In these changes the actual retinal image receives different *complements from the mind*. But the remarkable thing is that the complement and the image combine so completely that the twain are one flesh, as it were, and cannot be discriminated in the result" (*PP*, II, pp. 258–259). We make a mistake if we attempt to devise a distinction between (as Davidson puts it) the conceptual scheme and the content.

E. H. Gombrich, the psychologist of art, closely echoes James on the role expectation plays in perception. In his now classic campaign against the "innocent eye," *Art and Illusion*,[23] Gombrich, often invoking James's authority, stresses the active nature of perception. Not a passive registering of impressions, perception, as James discovered, involves an active expectation of certain forms. After describing several examples in which artists, while ostensibly faithfully recording the features of buildings, misconceive certain of their aspects, Gombrich outlines a theory of perception. Garland's engraving of Notre Dame, for instance, accurately represents the cathedral, but replaces its Romanesque, rounded windows with Gothic, pointed windows. Gombrich concludes that the artists approached their work with certain expectations and conceptions. In a very real sense they matched their impressions to what Gombrich calls a schema and James calls preperception.

In perception we begin with our expectation and we generally perceive that which conforms to our expectation. The individual "begins not with his visual impression but with his idea or concept ... The individual visual information, those distinctive features I have mentioned, are entered, as it were, upon a pre-existing blank or formulary. And, as often happens with blanks, if they have no provisions for certain kinds of

---

[23] Princeton: Princeton University Press, 1960.

information we consider essential, it is just too bad for the information."[24] As James insists, Gombrich too, using examples from the history of art, shows the conceptual influence on perception. In fact, he claims, corroborating O'Hear, that without such perceptual schemata we could not organize the flux of experience at all. Significantly, Gombrich argues that the exact schemata employed by an individual has little ultimate import because the whole process of perceiving (as well as "all culture and communication") depends on an incremental matching of impressions and schemata, "the interplay between expectation and observation, the waves of fulfillment, disappointment, right guesses, and wrong moves that make up our daily life."[25] Perceiving represents an hypothesis tested against further experience and amended accordingly. In entering a perceptual situation, we select our "most likely hypothesis" and submit it to the test of experience.[26]

Gombrich evinces James's influence also in what he labels "the theme song" of his book.[27] In many places in *Art and Illusion*, he insists that we cannot perceive ambiguity. He means that when presented with an image which we could perceptually interpret in various ways, Jastrow's infamous duck/rabbit for instance, we cannot perceive the ambiguity. We always immediately perceive the image in one way or the other. We can only infer the ambiguity by trying to perceive the image in the alternate way. If we can achieve the other interpretation, moreover, we still have a clear perception. Again, we must infer the ambiguity from the fact that we can alternate between two convincing interpretations. Even in cases where we intellectually know that we have no context by which to gauge the size or distance of an object, we nonetheless perceptually see the object with a presumed size and shape. "[T]o perceive means to guess at something somewhere, and this need will persist even when we are presented with some abstract configuration where we lack the guidance of previous experience."[28] Perceptually we tolerate no ambiguity and through our hypothesis supply the missing information.

[24] Ibid., p. 73.   [25] Ibid., p. 60.   [26] Ibid., p. 210.
[27] Ibid., p. 313.   [28] Ibid., p. 259.

To illustrate the importance of habit in perception, James undertakes a study of perceptual illusion. He argues that illusions arise when the mental contribution to perception leads to a misrepresentation of the object present to the senses. Illusion results from the intellect imposing a false interpretation on a perceptual situation. James distinguishes two sources of perceptual error.

The wrong object is perceived either because
(1) *Although not on this occasion the real cause, it is yet the habitual, inveterate, or most probable cause of "this";* or because
(2) *The mind is temporarily full of the thought of that object, and therefore "this" is peculiarly prone to suggest it at this moment.* (*PP*, II, p. 86)

Illusions of the first type occur when the mind interprets a stimulus in an habitual manner that in the present instance mistakes the cause of the sensory stimuli. In the second case the mind imposes, not an habitual, but rather an especially salient interpretation on the stimuli. In each case the mind supplies an erroneous interpretation of that with which the senses provide it. James explains, when analyzing the first sort of error, that we always perceive "the most probable object" (*PP*, II, p. 95). Later, after having discussed both sorts of error, he reiterates that "*just in proportion as an experience is probable will it tend to be directly felt*" (*PP*, II, p. 104). Presumably, James means probable as regarded from an individual's experience. Impersonal probabilities about the relative frequency of objects existing in the world are of no moment here. The individual perceives the probable in relation to her own past experience. Presented with sensory stimuli, the mind always supplies the associations habitually aroused by similar stimuli.

The second type of illusion, however, forces us to revise this explication. James calls it "suggestibility." Here the mind "is full of" thoughts of the object eventually perceived. Although James does not specify, we can surmise that he means that the objects occupy a fairly focal position in the fringe surrounding the center of the passing consciousness. When certain stimuli occur the mind jumps to supply the interpretation preoccupying it. Clearly, the mind here does not necessarily supply "the most probable" interpretation reflecting habitual associations. To properly account for both types of illusion, we must suppose that "the most probable" interpretation means most probable judged from the state of mind of the perceiver at the particular perceptual moment. "Most probable" cannot simply refer to objective probabilities in the world, nor to the subjective probabilities established in prior individual experience. It must refer to the vagaries of the individual's specific situation. For this reason I believe that contemporary philosophers who describe perception as what an individual (unself-consciously) assumes to be the best guess or best explanation of a perceptual situation more clearly represent this line of thought.[29]

James keenly appreciates the philosophical stakes riding on his position here. Historically, one repeated objection to idealism concerned "unconscious inference." Realists would rebuke idealists because, the realists claimed, idealism requires a faculty of unconscious judgment or inference. Realists sought to convince that we have no experience of this faculty and that it seems fanciful to posit it. This charge carries considerable persuasive force. It appeals to our suspicions that philosophy if unchecked multiplies (in this case) faculties without necessity. James takes especial care with this issue. One way to read the *Principles* interprets it as a sustained effort to run the gauntlet formed by empiricist, associationist psychology on the one hand and Kantian idealism on the other. Throughout the work he continually distinguishes his approach from those antipodes and lauds what he finds of value in each. James, accordingly, proves sensitive to the issue of unconscious inference. In fact, he discusses the issue twice and dedicates an entire subsection of a chapter to it. In both places he avers that the phrases "unconscious inference" or "unconscious reasoning" misdescribe perception. These labels mislead because they suggest a process similar to conscious reasoning. James insists we have no reason to suppose that any sort of three-term syllogism occurs uncon-

---

[29] Gilbert Harman, for instance, explicitly concludes that perception includes judgments about the best explanation of the way things look to the individual. He supports his claim with evidence from perceptual psychology, but mainly explores our intuitions about justification and knowledge, which indicate that our perceptions function as claims about evidence. Gilbert Harman, *Thought* (Princeton: Princeton University Press, 1973).

sciously. In other words perception does not include deduction from a major premise, as some had asserted. Rather, perception involves only two terms; a stimulus immediately suggests something to consciousness. James willingly refers to this process as "inference," but repudiates the description of it as unconscious. No mediate term exists unconsciously. Accordingly, he finds "immediate inference" a more fitting appellation.

On this crucial issue James again splits the idealists and empiricists. He agrees with the idealists that the mind contributes to perception and experience, but borrows the mechanism for this contribution from the empiricists. Habit, the association of ideas, rather than formal reasoning, conjoins the stimulus to the perception. The natural, habitual character of perception causes perception to feel immediate or direct.[30] James puts his finger on the motivation for direct realism when he notes that, "The sign and the signified melt into what *seems* to us the object of a single pulse of thought" (*PP*, II, p. 326, italics mine). As Proudfoot would have it, perceptual experience generally exhibits phenomenological immediacy, but that does not entail its theoretical (epistemological) immediacy. Essentially, James describes the cognitive element in perception as an inference, but an inference of a simple and specific type. Although phenomenologically immediate, perception involves habitual associations.

The inference to the best explanation in experience helps James account for one of what he will later, in the *Varieties*, term the "religious sentiments." In the chapter of the *Principles* entitled "Instinct," James enumerates many types of fear. Eventually, he lists "fear of the supernatural" as one specific type of fear. To explain it he once again points to the conceptual element of experience. He notes that science has "not yet adopted" supernatural beings and therefore attributes super-

---

[30] Rorty's brand of pragmatism relies on some such claim as James's here. In *Philosophy and the Mirror of Nature* (Princeton: Princeton University Press, 1979) he writes, "There is, to be sure, a place for the notion of 'direct knowledge.' This is simply knowledge which is had without its possessor having gone through any conscious inference. But there is no suggestion that some entities are especially well suited to be known in this way. What we know noninferentially is a matter of what we happen to be familiar with" (p. 106).

natural fear to a combination of circumstance and interpret-ation. "[W]e can only say that certain *ideas* of supernatural agency, associated with real circumstances, produce a peculiar kind of horror" (*PP,* ii, p. 419). Supernatural fear arises when the subject, in a particular situation, interprets the situation in supernatural terms. The experience itself includes the reference to a supernatural cause. James anticipates much later theory about religion when he links the supernatural interpretation to anomaly. He suggests that the *idea* of the supernatural enters into experience when an individual faces unusual circum-stances. For the *"intellectual"* element to enter maximally into experience, the individual must encounter "a vertiginous baf-fling of the expectation." In a more contemporary idiom, the naturalistic explanations of an event available to an individual appear inadequate and she must resort to the supernatural explanation. When an event baffles by its anomalousness, the individual turns to supernatural explanations. Anticipating the work of Mary Douglas[31] and Proudfoot, James extends his analysis beyond supernatural fear and asserts more generally that, "The idea of the supernatural involves that the usual should be set at naught" (*PP,* ii, p. 420). The very logic of the supernatural necessitates a strict bifurcation from the mundane or natural.[32]

Employing this fact about the logic of experience, Proudfoot plausibly characterizes religious experiences as experiences for which the subject believes she cannot account without reference to a religious cause. "A person identifies an experience as religious when he comes to believe that the best explanation of

---

[31] Mary Douglas, *Purity and Danger* (London: Routledge & Kegan Paul, 1966); Mary Douglas, "Self-evidence," *Implicit Meanings* (London: Routledge & Kegan Paul, 1975), pp. 276–318.

[32] I emphatically do not intend here to align myself with the common protective strategy which insists on the *sui generis* nature of religion and precludes naturalistic explanation. As will become clear, I promote the naturalistic explanation of religious phenomena. Herbert Fingarette in *Confucius – The Secular As Sacred* (New York: Harper and Row, 1972) provocatively argues against a universally unimpeachable distinction between the sacred and profane. He suggests that for Confucius "ex-plicitly sacred rite can be seen as an emphatic, intensified and sharply elaborated extension of everyday *civilized* intercourse" (p. 11, italics original).

what has happened to him is a religious one."[33] Proudfoot adduces the case of Stephen Bradley, quoted in James's *The Varieties of Religious Experience*, as an example.[34] Bradley's heart begins to race wildly and after searching for an explanation, settles for the religious interpretation. This account provides a textbook example of James's own term "suggestibility." Although James discussed suggestibility in the context of perceptual illusion (whereas Bradley's experience lacked a perceptual emphasis and James certainly didn't consider Bradley's experience an illusion), the fact that Bradley had recently returned from a revival meeting when he employed a religious interpretation of his experience illustrates James's point. Bradley's case proves so instructive because a process usually occurring instantaneously here happens consciously. Proudfoot argues that to ascribe an experience to someone (including ourselves) we must likewise ascribe to her certain specific concepts and beliefs. To express an experience in concepts presupposes that concepts in part compose the experience. Like Bradley's, any experience includes an implicit commitment about the best explanation of the experience and this commitment constitutes the experience.

James in the *Principles* describes experience as an indivisible amalgamation of sensory and intellectual elements. Perceptual experience involves an intellectual preperception or expectation and emotional experience (including fear of the supernatural) includes conceptual judgments. All experience, for James, represents an inference to the best explanation.[35] Even in his late works, he considers pure sensation an ideal limit or abstraction unattainable by waking adults. In *The Varieties of Religious Experience*, however, James presents a far less nuanced account of experience. At times he likens religious experience to sense perception. He characterizes it as a sense of something More, something beyond the mundane on the order of a sense of

---

[33] Proudfoot, *Religious Experience*, p. 108.

[34] William James, *The Varieties of Religious Experience* (New York: Collier Books, 1961).

[35] In this judgment James echoes Peirce who concluded in 1868 that "every sort of modification of consciousness – Attention, Sensation, and Understanding – is an inference" ("Some Consequences of Four Incapacities," *Charles S. Peirce: Selected Writings*, Philip Wiener, ed. [New York: Dover, 1966], p. 62).

presence. This analogy has become increasingly central to discussions of religious experience since James.[36] Proudfoot has observed, however, that when assessing the epistemic import of mysticism James treats it like sensation. James provides his conclusions about the epistemic import of mystical states of consciousness, their *"warrant for the truth,"* seriatim:

(1) Mystical states, when well developed, usually are, and have the right to be, absolutely authoritative over the individuals to whom they come.

(2) No authority emanates from them which should make it a duty for those who stand outside of them to accept their revelations uncritically.

(3) They break down the authority of the non-mystical or rationalistic consciousness, based upon the understanding and the senses alone. They show it to be only one kind of consciousness. They open out the possibility of other orders of truth, in which, so far as anything in us vitally responds to them, we may freely continue to have faith.[37]

Proudfoot observes that James's first conclusion includes both descriptive and normative elements. James rightly recognizes that beliefs formed on the basis of religious experience often wield considerable authority for the individual. Additionally, however, he asserts that mystical states provide warrant for the beliefs. Mystical states should authorize the beliefs that they, in fact, do.

As Proudfoot notes, however, James slips in his defense of this authority. He conflates perception and sensation. Moreover, he overlooks the importance of his conception of inquiry. In a passage Proudfoot partially quotes, James defends his first conclusion.

Our own more "rational" beliefs are based on evidence exactly similar in nature to that which mystics quote for theirs. Our senses, namely, have assured us of certain states of fact; but mystical experiences are as direct perceptions of fact for those who have them as any

---

[36] On the contemporary scene Alston, Swinburne, Franks Davis, and Gellman all exploit this analogy as does William Wainwright in *Mysticism* (Sussex: The Harvester Press, 1981). See chapter 5.

[37] James, *Varieties*, p. 331.

sensations ever were for us. The records show that even though the five senses be in abeyance in them, they are absolutely sensational in their epistemological quality, if I may be pardoned the barbarous expression – that is, they are face to face presentations of what seems immediately to exist.[38]

James draws an analogy between the epistemic structure of knowledge based on the senses and the putative knowledge based on mystical states. He claims that in both cases direct acquaintance warrants the beliefs. The language of this passage could easily appear in any of several recent epistemologies of religious experience. In chapter 5 we will encounter much prominent talk of "direct perceptions" which rationally base beliefs or of immediate "face to face presentations" which provide evidence. Unfortunately, James commits a two-fold error here. First, James neglects the fine analysis of sensation and perception he articulated elsewhere. Here he likens mystical states to both sense perception and sensation. Despite his discussion in the *Principles* and elsewhere, he talks as if there persisted in adults such an experience as pure sensation and treats religious experience *and* perception as if they too shared this "direct" nature, uninfluenced by concepts and beliefs. Second, he neglects his general theory of inquiry which empha-sizes how a potential belief coheres with everything else we believe and with further experience. A belief, for the more careful James, emphatically does not achieve warrant simply by its felt quality or intrinsic persuasiveness. We must in some sense reconcile our belief with all else we believe.

James strangely cleaves to his more usual view of warrant when discussing the authority of mystical states for those not experiencing them. Elaborating his second conclusion, he states that we must compare the mystic's asseverations against all else we believe and experience. "To come from thence [mystical consciousness] is no infallible credential. What comes must be sifted and tested, and run the gauntlet of confrontation with the total context of experience, just like what comes from the outer world of sense. Its value must be ascertained by empirical

---

[38] Ibid., p. 332.

methods, so long as we are not mystics ourselves."[39] One wonders what led James to add the last clause here. Certainly Peirce and James's importance rests in their insistence upon the ubiquity of interpretation. Both thinkers emphasize the conceptual element in all experience. James describes this stance, which following Schiller he came to call "humanism," most colorfully when he declares that the "Trail of the human serpent is thus over everything."[40] We must construe all cognition as hypotheses formed in the light of everything else we hold true. Perception, as we have seen, represents an hypothesis as to the best explanation of a perceptual event. On this analogy religious experience also represents an hypothesis as to the best explanation of an event. For James to confer warrant on the beliefs of the mystic because of the "directness" of the experience, while maintaining that the experience has no authority for those who did not undergo the experience, seems very strange indeed. One would imagine James linking warrant to "the gauntlet of confrontation" for all alike because in his other work James rejects direct experience.[41]

A passage in the *Varieties'* introductory lecture helps explain how James came to commit these blunders. When introducing his "empiricist criterion" for making spiritual judgments, he distinguishes first two and then three elements which contribute to an assessment of value. The first of the two he calls variously "immediate delight," "inner happiness," and "immediate luminousness." The second, the "good consequential fruits for life," he divides into "philosophical reasonableness" ("consistency") and "moral helpfulness" ("serviceability"). This tripartite criterion serves to structure the final lectures where the three correspond respectively to the lectures on mysticism, philosophy, and saintliness. In the empiricist criterion's original dual aspect, the second element represents truth. Whereas the first "stamps" a mental state as "good," the second passes

[39] Ibid., p. 334.
[40] *Pragmatism*, in *The Writings of William James*, John J. McDermott, ed. (Chicago: University of Chicago Press, 1967), p. 384.
[41] Richard Gale scolds James for this passage. He insists (as do I) that the evidence conferred by experience is observer-neutral. *On the Nature and Existence of God* (Cambridge: Cambridge University Press, 1991), pp. 287–288.

judgment on its truth. The diction here mirrors the language James employs several years later in *Pragmatism* and *The Meaning of Truth*, where he regularly defines truth in terms of a belief's "good consequences for life." In this first lecture James notes that the first part of the criterion for a spiritual judgment can conflict with the second. Significantly, he illustrates his point using mysticism as an example.

What immediately feels most "good" is not always most "true," when measured by the verdict of the rest of experience . . . The consequence of this discrepancy of the two criteria is the uncertainty which still prevails over so many of our spiritual judgments. There are moments of sentimental and mystical experience – we shall hereafter hear much of them – that carry an enormous sense of inner authority and illumination with them when they come. But they come seldom, and they do not come to everyone; and the rest of life makes either no connection with them, or tends to contradict them more than it confirms them. Some persons follow more the voice of the moment in these cases, some prefer to be guided by the average results.[42]

James believes mysticism a paradigmatic case of contradiction between immediate conviction and truth. The spiritual judgment rendered on mysticism will depend on the relative weighting of immediate luminousness and consistency.

The conclusions to the lectures on mysticism may bear the mark of this earlier passage. The inspiration to grant mystical experience the right to authority for the mystic might derive from James's discussion of spiritual judgments. The "sensational" or authoritative felt quality of the experience certainly matters in making a spiritual judgment because the criterion for a spiritual judgment includes immediate luminousness. The mystic would also have the right to privilege this quality because, as James argues in the first lecture, the mystic can give the first element of the empiricist criterion precedence over the second in making a spiritual judgment. James's conclusions in the chapter on mysticism seem to mean roughly that the mystic can and usually does privilege immediate luminousness over the gauntlet of confrontation, goodness over truth. The problems arise with James's conclusions because he labels them as conclu-

<hr />

[42] James, *Varieties*, p. 31.

sions about the "warrant for the truth" of mystical insights. As we have seen the "sensational" quality of mysticism cannot, on James's own view, count in the assessment of its truth. Nor does the first-person perspective have a different stance vis-à-vis truth than the third person in that assessment.

The conclusions drawn in the three chapters that correspond to the elements of the empiricist criterion corroborate this reading. James extols the morally helpful character of saintliness at the end of "The Value of Saintliness." He claims that "the saintly group of qualities is indispensable to the world's welfare."[43] The chapter on mysticism continually emphasizes mysticism's optimism, "inner authority and illumination." In the chapter on philosophy, however, James reluctantly announces that "intellectual processes" cannot "demonstrate ... the truth of the deliverances of direct religious experience."[44] These reported results, especially the last two, mirror the conclusions at the end of "Mysticism." The immediate luminousness of mysticism authorizes the mystic, but the failure of philosophy to render a verdict means "no authority emanates from them," "so long as we are not mystics ourselves." Religion's inability to satisfy convincingly the philosophical element of the empiricist criterion also explains why the other two fulfilled elements of the empiricist criterion, morally helpful saintliness and immediately luminous feeling, represent the more universal or "constant" features of religion for James.[45]

Nonetheless, James should not have labeled his three conclusions a discussion of mysticism's "warrant for the truth." O'Hear objects to James's conclusions about the epistemic value of mysticism for essentially the same reasons I have canvassed. Ironically, aside from a footnote where he acknowledges James's more plausible position in the *Essays in Radical Empiricism*, O'Hear's critique makes no reference to James's other work. O'Hear's position, however, resembles the one developed in the *Principles*. He likens perceptual judgments to theories because of the existing conceptual framework into which stimuli emerge. The authority adhering to perceptual

[43] Ibid., p. 297.   [44] Ibid., p. 355.   [45] Ibid., pp. 390–391.

beliefs cannot, therefore, arise simply from the experience, no matter how convincing. He faults James for this very error, allowing an experience's vividness to confer warrant on the belief evoked by the experience.

My criticism of James is precisely that in the Mysticism passage he fails to see that once we are able to deploy the distinction between our experiences and the objects we are taking them to be experiences of, the justification for our beliefs about the existence of what we think they are experiences of cannot be simply in terms of clarity, immediacy or apparent directness of the experiences.[46]

By treating experience as a theory, O'Hear cannot countenance any discussion of justification by phenomenological qualities alone. In the *Principles* James takes a like-minded view and declares that the material object hypothesis *"to pass for true, must at least include the reality of the sensible objects in it, by explaining them as effects on us, if nothing more. The system* [i.e. hypothesis] *which includes the most of them, and definitely explains or pretends to explain the most of them, will, ceteris paribus, prevail"* (*PP*, ii, p. 312). O'Hear explicitly invokes Gilbert Harman and argues that all experience including the most ordinary instances of perception represent explanations of data. In experience we naturally experience what we consider most plausible given what else we believe. In perception, "the impression and the object can be seen to be related as explicandum and explicans."[47]

Similarly, religious experiences, for O'Hear as well as for Proudfoot, exemplify the grammar of explanations. The felt qualities of an experience, therefore, do not entail the epistemic adequacy of the beliefs based on it. Justification for these beliefs depends crucially on the strength or goodness of the explanation constituting the experience. O'Hear, rightly I believe, claims that "epistemological justification goes hand-in-hand with explanatory power."[48] A belief achieves justification only if the reasons given for it contribute to the best explanation of the data in a given situation. This approach importantly recognizes the provisional nature of justification. What an individual deems the best explanation of an event may change with the

---

[46] O'Hear, *Experience*, p. 37.   [47] Ibid., p. 32.   [48] Ibid., p. 37.

addition of further information. The total evidence that a culture possesses about a class of events may change with the adoption of new theories. The individual's implicit inference to the best explanation always remains provisional with regard to a broader context and, likewise, this wider judgment about the adequacy of explanations always remains provisional with regard to shifts in the theory adopted by a community.

James's analogy in the *Varieties* comparing mystical experience to sensory and perceptual experience influenced the shape of subsequent apologetics based on religious experience. The fuller analysis of experience he gives elsewhere, however, provides the tools to undermine the position he takes there. Throughout I will understand experience along the lines he draws in his better work.

EXPLANATION

In the last section I contrasted two lines of thought about experience in William James's philosophy. James's more fully articulated and carefully defended view characterizes experience in general as a response to stimuli. This response exhibits the logic of an inference to the best explanation and pragmatically reflects our interests, beliefs, and values. We experience what we infer to be the best explanation of an event. This inference usually does not occur consciously and we can only observe its working indirectly, as when reflecting on a mistaken judgment. We might best construe these inferences as habitual associations. Specifically religious experiences include, therefore, a tacit commitment to a religious explanation of the event causing the experience. James also suggests that anomaly plays a role in the genesis of supernaturally explained experiences. If we admit, however, that experience includes an embedded claim about the best explanation of an event another philosophical tar pit opens before us. To elucidate our conclusion properly we must at least attempt some rudimentary explication of the concept "explanation." I intend to adopt a theory of explanation adumbrated in the *Principles* by James himself. James claims that the explanation which

informs experience is tacitly judged best because of its suit-
ability for one's interests.

The conceived system, to pass for true, must at least include the reality of the
sensible objects in it, by explaining them as effects on us, if nothing more . . . That
theory will be most generally believed which, besides offering us
objects able to account satisfactorily for our sensible experience, also
offers those which are most interesting, those which appeal most
urgently to our aesthetic, emotional, and active needs. (*PP*, II, p. 312)

James argues that explanatory power obtains relative to interests and beliefs. Such a pragmatic view of explanation has
recently become increasingly accepted.

The prominence philosophy of science has enjoyed in the
later half of this century has led to notorious debates about the
nature of scientific explanations. In keeping with the tenor of
twentieth-century analytic philosophy, philosophers often
viewed the alleged virtues of scientific explanation as transfer-
able to explanations generally. Philosophers believed the
qualities supposedly manifested by accepted scientific
explanations emblematic of good explanations in all domains.
O'Hear, for one, succumbs to this exaltation of scientific
explanations. During the past thirty-five years, the deductive-
nomological model of explanation, still referred to as "the
received view," has come under increasing criticism. The
deductive-nomological model (a.k.a. the Hempel-Nagel model)
maintains that a tenable explanation must provide for the
explanandum by deducing it from a universal statement and the
initial conditions. Aside from specific difficulties which the
model cannot alleviate, the generally accepted relation between
science and the rest of culture has changed. Whereas in the
heyday of American analytic philosophy, philosophers believed
that they could delineate some formalizable criteria for adequate scientific explanations which they would then extol as
paradigmatic of rationality, recently many philosophers have
adopted a new stance. They view scientific explanations as
continuous with the sort of explanations we employ in all other
areas of culture. On this count the deductive-nomological
model drives a wedge between scientific explanations and
explanations more commonly employed. Many of the explana-

tions we consider satisfactory in our quotidian affairs certainly do not invoke, in O'Hear's words, "universal statements or laws of nature asserting that all members of a certain class have . . . [a certain] property . . ."[49] Many of our explanations do not resemble deductions at all.

Bas van Fraassen has avowedly developed an account of explanation that equally accommodates mundane and scientific explanations. The deductive-nomological model bills explanation as one sort of description *simpliciter.* The explanatory power of a theory inheres in the type of description given – one employing universal statements and boundary conditions. Van Fraassen, however, makes a move quite similar to one William James makes in the *Principles.* James debunks the scholastic doctrine of essences. He insists that, "*There is no property* ABSOLUTELY *essential to any one thing*" (*PP,* II, p. 333). The practical nature of inquiry necessitates that certain features of a fact or object acquire a prominence in our thinking. The many properties of a thing can individually gain or recede in importance when the practical interest we have in the thing changes. When we attempt to describe its essential properties some practical interest or activity always informs our conception of it and guides our selection. James claims, therefore, that essences are essentially (as it were) teleological. They reflect our common purposes but, "Meanwhile the reality overflows these purposes at every pore. Our usual purpose with it, our commonest title for it, and the properties which this title suggests, have in reality nothing sacramental. They characterize *us* more than they characterize the thing" (*PP,* II, p. 334). James realized that essences (and explanations) make reference not only to the object or fact, but also to a context of human interest.

Likewise, van Fraassen believes that the most vexing difficulties left unsolved by the deductive-nomological model arise because explanatory power involves more than simply a specified sort of description. He believes that explanatory power provides descriptive information *referring to the context of the human interest* in the fact requiring explanation.

---

[49] Ibid., p. 32.

The discussion of explanation went wrong at the very beginning when explanation was conceived of as a relationship like description: a relation between theory and fact. Really it is a three-term relation, between theory, fact, and context. No wonder that no single relation between theory and fact ever managed to fit more than a few examples![50]

Van Fraassen basically argues, as James argues, against one sufficient essence, against the notion that one definitive description suffices for an explanation of a fact. James and van Fraassen emphasize the pragmatic aspects of their topics. They attend to the users of words and symbols and the practical applications to which individuals put them. The deductive-nomological model cast explanations as descriptions patterned on *arguments*. Van Fraassen considers explanations *answers*.[51] This characterization naturally catches the relational aspect of answers whose content depends crucially on the context in which the question arises. He likens the difference between explanations and descriptions to that between daughters and women. All explanations are descriptions as all women are daughters, but both "explanation" and "daughter" make reference to a relation whereas "description" and "woman" do not.[52] Attending to this relational aspect in explanation helps to surmount the obstacles tripping up models of explanation based on the two-term conception.[53]

Van Fraassen, to repeat, characterizes explanations as

---

[50] Bas van Fraassen, *The Scientific Image* (Oxford: Clarendon Press, 1980), p. 156.

[51] In *Four Decades of Scientific Explanation* (Minneapolis: University of Minnesota Press, 1989), Wesley Salmon accordingly classifies van Fraassen's views on explanation as an "erotetic conception."

[52] Despite differences about the status of explanatory entities, Rorty shares van Fraassen's view of explanation as redescription. His discussion of the topic evinces both a style and philosophical pantheon contrasting with those of van Fraassen. In his characteristic manner Rorty declares, "from a Wittgensteinian or Davidsonian or Deweyan angle, there is no such thing as 'the best explanation' of anything; there is just the explanation which best suits the purpose of some given explainer. Explanation is, as Davidson says, always under a description, and alternative descriptions of the same causal process are useful for different purposes. There is no description which is somehow 'closer' to the causal transactions being explained than the others." ("Is Natural Science a Natural Kind?," *Objectivity, Relativism and Truth* [Cambridge: Cambridge University Press, 1991], p. 60).

[53] Van Fraassen concentrates on the asymmetries of explanation and the rejection of explanation requests.

answers. Answers to what? Answers to why-questions. This
stance, of course, requires that we can reformulate any actual
explanation request in the idiom of a why-question. Many
doubt the success of such translations. Wesley Salmon, for
instance, claims that explanation requests sometimes take the
form of either how-possibly or how-actually questions and that
one cannot without change in meaning reformulate these
requests into why-questions. As for how-possibly questions,
Salmon is not referring to a "conditions for the possibility
of ... " question. Rather, he describes a situation in which,
faced with a highly improbable event, we might ask an expert to
explain how the event could possibly have occurred. The
response to this request will count as an explanation, but will
not necessarily answer the related why-question. A valid answer
to a how-possibly question will come from a range of equally
valid alternatives, only one of which provides a valid answer to
the why-question. Similarly, Salmon believes that how-actually
questions ask for different information than why-questions. As
an example, he adduces the two questions: "How did there
come to be mammals (other than bats) in New Zealand?"
(answer – Because humans came in boats) and "Why are there
mammals in New Zealand?" (answer – Because the humans
wanted to see what they could see – or some such explanation).
The first requests a causal explanation and the latter requests a
reason.

Because a contextually relevant description not only answers
why-questions, but also how-questions, I see no reason to abort
van Fraassen's explication of explanation even if one cannot
translate all how-questions into why-questions. Philip Clayton
captures both the contextual and descriptive aspects of explanation in his initial characterization of explanation. "In general,
then, an explanation makes some area of experience comprehensible to a number of individuals, either by presenting it in
terms of its components or details (analysis), or by placing it
into a broader context within which its meaning or significance
becomes clear (synthesis)."[54] With this view of explanation,

---

[54] Philip Clayton, *Explanation from Physics to Theology* (New Haven: Yale University Press,
1989), p. 2.

Clayton sagely advises that one broadly construe the class of why-questions to include some questions phrased as how-questions. To do so hardly endangers a pragmatic analysis of explanation.

Nonetheless I believe one *can* translate how-questions into why-questions. First, a how-possibly question, as Salmon describes it, really amounts to a request for a possible response to a why-question. How-possibly questions request a possible explanation. If explanations represent answers to why-questions, then strictly by substitution we can translate a how-possibly question as a request for a possible answer to a why-question. This schema makes sense in practice too. When asking how the implausible event could possibly have occurred, we simply ask for an hypothetical as opposed to a definitive answer to the why-question.

Second, as for how-actually questions, I agree with Salmon that a given how-actually question may ask a different question than a correspondingly formulated why-question. This fact, however, does not seriously endanger van Fraassen's theory because it does not show that the how-actually question cannot be translated into a why-question. In fact, while a given how-actually question may request a different sort of answer from a corresponding why-question, one can usually interpret either question in either of the two ways. Divorced from any explanatory context, one could understand either of the two questions about New Zealand, for instance, to request either of the explanations given. To focus on the point at hand, both explanation requests could be issued with the why-question (but in different contexts).

Salmon also draws the important distinction between explanation-seeking why-questions and evidence-seeking why-questions. An explanation-seeking why-question inquires into the cause of an event or state of affairs. An evidence-seeking why-question, on the other hand, inquires into the reason(s) for believing that a fact obtains. Clearly, these two requests for information differ substantially. The latter more closely resembles a request for the justification of a belief. Although I believe that explanation plays a crucial role in justification, we must, nevertheless, keep clear about the fact that van Fraassen's account of explanation based on why-questions concerns only explanation-seeking why-questions, questions requesting reasons for the occurrence of an event.

Further, Salmon also reminds us to distinguish explanation-seeking why-questions from rhetorical why-questions. He believes some why-questions do not actually request information.

There are, however, why-questions that do not seem to be calls for explanations. One might ask, in a time of grief, why a loved one had died. Such a question is not intended to evoke an explanation; it is a cry for sympathy. Exclamations and tears may constitute a far better response than would any factual proposition. Indeed, the grieving individual may be fully aware of the scientific explanation of the demise. Other why-questions seem best interpreted as requests for moral justification.[55]

Salmon concludes that contextual factors provide clues about which why-questions actually present requests for information and which have merely rhetorical intent. While this distinction highlights an important consideration, the line dividing explanation requests from rhetorical questions slides evasively underfoot. Van Fraassen's model of explanation, avowedly not limited to scientific explanation, can straightforwardly accommodate many such "rhetorical" why-questions. Granted that the why-question concerning the death of a loved one does not request a scientific explanation, it may yet function as a genuine request for explanation. Job's why-question, for instance, surely had more than rhetorical intent. Either a theological explanation may provide the answer (i.e. "God has his reasons" or "Bad karma") or we reject the explanation request and provide sympathy because on our best theories we have no answer. Similarly, the request for moral justification (though it will most often take the form of an evidence-seeking why-question) can also involve genuine explanation-seeking why-questions, albeit not requests for scientific explanation. They seek an explanation in terms of the moral reasons explaining a moral state of affairs. A student might say, for instance, "I fully believe that plagiarism is morally wrong and require no evidence to bolster

[55] Salmon, *Four Decades*, p. 136.

that belief, but please explain to me precisely why plagiarism is morally wrong." Essentially, this explanation request seeks answers in an ethical context rather than a scientific one and van Fraassen's theory aims to explicate explanations in any context.

Van Fraassen identifies a why-question by three crucial elements. He labels these the topic, the contrast class, and the relevance relation. The topic consists in the proposition about which the why-question asks. For instance, in the question "Why does the liquid taste like tangerines?" the topic would be "The liquid tastes like tangerines." The contrast class represents the range of alternatives against which that which we ask about obtains. In our example we can specify three different contrast classes. We might wish to know why the liquid tastes like tangerines rather than the solid, the gas, etc. Alternatively, we might wish to know why the liquid tastes like tangerines rather than smelling like tangerines, feeling like tangerines, looking like tangerines, etc. Finally, we might wish to know why the liquid tastes like tangerines rather than like apples, like plums, like chili, etc. Obviously, the context in which we ask our question will determine the contrast class against which the topic of our why-question stands. The relevance relation determines which events in the total causal picture pertain to the inquiry. In our example different explanations will result depending on our interest in the topic. In the lab the appropriate explanation might make reference to chemical and physical properties. In the boardroom the appropriate explanation might involve marketing studies on the popularity of synthetic fruit flavors. In the courtroom the appropriate explanation might invoke patent laws. Again, the context in which the why-question arises determines the relevance relation, the pertinent sorts of explanations.

Van Fraassen intends the relevance relation to pick out the intentional stance from which an inquirer asks a why-question. In my example we can ask about the cause of the tangerine-flavored liquid seeking chemical explanations, legal explanations, economic explanations etc. To explain in terms of atomic structure why the liquid tastes like tangerines is *irrelevant* when

the liquid in question is a Dole product and the question arises
in a boardroom in Del Monte, Inc.'s marketing division. In van
Fraassen's example one can seek the cause of a car crash from
multiple perspectives including the mechanical, the psychological, the legal etc.[56] The legal explanation has little value for the
mechanic seeking to repair the car. Van Fraassen insists that a
given topic can instantiate a multitude of why-questions. To
look to either the contrast class or the relevance relation alone
avails little. "Instead we must say of a given proposition that it is
or is not relevant (in this context) to the topic with respect to
that contrast class."[57] We cannot specify the particular request
for explanation without attending to both the contrast class and
the relevance relation. Essentially, on van Fraassen's view an
explanation offers a relevant reason in favor of the topic given
the contrast class.

A pragmatic theory of explanation such as van Fraassen's
entails a number of important consequences. Let me point to a
few. A legitimate request for explanation depends crucially on
our background knowledge and theories. Even a dyed-in-the-
wool scientific realist such as Richard Boyd recognizes that
"our theoretical knowledge tells us what sorts of explanations
are possible and what standards are to be used to judge
them."[58] Our current understanding of the world directly
influences, not only our evaluations of competing explanations,
but also the sorts of explanations we seek. Accordingly, the
explanations we find in one scientific discipline or area of
culture often have very little in common with explanations
found elsewhere.[59] In a justly famous article Theodore Mischel
anticipated the recent turn to pragmatic factors in explanation.
He clearly and concisely argued each of the points just raised.
An explanandum depends crucially on an epistemic context

[56] Van Fraassen borrows this example from Norwood Russell Hanson.
[57] Van Fraassen, *The Scientific Image*, p. 142.
[58] Richard N. Boyd, "Lex Orandi est Lex Credendi," *Images of Science*, Paul Churchland
    and Clifford Hooker, eds. (Chicago: University of Chicago Press, 1985), p. 29.
[59] Edward Schoen writes, "Even though cultural climate and audience composition
    may be kept rigidly invariant, the structure of explanations that are considered
    rigorously scientific within the confines of one discipline often are looked upon with
    extreme skepticism or even repudiated when introduced into the sphere of another
    science" (*Religious Explanations* [Durham: Duke University Press, 1985], p. 54).

which also influences possible explananses. "The point is that when we identify X as something that needs explaining we do so against a framework of beliefs, a background of expectations about how things of that sort ought to behave; and this background also determines the kind of considerations that could figure in an intelligible explanation of X."[60] A scientist's theories, and more generally a person's background beliefs, provide rules by which to determine that which requires explanation. The anomalous with regard to the set of background beliefs requires explanation. The background beliefs also guide considerations of plausibility in comparing explanations.

Mischel echoes Kuhn and foreshadows Rorty when he argues that the rules involved in pinpointing explananda and evaluating explananses have a primarily sociological basis. "We [must] think of the basic rules which guide scientific inquiry at a particular period in history as rules which define an accepted (social) practice of explaining."[61] Because of all these contextual factors, Mischel insists that "the acceptability of an explanation must depend not only on its relation to the facts, but also on its relation to the rules of scientific activity as it is practiced in different periods, rules which regulate the way the facts are to be ordered and understood."[62] These rules of scientific practice clearly bear a loose resemblance to Kuhn's famous "paradigms." Both accounts make sense of the historical changes in explanatory practice which Kuhn brought to light in *The Structure of Scientific Revolutions*.[63] In similar fashion to Kuhn, Mischel attributes shifts in explanatory practice to pragmatic factors. A practice yielding certain attractive "fruits" can win allegiance. Obviously, as William James repeatedly claims, these "fruits" appear attractive relative to our larger pragmatic interests.

The unavoidably pragmatic factors in explanation lead to the position that the goodness of explanations depends crucially on

[60] Theodore Mischel, "Pragmatic Aspects of Explanation," *Philosophy of Science* 33 (1966), p. 42.
[61] Ibid., pp. 42–43.   [62] Ibid., p. 43.
[63] Thomas Kuhn, *The Structure of Scientific Revolutions*, 2nd edn. (Chicago: University of Chicago Press, 1970).

context. We both formulate and judge explanations in light of our ever changing background beliefs. These facts lead Clayton to designate coherence (a term we will discuss in chapter 3) the "umbrella criterion for explanatory adequacy." "Coherence requires the systematic interdependence or 'fit' of the various components of an explanatory account, both internally (call it the consistency criterion) and externally – with the situation (pragmatic criteria), with the data implied and expressed by the explanandum (the correspondence criterion), and with the broader context of experience (the comprehensiveness criterion)."[64] Clayton demonstrates the complexity and embeddedness of the relation between explanation, context, and background beliefs. A look at the pragmatic aspects of explanation leads to an understanding of explanation which emphasizes the coherence between an explanation and the myriad contextual factors impinging on it.

Because I place an emphasis on the explanatory element of experience, I have defended an explication of "explanation." By advocating a pragmatic account of explanation I do not mean to suggest that experience answers an explicit why-question with well-formed relevance relations and contrast classes. Rather, stimuli pose a tacit why-question and our pragmatic interests, conditioned by our historical context, supply equivalents to a relevance relation and contrast class. Really, I simply mean to claim that experience exhibits this same logic, but without any explicit mechanism. I would call these trivial explanations but for the far from trivial role they play in justification.

---

[64] Clayton, *Explanation*, p. 48.

CHAPTER 3

Justification by reasons alone

When philosophers use a word – "knowledge", "being",
"object", "I", "proposition", "name", – and try to grasp
the *essence* of the thing, one must always ask oneself: is the
word ever actually used in this way in the language-game
which is its original home? –

What *we* do is to bring words back from their metaphysical to their everyday use.

Ludwig Wittgenstein (*Philosophical Investigations*, no. 116)[1]

In chapter 2 we established that the logic of experience
implicitly requires a commitment to an explanation. Experiences include inferences to the best explanation, albeit
inferences of an informal sort. By emphasizing the pragmatic
aspects of explanation, we also gestured toward an explication
of explanation. With this partial understanding of experience,
we must now, if we wish eventually to assess the justification of
religious beliefs by religious experience, undertake a theory of
justification. A theory of justification commonly includes two
elements: a metaepistemological stance on the conceptual
analysis of justification and a substantive view of how justification works. Undoubtedly, this convention reinforces a facti-
tious distinction. One's understanding of the concept of
justification clearly carries implications for one's substantive
theory and *vice versa*. The history of the concept, as we will see,
amply illustrates this interdependence. Nonetheless, to divide
the material along these lines has heuristic merit. Accordingly, I

---

[1] *Philosophical Investigations*, 3rd edition, G. E. M. Anscombe, tr. (New York: Macmillan
Publishing Co., 1958), p. 48.

will first discuss the concept of justification and then apply it to the issue at hand: how a belief becomes justified.

THE CONCEPT OF JUSTIFICATION

The genealogy of the concept of justification favored by many epistemologists reaches back to the Socratic questions asked in Plato's *Theaetetus*. Despite the considerable venerability this antecedent lends to the concept, the complex of concerns and issues surrounding the contemporary interest in justification derives more directly and with little modification from the problems vexing early modern philosophy. Although recent developments in epistemology surely mark improvement, I believe the form epistemology currently takes remains beholden to superannuated concerns which render it irrelevant at best and misleading at worst when employed to help resolve disputed questions. Emphasizing our interests and excising the vestiges of the obsolete should clarify the salient features of justification. A few remarks highlighting the dependence of the regnant analysis of justification on early modern problems should illustrate my point.

Almost two decades ago Alvin Goldman distinguished two prominent functions the concept of justification serves.[2] He delineated both a theoretical and a regulative enterprise wherein we employ the concept of justification. Previously, he felt, philosophers had not sufficiently noted the autonomy of the one from the other. The theoretical interest in justification reflects a preoccupation with the standard analysis of knowing. Philosophers pursue the topic of justification hoping to identify that feature which distinguishes merely true belief from knowledge. Knowledge, so the argument runs, consists in true, justified belief (with the possible addition of a fourth necessary

---

[2] Alvin Goldman, "The Internalist Conception of Justification," *Midwest Studies in Philosophy*, 5 (Minneapolis: University of Minnesota Press, 1980), pp. 27–51. Goldman's distinction differs in important ways from the distinction Roderick Firth made about the same time in his American Philosophical Association Presidential Address "Epistemic Merit, Intrinsic and Instrumental," *American Philosophical Association Proceedings and Addresses*, pp. 55, 5–23.

condition to eliminate a class of problematic cases first identified by Edmund Gettier and now called Gettier examples). This theoretical interest constitutes a largely descriptive task, unpacking the necessary and sufficient conditions for knowledge.

More prescriptive interests, on the other hand, motivate the regulative use of justification. Here, philosophers aim to arrive at principles or criteria by which to decide what to believe, a general guide for epistemic progress. Historically, the desire to formalize scientific method, to instruct scientists on proper epistemic conduct in inquiry, has inspired the regulative use of criteria of justification. Goldman rightly observes that Descartes intended his criterion of clarity and distinctness to serve this second function. Goldman neglects to mention, however, that Descartes also espoused a position quite similar to the standard analysis of knowing. The origin of the modern study of justification explains why philosophers generally conflate the theoretical and regulative functions.

In Descartes we observe the historical rationale for the shape that contemporary studies in justification take. In the *Meditations* Descartes attempted to discover a ground for scientific inquiry impervious to skeptical assault. Recent historical work documents the depth of the epistemological crisis accompanying the revival (and subsequent transformation) of ancient skepticism. Increasingly, the limits of Scholastic "science" became clear as well. Descartes sought to provide an account of inquiry more sound than Scholastic models and unthreatened by skeptical argument. One cannot exaggerate the importance of skepticism in the formation of the epistemological period in philosophy. It set the constraints on Descartes's project and thereby has shaped the way we view epistemology ever since. Despite avowed efforts to reject it, skepticism continues to exercise a phantom control over the questions epistemologists ask and the approaches they take.

Consider the specifications for an epistemology which the threat of skepticism imposes. Taking the skeptical challenge seriously forces one's hand in an inquiry into knowledge. Because skepticism purports to demonstrate that our confidence in even our most uncontroversial and universally accepted beliefs is unfounded, one cannot begin epistemological reflection with particular examples of things we know and then continue the inquiry into knowledge inductively from there. Rather one must first formulate an infallible criterion of knowledge and apply that criterion to candidates for knowledge. Skepticism, in other words, precludes the possibility of a *particularist* approach to knowledge. To wit, it impugns our ability to identify particular examples of knowledge and, therefore, one could never begin with exemplars to formulate views about knowledge. A serious attempt to meet (rather than reject) the skeptical challenge requires that one first find a *method* immune to skeptical doubt and employ it universally as a criterion to identify which beliefs in fact qualify as knowledge. Whereas particularism ignores, rejects, or undermines the skeptical challenge, methodism confronts and tries to overcome skepticism.[3] By endeavoring to overcome skepticism, Descartes committed himself to a methodist approach.

Methodism explains the historical conflation which Goldman remedies. It obviously lends itself to a conception of epistemology as the discipline which identifies and formulates general, regulative principles of epistemic advancement. Prior to engaging with any particular data or information, epistemology provides criteria for amending one's body of knowledge. Descartes, as Goldman notes, arrived at the famous criterion of clarity and distinctness. Methodism also, however, leads to the sort of views about knowledge represented by the standard analysis. From the point of view of methodism, only beliefs justified in terms of the method qualify as knowledge. The term "knowledge" can only pertain to beliefs certified by the criterion. Knowledge therefore requires justification. Descartes makes this point quite unequivocally in the fourth meditation.

---

[3] Chisholm introduced this terminology in "The Problem of the Criterion," *The Foundations of Knowing* (Minneapolis: University of Minnesota Press, 1982), ch. 5. He doesn't view the issues in quite this light however. As I note below, he casts skepticism, methodism, and particularism all as answers to the problem of the criterion. Ernest Sosa, Chisholm's colleague, treats methodism and particularism as manners of commencing a theory of knowledge in "The Raft and the Pyramid," *Midwest Studies in Philosophy*, 5, p. 4.

If, however, I simply refrain from making a judgment in cases where I do not perceive the truth with sufficient clarity and distinctness, then it is clear that I am behaving correctly and avoiding error. But if in such cases I either affirm or deny, then I am not using my free will correctly. If I go for the alternative which is false, then obviously I shall be in error; if I take the other side, then it is by pure chance that I arrive at the truth, and I shall still be at fault since it is clear by the natural light that the perception of the intellect should always precede the determination of the will.[4]

Descartes's methodism with its regulative criterion leads him to explicitly deny that accidentally true belief qualifies as knowledge. Knowledge properly so-called for Descartes must bear the seal of the regulative method. For the philosopher exercised by skepticism, therefore, the regulative and theoretical functions of justification prove far from unrelated. They represent flip sides of the same methodist coin.

Although contemporary epistemologists undoubtedly consider skepticism an extraordinarily important question in the theory of knowledge, most no longer consider it the paramount concern; indeed most philosophers on the scene relegate skepticism to a position of secondary or tertiary importance. They consider their theoretical or regulative views about justification, for instance, as legitimate philosophical concerns apart from the issues which skepticism raises. No doubt this claim is true. They do not however pay enough heed to the generating circumstances of their problematic. Apart from the methodist rejoinder to a skeptical challenge, the conflation of the theoretical and the regulative functions of justification requires some justification of its own. When one no longer permits skeptical doubts to dictate the course of epistemology, what reason does one have for thinking that an elaboration of the conditions under which true belief qualifies as knowledge also serves to provide criteria for conducting inquiry properly? That the regulative function of justification, furthermore, requires criteria also needs some justification. Both the standard analysis of knowledge (that justification represents a necessary condition

---

[4]   *The Philosophical Writings of Descartes*, vol. II, John Cottingham, Robert Stoothoff, and Dugald Murdoch, trs. (Cambridge: Cambridge University Press, 1984), p. 41.

of knowledge) and the impetus behind a criterial conception of justification found their inspiration in the skeptical challenges of the early modern period, yet atavistically survive today.

The skeptical challenge also conditions other inveterate aspects of philosophical discussion about justification. Faced with radical doubt about the ability to know anything, one naturally begins an investigation into knowledge with one's own directly accessible states. The approach to knowledge must commence from the individual's perspective because skepticism impugns the very existence of others. It forces the epistemologist to begin with the resources available to the individual and thereby enjoins a methodological solipsism. Justification must pertain solely to an individual's epistemic state. Similarly, because skepticism calls into question the existence of an external world, one must begin inquiry from a position within the mind. Justification, therefore, must obtain solely in relation to one's internal states. Descartes, of course, perfectly illustrates these strictures. The mental clarity and distinctness of an *idea* provide justification for the individual. These preoccupations remain today. Justification refers to the epistemic situation of an individual and until quite recently always obtained in light of an individual's beliefs or psychological states.

Epistemologists have come to call this latter feature of justification "internalism." Facts about an individual's mind confer justification on a belief. The literature reflects different varieties of internalism. Their differences depend on which features of the individual's psychology can contribute to justification: beliefs alone or beliefs and experiences, etc.[5] Externalism, on the other hand, locates the justification-conferring fact outside the mind of the individual and does not even require the individual to have any access to the information.[6] Although epistemologists no longer focus on

[5] See William Alston, "Concepts of Epistemic Justification" and "Internalism and Externalism in Epistemology," *Epistemic Justification* (Ithaca: Cornell University Press, 1989), for taxonomies of internalism.

[6] Lawrence Bonjour describes externalism in such terms: "This relation, which is differently characterized by different versions of the view, is such as to make it either nomologically certain or else highly probable that the belief is true. It would thus provide, *for anyone who knew about it*, an undeniably excellent reason for accepting such

skepticism, it continues to shape the parameters of their questions. Justification applies to individuals and, on most accounts, supervenes on exclusively mental facts.

The early modern concern with skepticism also contributes to the way we assimilate epistemology to ethics. The relation between epistemic appraisal and ethical appraisal has long constituted a topic of philosophical discussion. Because the threat of skepticism forced a methodist epistemology, one construal of the relationship has historically predominated. Methodist approaches specify criteria to regulate doxastic progress. They enumerate principles to apply when assessing potential beliefs. Naturally, in such a situation the inquirer can either apply the principles or fail to apply the principles and, if applying the principles, can either apply them correctly or incorrectly. The inquirer can thus conduct his doxastic affairs rightly by fulfilling obligations or wrongly and, if wrongly, incurs blame for his failure. Methodism, therefore, casts epistemic appraisal as a natural analogue to the variety of ethical appraisal which emphasizes duty, obligation, right, and blame. When applied to epistemic matters William Alston and others refer to this variety of appraisal as a "deontological concept of justification." Alston acknowledges that here he uses the term "deontological" in a non-standard way because in ethics (whence the term comes) "deontological" contrasts with "teleological" where both employ the concepts of duty, obligation, blame, and the like.[7] Alston seems to use "deontological" the way others, in the spirit of Sidgwick, use the epithet "right-based ethic."[8] A right-based ethic explicates the good in terms of the right. The good action conforms to duty or obligation regardless of one's personal inclination. This ethic considers right an imperatival notion. A good-based ethic, on the other

a belief. But according to proponents of the view under discussion, the person for whom the belief is basic need not (and in general will not) have any cognitive grasp of any kind of this reason or of the relation that is the basis for it in order for this basic belief to be justified; all these matters may be entirely *external* to the person's subjective conception of the situation" ("Externalist Theories of Empirical Knowledge," *Midwest Studies in Philosophy*, 5, p. 55).

[7] Footnote 4 of "Concepts of Epistemic Justification."

[8] Henry Sidgwick, *The Methods of Ethics*, 7th edn. (London: Macmillan, 1907), ch. 1.9.

hand, defines the right in terms of the good and believes the good intrinsically attractive. Methodism, therefore, leads to a right-based epistemology, what Alston calls a deontological concept of justification, and most philosophers have conceived of justification in this light. Descartes compounded the emphasis on a deontological conception in the *Meditations* with his Augustinean epistemological theodicy. By emphasizing human free will and doxastic sin, he obviously presupposed a deontological view of justification.

Skepticism, we have seen, contributed much of the shape and much of the content to the contemporary discussion of epistemic justification. Skepticism itself, however, as a topic of both philosophical and general concern has receded in importance. The skeptical crisis in early modern philosophy found resolution without a definitive refutation of skepticism and it no longer carries the profound cultural importance it once did. Science, for instance, as an institution has established itself through its achievements, thereby obviating any clamor for its grounding. It no longer operates criterially (if it ever really did) and eschews any role as an answer to skepticism. Although many today, following Wittgenstein, plausibly suggest that universal skepticism would not hold enough constant to make sense of its own doubt, even those who see no convincing answer to the skeptic generally do not fret that they have no direct means of combating universal skepticism. Skeptical doubts have become, in Burnyeat's telling phrase, "insulated" from "the ordinary business of life."[9] If we recognize, therefore, that skepticism need not exercise an insidious control over our theory of knowledge, an entirely different view of justification arises, one that conforms more closely to a non-philosophical idiom of justified belief.[10] Concomitant with the rejection of the skeptical challenge as a major concern, we can reject methodism and take a particularist approach in the theory of

---

[9] M. F. Burnyeat, "The skeptic in his place and time," in *Philosophy in History*, Richard Rorty, J. B. Schneewind, and Quentin Skinner, eds. (Cambridge: Cambridge University Press, 1984), p. 225.

[10] I leave open the (in my view, strictly terminological) question whether my views on justification comprise a different analysis of justification or a new concept.

knowledge.[11] Epistemology can then begin, as do most areas of research, by supposing that its object uncontroversially exists. We can begin with examples of knowledge and fashion our epistemological and metaepistemological views from that standpoint. If we accept that we can have knowledge that we have not previously certified by some criterion, the traditional ideas about justification seem superfluous or excessive.

More precisely, the traditional requirements for a theory of justification lose their rationale without methodism. We have no reason to suppose that an analysis of the one concept will fulfill both the theoretical and the regulative functions. When we consider the theoretical and regulative questions independently, we find that the traditional concept is a hybrid which consequently imports to each function elements inessential to the fulfillment of that function. In divorcing the two functions, as particularism enables us to do, we find that the independent answers to each of the two questions can take a much simpler shape. To believe that knowledge exists prior to method may not weaken the desire for some strategy for regulating belief acquisition, for instance, but it offers no support for elaborating a purely formal set of criteria. The very many and different sorts of knowledge accepted (and the very many and different sorts of beliefs up for debate) prior to any regulative inquiry would leave any resulting procedural guidelines extremely general and flexible. A criterial regulative conception of justification makes sense when confronted with the task of building knowledge up from virtual scratch, but without a skeptical constraint, criteria do not sufficiently account for the complexity of our epistemic situation. In any real inquiry formal principles prove far too cumbersome for reliable use and lead to many profoundly troubling conclusions.

Most contemporary particularists, virtually all heavily influenced by Chisholm, the self-avowed particularist, remain, however, in the thrall of skepticism. Chisholm views skepticism, methodism, and particularism all as responses to the problem of

---

[11] Ironically, particularism resembles in some respects the sort of philosophical *ataraxia* historically advertised by classical skepticism. It eliminates dogmatism in favor of fallibilism and values conventional beliefs highly.

the criterion: the problem of non-circularly arriving at a criterion by which to judge candidates for knowledge. In this formulation Chisholm and his followers falsely couch the issues, however, and grant skepticism too great a role. The problem of the criterion, historically and by its very nature, issues a skeptical challenge. It demands a universal means of establishing that we know what we know. Methodism accepts the challenge. Particularism, on the other hand, need not address itself to answering the problem of the criterion. It need not generate criteria for judging possible knowledge. If it does, then it squanders its liberating value. I suggest that a more adequate schema of the available options in epistemology begins not with the problem of the criterion, but simply opposes skepticism and methodism as a related complex to particularism. In this case particularism has no interest in formal evaluative criteria or principles.[12]

Rather than considering particularism an opportunity to evade skepticism, Chisholm and his followers take inspiration from Thomas Reid's Scottish "common sense" philosophy and employ particularism to develop criteria of epistemic goodness. The particularist principles (as I will call them) which result license beliefs of certain kinds, formed in approved ways, subject to defeating conditions. Particularist principles, unfortunately, prove far from benign. They divorce regulative epistemology from the best knowledge we might bring to bear on individual cases of belief formation by relegating that knowledge to a solely overriding role. Particularist principles handicap epistemic progress by rendering our doxastic resources secondary, if not supererogatory. It is no coincidence that religious epistemologists make heavy use of such principles when their apologetic aims get most controversial. They seek to justify religious beliefs autonomously, isolating them from our other beliefs. The epistemologies considered in chapter 5 all

---

[12] Hilary Putnam has argued that any criterial conception of justified belief refutes itself because, through the criteria alone, one cannot justify the claim that the criteria in fact determine the justified. I see this observation as pointing to the problem of the criterion. *Reason, Truth and History* (Cambridge: Cambridge University Press, 1981), ch. 5.

employ strategies of this type. Plantinga too argues for particularist principles of properly basic belief (i.e. justified beliefs
believed on the basis of no others).[13] His traffic in particularist
principles seems needless apart from their utility for a protective
strategy. By contrast, I believe justification should function at
the level of a disputed belief itself and make use of all the
available information, rather than functioning at one remove to
defend the right to hold *prima facie* certain species of beliefs. By
interposing this layer of epistemological apparatus between a
disputed question and our knowledge, particularist principles
place roadblocks in the path of inquiry. Peirce, who repeatedly
expressed admiration for Reid's common sense philosophy,
nonetheless recognized in it a conservative tendency to interfere
with inquiry. Accordingly, he labeled his own view "critical
common-sensism" and declared, "Common Sense is to be
trusted only so far as it sustains critical investigation."[14] Below I
elaborate further on my aversion to epistemologies which treat
beliefs as justified until defeated.

Aside from obviating regulative principles, particularism
removes the major impetus to subscribe to the standard analysis
of knowledge. In the absence of any skeptical worries the
standard analysis of knowledge appears, on deep reflection,
excessively stringent. The traditional theoretical function of
justification serves to prevent beliefs uncertified by regulative
criteria from wearing the mantle of knowledge. If from a
particularist starting point, one acknowledges knowledge prior
to establishing a method for achieving knowledge, then we must
jettison the standard analysis of knowledge and cede the
ubiquity it grants justification. The complex history of the
concept, buried in the diversity of our usages and intuitions,
leaves me suspicious of any "essentialist" attempt to analyze
knowledge in terms of universally necessary and sufficient
conditions.[15] For most of our purposes and contexts of usage we

---

[13] Alvin Plantinga, "Is Belief in God Properly Basic?," *Nous* 15 (1981), pp. 41–51.
[14] Letter to Lady Welby, May 20, 1911, *Charles S. Peirce: Selected Writings*, Philip Wiener,
     ed. (New York: Dover Publications, 1966), p. 426.
[15] See Jeffrey Stout, *The Flight from Authority* (Notre Dame: University of Notre Dame
     Press, 1981), part i.

can explicate knowledge as merely true belief.[16] Such a recognition rightly places the approbation, which the honorific term "knowledge" confers, on the belief rather than the believer. To call a belief knowledge amounts, in most contexts, to claiming that it is a good belief to have, not that the believer did a good job in forming it. In fact, in many settings ill-gotten gains *can* constitute knowledge. From a particularist point of view, the excellence of a belief's justificatory pedigree comprises an independent virtue from that of its consisting in a bit of knowledge.[17]

Even those unwilling to accept my view of knowledge (and I imagine this group to include most professional philosophers) could nonetheless accept my suggestion that we reject the standard analysis of knowledge and decouple justification from knowledge. Nothing of importance for my argument rests on my willingness to describe certain occasions of merely true belief as knowledge. That which "epistemizes" true belief (i.e. makes it knowledge), if some such property is indeed necessary, need not be justification and, as Goldman himself argued, need not be something epistemically internal to the believer. It is skepticism that introduces those constraints on a theory of knowledge. Plantinga, for instance, in his most recent work uses the term "warrant" to describe that which, when added to true belief, yields knowledge.[18] He argues that justification is neither necessary nor sufficient for warrant, but allows that justification is nonetheless a valuable state of affairs. Plantinga's account of warrant, it furthermore turns out, is externalist. Regardless, therefore, of the plausibility of my analysis of knowledge, a particularist approach to epistemology enables us to ask the regulative question about how best to conduct inquiry without conditioning our answer by expecting it also to answer the theoretical question about the conditions necessary and sufficient for knowledge. When we then approach the regulative

---

[16] I will avoid here the complicated issue of degrees of belief.

[17] The preceding several sentences reflect in content and diction the influence of Isaac Levi.

[18] Alvin Plantinga, *Warrant: The Current Debate* (New York: Oxford University Press, 1993).

question about how best to conduct inquiry, moreover, I think we find no reason to suppose that principles or criteria of *prima facie* acceptability form part of the answer.

Rejecting the standard analysis of knowledge frees epistemology from countless difficulties and ultimately renders it more reasonable. It obviates, for instance, the Gettier problem, that true, justified belief is not sufficient for knowledge. Such an end-run around the problem may not satisfy some, but its links to skeptically inspired epistemology convince me that the whole question is wrong-headed. Less obvious and more radical consequences accrue with the reassignment of a role for justification. Justification, rather than functioning as a component of knowledge, will come into account only relatively rarely when genuine doubt about knowledge surfaces. Genuine, uninsulated doubt exhibits a fairly direct connection with conduct which, while difficult to specify precisely, is missing in feigned or merely "philosophical" doubt. To defend some candidate for knowledge, one must provide a justification for believing it true. Construed in this way, justification will always consist in the giving of apposite and weighty reasons to resolve doubt. Because genuine inquiry always presupposes doubt, justification will play a role wherever anyone undertakes an inquiry. This fact, that inquiry requires justification, lends misplaced support to the traditional view, that knowledge requires justification. The less extreme view only requires justification in the absence of knowledge or when in genuine doubt about knowledge. Charles Larmore takes a similar view of justification and labels his view "contextualist." His usage has great appeal, but others have employed this term for much more traditional theories.[19]

A commitment to the standard analysis of knowing (even by those who hesitate to embrace it explicitly) yokes epistemology to misguided claims about justification. This commitment, for example, coupled with the observation that one can know things without the ability to give reasons for what one knows,

---

[19] *The Morals of Modernity* (Cambridge: Cambridge University Press, 1996), pp. 61–63; Mark Timmons, "Outline of a Contextualist Moral Epistemology," *Moral Knowledge?*, Walter Sinnott-Armstrong and Mark Timmons, eds. (New York: Oxford University Press, 1996), pp. 293–325.

necessitates the rejection of the view of justification as "higher-order thinking" (i.e. the giving of reasons).[20] It supports theories which posit something mysterious labeled "immediate justification" wherein a belief, if formed in the appropriate way, can achieve justification without the mediation of any other beliefs or reasons.

The commitment also leads to a related position implicit in much of the literature of justification. Nicholas Wolterstorff and Alston make it explicit. Wolterstorff sounds this "caution": "For one thing, *being justified* in one's belief that so-and-so is different from *justifying* one's belief that so-and-so. To be justified in believing that so-and-so is to be in a certain *state*. To justify one's belief that so-and-so is to perform a certain *action*."[21] Alston similarly exhibits a penchant for disambiguating "the process-product ambiguity" between the quality of being "justified" and the act of "justification" and claims that the former exercises logical priority because the latter aims to demonstrate that a belief resides in the former.[22] They want to claim that beliefs can be justified prior to the act of justification and that one can be justified in holding a belief without reasons to justify it. This move reflects the mistake committed at the very outset. Justification need not accompany knowledge. I believe we should label a belief justified only if someone *has* justified it. The issue of justification never arises for most of our beliefs and knowledge.

The epistemological sacred cow, that justification forms a necessary component of knowledge, invites conceptions of justification like these that divorce it from anything like its non-philosophical uses. In common parlance one would rarely, if ever, say a belief is justified without having in some sense (even if only interiorly) justified it with reasons.[23] The whole logic of methodism (which inspired the concept) reflects this fact: for the

---

[20] Alston mounts this argument against Sellars in "What's Wrong with Immediate Knowledge?," *Epistemic Justification*, p. 70.

[21] Nicholas Wolterstorff, "Can Belief in God Be Rational If It Has No Foundations?," *Faith and Rationality*, Alvin Plantinga and Nicholas Wolterstorff, eds. (Notre Dame: University of Notre Dame Press, 1983), p. 157.

[22] William Alston, "Two Types of Foundationalism," *Epistemic Justification*, pp. 19–38.

[23] I allow the possibility of derivative locutions belying this generalization.

methodist a belief is not justified until she justifies it in terms of the method. Everywhere but in our philosophy we believe the act of justifying something more basic than the state of being justified. Without the standard analysis of knowledge, we have no reason to believe the state of being justified more basic than the act of justifying.[24] We in fact accept the converse, that the state of being justified depends on the act of justifying. The "work-day" (as Ryle would call it) conception of justification I propose bases it on the giving of reasons. Alston calls positions such as mine which limit justification to the giving of reasons (i.e. identify grounds and reasons) "discursive theories."

Epistemologists often compare justified belief to justified action and analyze justified action as an action which does not have any proscriptions against it. To me this description of justified action does not conform to standard usage. A justified action is one for which justifying reasons have been offered. A justified seizure of property or a justified use of force include justifying reasons. They are not justified simply by the absence of proscriptions against them. No one would call an action justified unless she had reasons in mind. The use of force by the police, for example, is not deemed justified until they have offered convincing reasons why they needed to exercise force. One might ask, in response, what quality inheres in the formation of a belief which later enables one to justify it. The answer, of course, is the availability of good justifying reasons. This availability of good reasons prior to the act of justification should not, however, tempt us to say that the belief was immediately justified from the time of its formation. The availability of good reasons prior to the act of justification merely means that the belief was *justifiable*.

Unsurprisingly, others have revisited the seventeenth-century

---

[24] Although I believe he chooses unwisely, Alston recognizes the connection between the analysis of knowing and the relative priority of the state of being justified and the activity of justifying: "We will be concentrating on the 'be justified' side of this distinction, since that is of more fundamental epistemological interest. If epistemic justification were restricted to those cases in which the subject carries out a 'justification', it would *obviously* not be a necessary condition of knowledge or even of being in a strong position to acquire knowledge" ("Concepts of Epistemic Justification," *Epistemic Justification*, p. 83).

skeptical crisis to explain the strange insignificance of reason-giving in contemporary epistemology. Richard Rorty, as one example, famously traces the vagaries of generally accepted notions about justification to an early modern empiricist confusion.[25] Epistemology, from its very inception, has conflated two very different issues: a causal explanation of the mental processes operative in an individual's acquisition of knowledge and the justification of belief. Locke, he argues, attempted to answer skepticism through a mechanistic explanation of mentality. To justify a belief, one offers a causal account of the belief's formation in mental space. A belief's pedigree relative to other features in mental space confers justification on it regardless of its status in the public space of reasons. Although in this critique he never questions the standard analysis of propositional knowledge, Rorty believes that epistemology's very impetus rests on this confusion of the justificatory space of reasons with the causal space of explanation. Epistemologists naturally, therefore, neglect discursive theories and focus on the individual. He plausibly argues that epistemology continues to harness justification to the causal circumstances of a belief. A belief formed in an appropriate way can, in advance of any reasons given in its support, count as justified. Even after the rejection of skepticism, epistemology perpetuates the fallacy Rorty identifies.

As a case in point, one increasingly reads the phrase in the literature that beliefs are "innocent until proven guilty." The pragmatists employed it and recent inheritors and expositors (including Chisholm) suggest it means that beliefs are justified until a justifiable doubt overrides their justification. Both particularist principles and the distinction between being justified and the act of justification serve to support this same view. Without engaging in exegesis, I believe that the pragmatists intended to demonstrate that justification involves only very local regions of our doxastic scope at any one time. They sought to minimize the role of justification while retaining an open path for genuine inquiry. To gloss the pragmatists as

---

[25] Richard Rorty, *Philosophy and the Mirror of Nature* (Princeton: Princeton University Press, 1979), ch. 5.

maintaining that beliefs are justified until overridden obscures their interest in epistemic advancement. As Peirce's insistence on a qualified, *"critical"* common-sensism (i.e. one that sustains "critical investigation") evidences, they believed that to grant our beliefs positive justificatory status in advance of inquiry in fact retards inquiry. To declare beliefs justified until shown otherwise lends unfair prestige to the beliefs we currently hold.

I agree that pragmatically we need a reason that appeals to our other beliefs to truly doubt a given belief, but that fact in itself does not confer justification on beliefs we have yet to justify. To suggest it does legitimates conservatism in epistemic appraisal. Conservatism, while descriptively accurate psychology (we tend to minimize change when revising beliefs), functions as a protective strategy when enlisted in the prescriptive enterprise of regulative epistemology. A principled allegiance to that which one already believes does not necessarily result in epistemic improvement. The inquirer who flouts current opinion may well adopt a belief better justified than the belief retained by the conservative.[26] In fairness a belief only becomes justified when it has *been* justified, when, that is, someone provides good reasons in its support. Conservatism, construed as a regulative principle, can only function to block inquiry.

To cut the Gordian knot into which contemporary epistemologists have tied the concept of justification, one only need repudiate the standard analysis of knowledge.[27] In that case, the fact that we can know things without the ability to give reasons does not require that we countenance immediate justification. It only means that we cannot always justify our knowledge, something we do not normally try to do.

---

[26] Keith Lehrer in his 1974 book, *Knowledge* (Oxford: Oxford University Press, 1974, ch. 7), also questions the wisdom of emphasizing conservatism in a model of justification.

[27] J. S. Mill remarkably both embraces the standard analysis of knowing and takes the position I advocate here that one justifies a belief by offering reasons. He claims that no true opinion held by a person "deserve[s] the name of knowledge, except so far as he has either had forced upon him by others or gone through of himself the same mental process which would have been required of him in carrying on an active controversy with opponents" (*On Liberty* [Indianapolis: Hackett, 1978], p. 43. See also pp. 34 and 50). Mill severely restricts the range of knowledge and excludes much that most of us would unhesitantly include.

Restricting the role of justification solves yet another difficulty inherent in the standard analysis of knowledge. In some persons the conditions necessary for the very possibility of justification do not obtain, and yet we often ascribe knowledge to such persons. Broadly and non-controversially stated, justification functions to insure the rationality of beliefs. A requirement that one justify a belief imposes responsibility for the rationality of accepting the belief (especially so in deontological models). When included as a condition of knowledge, such a responsibility conflicts with our tendency to treat children and the insane as knowers. We usually absolve children and the insane from responsibility for their actions because of their limited powers of reason. How then, if knowledge includes justification as a condition, can they know? Separating justification from the analysis of knowledge and limiting it to discursive reason-giving evades the problem. On this view children and the insane may know something, but yet lack the reasoning capacity properly to justify the belief to others. Whereas anyone may know, justification need only pertain to the province of the sufficiently rational.

Aside from the pressures alleviated by repudiating the standard analysis of knowledge, a few other features of justification can take a more germane and compelling shape once our perspective shifts from a concern with skepticism and its consequent, methodism. For one, although questions about what beliefs an isolated knower should rationally adopt given that individual's psychological boundary conditions always have value, without the solipsistic constraint introduced by skepticism, epistemology can more fully address belief formation among groups.[28] Really, this question proves far more useful. What should someone rationally believe given the best information available at large? Epistemology of the sort I find

[28] One cause of the rift between contemporary continental and analytic philosophy derives from the looser way in which continental philosophers employ the term "epistemology." They have long demonstrated more interest in belief formation in societies than in belief formation in the individual. Recently, Goldman has used the term "social epistemology" to capture much of the sense of what I mean here. See "Argumentation and Social Epistemology," *The Journal of Philosophy*, 91 (1994), pp. 27–49.

unsatisfactory informs us that an hypothetical believer with a stipulated configuration of mental properties has, *ceteris paribus*, properly fulfilled a duty in arriving at belief X. Essentially, it tells us about the rationality of the believer, but nothing intrinsic about the goodness of the belief. A more social construal of justification, based on the giving of reasons, can tell us, on the other hand, both about the rationality of the believer (through the reasons the believer offers) and about the intrinsic goodness of the belief (through the outcome of the justification).

Ironically, the classic proponents of early modern methodism, designing to facilitate the growth of scientific knowledge, sought to overcome epistemic individualism. Descartes and Bacon, for instance, both intended their methods to create a division of intellectual labor. Epistemic advancement would no longer require the sustained effort of individual genius. Anyone of reasonable intellectual caliber could apply the method in any one of many diverse fields and make epistemic progress. Despite their efforts (and science *has* become a communal effort, even if not modeled on their methods), the specter of skepticism has haunted epistemology and left it primarily concerned with individual epistemology.

The traditional emphasis on the isolated individual and the more pressing interest in the wider question represent two conflicting inclinations in our intuitions about justified belief. I sense that we usually fail to attend self-consciously enough to them and introduce an ambiguity into our philosophical discussions of justification. Sometimes when we ask about justification we wish to know whether someone arrived at a belief rationally, using the evidence available to her. Essentially, this question concerns the justification she has for her belief given the constraints of her circumstances and epistemic position. Other times when we ask about justification we wish to know, regardless of whether it makes sense for some particular person to hold the belief, if the belief is justified in a more universal sense. We want to know whether the belief is justified on all the available evidence, not just whether the belief represents a reasonable addition to the belief structure of one individual with her individual vagaries. I propose that we reserve the term "individual justification" for justification pertaining to the individual psychology and evidence available to the believer (someone giving himself reasons). "Social justification," then, will refer to the second or more social sense of justification, the merit a belief has apart from the particular situation of an individual.[29] Of course, we can ask about the justification a belief has for some group of people given their epistemic circumstances or we can ask that question about a belief, but not in principle limit the social justification to any group. In general individual and social justification represent distinct epistemological desiderata, but, in the second portion of this chapter, I will claim that social justification presupposes individual justification. The activity of socially justifying a belief presupposes individual justification.

The conception of justification for which I have argued here strongly denies externalism. As a discursive theory it limits the justifying grounds for a belief to the giving of reasons. Externalism, conversely, permits justifiers or reasons of which the believer need have no cognizance. Fundamentally alien to my view, such a conception allows facts entirely external to minds to provide justification for beliefs. The property or properties that epistemize true belief (if there is such a property or properties) may well be epistemically external to the believer, but justifications for a belief must be epistemically internal to the believer. Discursive theories are paradigmatically internalist, but an account of social epistemology must reinterpret internalism. The "internal" in internalism standardly refers to the interior of an *individual's* mind. A discursive theory of justification in social epistemology, such as mine, must construe internalism to mean that the justifying grounds of beliefs take the form of publicly offered reasons.

Finally, conceiving of justification apart from any overriding worry about skepticism influences how one relates it to ethics. If methodism compels one to adopt a deontological conception of

---

[29] Unfortunately, Goldman (ibid., p. 39) employs the distinction between "personal justification" and "social justification" to explain the distinction between "being justified" and "the act of justification" which I have rejected. He, therefore, limits the giving of reasons to social justification.

justification, particularism frees one from it. Methodism appraises beliefs according to whether or not one properly and successfully applied the method to them. It naturally, therefore, results in a theory of justification focused on obligations and blame etc. Particularism of the variety here espoused, on the other hand, naturally lends itself to an analogy with good-based ethics.[30] A belief achieves justification if supported by *good* reasons. A good-based theory of justification integrates, not identifies, epistemological values with ethical values in an overall philosophical anthropology or conception of human flourishing. I shall have a great deal more to say about these issues in the next part of this chapter. Suffice it to say here that a good-based theory of justification nicely complements similar current moves in ethical theory. Elizabeth Anscombe in "Modern Moral Philosophy"[31] and Iris Murdoch in *The Sovereignty of Good*[32] have done much to rehabilitate *eudaimonian* conceptions of ethics. Both suggest that the modern right-based ethical vocabulary seems impoverished in comparison with ancient philosophy. Anscombe, moreover, identifies right-based ethics as a vestige of the Christian law conception of ethics. It represents a philosophical tendency no longer architectonic with the prevailing world-view. Descartes's epistemological free will theodicy highlights for the contemporary reader a corresponding anachronism in epistemology. Deontological theories of justification derive from obsolete philosophical agendas.

In sum: the concept of justification relevant to contemporary issues and not beholden to archaic skeptical cavils functions autonomously from knowledge. In fact, it comes into account when doubt arises about knowledge. It consists in the giving of reasons. Accordingly, a belief is justified only if someone has actually justified it. Justification, furthermore, need not pertain only to the epistemic situation of an individual; one can

---

[30] Plantinga asserts in *Warrant: The Current Debate* that internalism is unmotivated without a deontological conception of justification. Clearly, I find his claim unsupported.

[31] G. E. M. Anscombe, *Ethics, Religion and Politics* (Minneapolis: University of Minnesota Press, 1981), pp. 26–42.

[32] London: Routledge & Kegan Paul, 1970.

consider it primarily a social, discursive practice. Finally, one judges justification in light of the goodness of the reasons given.

A THEORY OF JUSTIFICATION

The philosophical literature about justification debates the relative merits of two major types of substantive theories: foundations theories and coherence theories. My commitment to a discursive conception of justification (that is, one which requires the giving of reasons for justification) rules out foundations theories because they rely on some class of immediately justified (foundational) beliefs whose justification obtains in virtue of no other beliefs and which transfer justification to beliefs based on them. Particularist principles, as one example, contribute to a foundationalist epistemology because they issue immediately justified beliefs. I reject all such foundational models because they misconstrue justification when they base it on something non-doxastic. Only beliefs can legitimately justify beliefs.[33]

Coherence theories, conversely, see that justification properly describes a relation between beliefs. In a coherence model of justification, a belief achieves justification through its coherence with some set of beliefs. The precise explication of the coherence relation and the set with which the belief must cohere varies greatly among the many alternative theories. For my purposes, I find a suitably amended explanatory coherence model of justification most fruitful and plausible. Such a model bridges and binds the logic of experience and the logic of justification. Experiences, to summarize the conclusion of chapter 2, include an implicit claim to represent the best explanation of a stimulus. An explanatory coherence model

[33] See Donald Davidson, "A Coherence Theory of Truth and Knowledge," *Truth and Interpretation*, Ernest LePore, ed. (Oxford: Basil Blackwell, 1986), p. 311. "The relation between a sensation and a belief cannot be logical, since sensations are not beliefs or other propositional attitudes. What then is the relation? The answer is, I think, obvious: the relation is causal. Sensations cause some beliefs and in *this* sense are the basis or ground for those beliefs. But a causal explanation of belief does not show how or why the belief is justified." John McDowell, in his Locke Lectures, *Mind and World* (Cambridge: Harvard University Press, 1994), conducts a sustained, sympathetic, yet critical, reflection on Davidson's way of thinking about these issues.

awards justification to the beliefs comprising the best total explanatory account of the relevant phenomena. The logic of justification thereby appraises the claims made according to the logic of experience. I appreciate this picture because it weds explanation and justification, two issues often artificially separated in philosophical works on religious experience.[34]

The bulk of this next section will tailor an explanatory coherence model to suit the conception of justification outlined in the first section. Simply, I maintain that the goodness of reasons consists in explanatory coherence. Good reasons indicate how a belief coheres with others we hold in the best overall explanatory account of the phenomena in question. Good reasons can even account for the erroneousness of competitor beliefs. Bad reasons, conversely, can fail to justify even without well-articulated competition. These judgments, of course, presuppose values, in this case epistemic values. I prefer to think of our epistemic values as one species of our values, akin to our ethical values, both of which contribute to our ideal of human flourishing.

Over the years Gilbert Harman has most fully and persistently propounded an explanatory coherence model. His work has proved enormously influential and controversial.[35] He has an essentially dual ambition. He seeks both to explain the process by which an individual revises her beliefs and to provide a model of justified belief. By (as he puts it) turning skepticism on its head, he aims to solve both problems. He advocates that in epistemological inquiry we begin with non-controversial examples of knowledge. Rather than wondering how knowledge is possible, he employs "the strategy of using intuitive judgments about when people know things in order to discover principles of reasoning that justify belief."[36] His method admittedly amounts to an appeal to psychologism. He believes, in other words, that by examining examples of inferences we

---

[34] See chapters 5 and 7.

[35] One can locate his position fairly easily in two of his books: *Thought* (Princeton: Princeton University Press, 1973) and *Change in View* (Cambridge, MA: M.I.T. Press, 1986). My exposition will make use of both.

[36] Harman, *Thought*, p. 116.

accept, we can discover the valid principles of reasoning and justification. With only minor allowances a descriptive account of the rules of belief revision can function as a normative account as well. In this sense his theories exemplify naturalized epistemology. Ultimately, he pictures reasoning or belief revision as an inference to the best overall explanatory account or maximally coherent explanatory view. Beliefs arrived at in this manner remain justified until defeated.

Despite its avowed repudiation (not refutation) of skepticism, Harman's psychologism unfortunately remains tied to skepticism in important ways. While admirable for his particularist stance, Harman nonetheless positions his work in relation to the set of epistemological issues ultimately traceable to early modern skepticism. It obviously still focuses on the individual's reasoning. Although presumably the "intuitive judgments" have a social element, he cannot adequately convey the essentially social nature of justification. Additionally, by seeking to determine the mental processes that justify uncontroversial knowledge, it exhibits allegiance to the standard analysis of knowing. He focuses centrally on the Gettier problem. Finally, psychologism of this sort (and naturalized epistemology generally) commits the central epistemological fallacy, derived from skepticism, to which Rorty objects. It conflates the causal story of mental processes with public justification by reasons. Harman's ambition simultaneously to explain belief revision and provide a model of justified belief perfectly exemplifies Rorty's complaint. All these factors result in particularist principles with their attendant drawbacks. Harman imports, for instance, conservatism (he calls this maxim "The Principle of Positive Undermining"), a feature of belief revision, into a theory of justification and the unsatisfactory results described in the first section of this chapter ensue.

Essentially, Harman's coherentism relies on assumptions inappropriate to coherentism rightly construed. Historically, the foundationalist picture of justification arose concomitantly with methodism. If one feels, as did Descartes, compelled by the challenge of skepticism to certify every belief in terms of a method before conferring the title "knowledge," one naturally pictures the structure of knowledge as comprised of a class of beliefs immediately justified in light of the method and a much larger class of beliefs whose justification relies on the former class. Coherentism, as an historical phenomenon, arose as an alternative to this skeptically inspired foundationalism. Peirce, who is often credited with first explicitly formulating a coherentist account of knowledge, wrote his early articles in a "spirit of opposition to Cartesianism" and describes skeptical doubt as mere "self-deception."[37] In true particularist spirit, he sought to address the regulative function of justification in inquiry occasioned by genuine doubt. For a coherentist account to require justification as a condition of all our knowledge, therefore, betrays its historical impetus. A coherentist who embraces particularism, as did its originators, need not consider justification necessary for knowledge, but rather necessary only for inquiry.

If we disavow Harman's interest in the analysis of knowledge and his attempt to cantilever a theory of justification entirely out of individual psychology, we can escape the common objections to explanatory coherence theories. Our discursive theory that limits the role of justification proves harder to assail. Lehrer, for instance, presents one interesting argument in the form of a *reductio*. He points out that a maximally coherent system leaves nothing unexplained and argues that the explanatory coherence model of justification requires some safeguard against the depletion of unexplained observational facts under the pressures of explanatory coherence.[38] Lehrer claims that the coherentist could simply declare unexplained facts false and thereby increase the overall coherence of his view.

The coherentist has at least a couple of responses. Harman's appeal to conservatism answers this charge, but as I have repeatedly indicated I have reservations about conservatism as a principle of justification. Harman's "Get-back Principle,"

---

[37] "Some Consequences of Four Incapacities," *Charles S. Peirce: Selected Writings*, pp. 39–72.

[38] James Cornman, in his influential paper, "Foundational versus Nonfoundational Theories of Empirical Justification," *Essays on Knowledge and Justification*, George Pappas and Marshall Swain, eds. (Ithaca: Cornell University Press, 1978), also levels this objection at the explanatory coherence model.

that one should not reject a belief one can easily get back, surely has an application here as well.[39] He may conceivably have first invoked it in response to this very problem. In surmounting Lehrer's objection, Anthony O'Hear employs a retort akin to the Get-back Principle.[40] He takes sensory experiences as the primary data requiring explanation. One cannot, therefore, simply delete the inexplicable. Another potential answer to the charge that coherence theories tend to the depletion of observation sentences challenges the suppressed claim that unexplained facts necessarily diminish the coherence of one's view. Any observation sentence includes the low-level explanation of experience which answers why one sees what one does or believes one sees what one sees. Unexplained regularities, moreover, can also add to coherence. Harman adduces the example of the explanatory relation between the barometer falling and a storm developing. One need not understand the causal mechanism in this case for the one fact to have explanatory value for the other. In other words, Lehrer's objection focuses too exclusively on higher-level or scientific explanations which leave something unexplained. Any observation statement, even one which complicates scientific theory or remains theoretically unexplained, can add to explanatory coherence through its pragmatic contribution to different sorts of explanation.

Harman and O'Hear's answers seem arbitrary and my own tentative suggestion does not fully convince me. Fortunately, my proffered view of justification evades this difficulty. On my model one only need justify a belief in the case of genuine doubt. To justify a belief one must offer good explanatory reasons, reasons that, when viewed against the background of all one does not currently doubt, contribute to the best overall explanatory account of the phenomena in question. Justification, on my model, is not a matter of assessing how well a belief coheres with a maximally coherent set, but rather of judging reasons in support of beliefs for their explanatory goodness. Accordingly, on this model one feels no temptation to

[39] Harman, *Change in View*, p. 58.
[40] Anthony O'Hear, *Experience, Explanation and Faith* (London: Routledge & Kegan Paul, 1984), p. 38.

systematically delete observation sentences to create a maximally coherent belief system. One would only reject an observation sentence if someone's reasons to do so contributed to the best explanatory account in light of our background knowledge. In fact, scientific practice seems to conform to this view. When deciding whether to reject observational data or theory, scientists weigh reasons for either option and choose whichever makes more explanatory sense in light of what they hold constant.

Lehrer also raises what Nelson Goodman has called "the classic and chilling objection" to coherence theories.[41] He asks with which belief system must a belief cohere for justification, the maximally coherent system which an individual can conceive or that maximally coherent system which might lie beyond the individual's ken. Lehrer believes either answer makes trouble for the coherence model. At this expository stage he must choose, but judging from his evaluative remarks, we could treat this presentation as a dilemma:

> One problem with the first answer is that a man might turn out to be completely justified in believing something because of his inability to conceive of a system having a maximum of explanatory coherence with which his belief fails to cohere. One drawback of the second answer is that according to it a man might be completely justified in believing something even though it fails to cohere with systems he understands: his belief may cohere with a system of beliefs having a maximum of explanatory coherence which he is unable to comprehend.[42]

In his exposition of the coherence model, Lehrer chooses to represent it along the lines of the first alternative, that for justification a belief must cohere with the maximally coherent belief system available to the individual. In this passage he clearly views this feature as a liability of the theory. Later in his chapter he expands on these concerns.

Even if one supposes that two individuals have equally maximally coherent systems, those systems may be inconsistent. This fact, he avers, calls into question the very notion of

[41] *Ways of Worldmaking* (Indianapolis: Hackett, 1978), p. 124.
[42] Lehrer, *Knowledge*, p. 163.

justification Harman employs in his explanatory coherence model. Lehrer explains:

> As for the ... suggestion that complete justification be made relative to a system of beliefs, there remain two objections. First, and perhaps most important, the question of whether a man is completely justified in believing that *p* is not answered by the announcement that he is completely justified in believing it relative to a system *B* . We must ask whether a man who is completely justified in his belief relative to system *B* is completely justified in his belief. In other words, is system *B* a system to which a man may appeal to completely justify his beliefs? If *B* is but one of a set of systems having maximal explanatory coherence which are inconsistent with each other, then we have no way of answering this question.
>
> We are left with the problem of inconsistent *systems* of beliefs having a maximum of explanatory coherence, and consequently, inconsistent beliefs being completely justified by such systems ... No relation between statements suffices to guarantee complete justification. In addition to relations between statements, some other feature must be an ingredient of justification.[43]

The problem of inconsistent justified beliefs leads Lehrer to conclude that a mere relation between beliefs proves inadequate for justification. I too believe that justification does not essentially depend on the coherence relations between beliefs in an individual's mental space, but draw a different conclusion from the possibility of inconsistent justified beliefs.

This possibility simply points to the pragmatic nature of justification. Justification works to convince others of our epistemic goodness. One offers reasons contributing to the best explanatory account relative to the beliefs and interests of one's interlocutors. A belief's justification always obtains relative to a set of background beliefs and a body of values. One can justify a belief, therefore, to oneself, another individual, one's intellectual peers, a culture, or an era. If we have any interest in a social justification, the reasons offered in defense of a belief must exemplify shared epistemic values regarding good explanations and good ways of believing. In evaluating the reasons given for a belief, one must relate those reasons to these deeply held and unarticulated values partially comprising an ideal of human

[43] Ibid., pp. 181–182.

flourishing. Epistemic values help determine which of a number of competing explanations and beliefs represents the good in the way of belief. Even with no other acceptable competitors on the field, they can detect bad explanations. As I understand it, therefore, justification reflects the general logic of scientific explanation. Both presuppose contexts which fix relevance, prior beliefs, and openness to intersubjective criticism and demand public reasons offered against a background of shared values and ideals. The contextual nature of justification also accounts for the reluctance we sometimes feel about granting that a belief which *we* consider false is in *any* sense justified, even when the believer has offered himself good reasons. We feel uncomfortable because the belief is not justified for us.

To construct timeless canons of explanatory goodness for universal application overlooks both the pragmatic element (interest-relativity) in explanation and the historical and cultural relativity of epistemic values.[44] We cannot enumerate any formal criteria of justified belief. No syllogism can arbitrate justification. Determining whether a belief is justified proves neither so simple nor so final. In controversial cases we must argue for our stance. Justification in such circumstances necessarily includes debate between interlocutors who have much in common. In this way to speak of an explanatory coherence model can mislead because canons of explanation and criteria of coherence have histories. Any candidate belief for justification must conform to an ideal of human epistemic flourishing.[45] Ideals of human flourishing, however, bear the distinctive marks of time and place, era and culture. A picture

---

[44] Paul Thagard in "The Best Explanation: Criteria for Theory Choice," *Journal of Philosophy*, 75 (1978), pp. 76–92, examines actual cases of scientific reasoning and distills three criteria which they exhibit. Science, he maintains, judges theories in terms of consilience, simplicity, and analogy. A comparatively good theory will explain in a way analogous to other successful explanations more classes of facts with fewer *ad hoc* assumptions. Needless to say, however, the criteria manifested in scientific practice need not carry over to our other pragmatic concerns. Criteria developed historically in the scientific domain may not prove entirely applicable elsewhere in our lives or in the lives of those spacially or temporally removed from us.

[45] The inspiration for much of what follows comes from Hilary Putnam's recent work, *Reason, Truth and History* and *Realism with a Human Face* (Cambridge: Harvard University Press, 1990).

such as this one allows that the justificatory status of a belief can vary from culture to culture and from one historical epoch to another. Beliefs justified in one context can conflict with beliefs justified in another.

Ideally, however, one can always trump these justifications, broaden the inquiry and ask the higher-gauge question about justification *tout court*. I mean by this claim that we can always seek the most encompassing perspective from which to judge a belief. Justification cannot, of course, occur abstracted from any and all context, but we can seek common ground to establish the widest possible shared context. Despite the dramatic extent to which cultures or historical epochs can differ, and even the extreme segmentation within an individual's catalogue of beliefs,[46] I nonetheless see no merit in the general thesis that rationality cannot commensurate across the various domains. We cannot arbitrarily limit the scope of possible justifications and claim that the practice of reason-giving only succeeds among those who share one arena of concern or parochial culture. Such a doctrinaire relativism overlooks the enormous reservoir of shared beliefs and values which in many cases provides the common ground on which we stake our arguments. Granted that the Yoruba, for example, justify certain beliefs to themselves, they can, when confronted with alien beliefs justified relative to another epistemic context, attempt to justify their beliefs in light of what they share with the defenders of the alien beliefs. Justification obtains relative to values, but we can specify no limits in advance to whom we share enough with to justify our beliefs. We must always allow for a dialogue between persons and cultures with different values to offer reasons in defense of their beliefs and values.

The fact that epistemic standards depend on values,

---

[46] Despite the postmodern emphasis on the fragmented self, William James may have best captured this aspect of mentality in the chapter "The Perception of Reality," in *The Principles of Psychology* (New York: Dover Publications, Inc., 1950). Alfred Schutz, "On Multiple Realities," *Collected Papers* vol. 1 (The Hague: Martinus Nijhoff, 1962) imported "finite provinces of meaning" from James into phenomenology. Ernest Gellner, "Concepts and Society," *Rationality*, Bryan Wilson, ed. (Oxford: Basil Blackwell, 1970, pp. 18–49), presents the most vivid account of the dangers of failing to attend to the multiple perspectives constituting a belief system.

therefore, does not mean that anything goes. We normally do possess the leverage to evaluate beliefs and ideals. No "form of life," discourse, or "world" remains isolated in principle, protected, immune from criticism. We extend tolerance to beliefs or ideals when nothing significant rides on the issue (political toleration is, of course, another, more complicated matter). When we consider a belief or value and feel concern about its implications, we often deliberately seek reasons to repudiate it. If we judge the consequences of a belief or value important, we no longer deem the preference subjective or culturally relative. Not always will we attempt to discern an objective correctness (in light of shared values) in matters of preference; only when we regard the implications as serious.

Epistemic values along with ethical and other sorts of values all form species of the good. They all contribute to an ideal of human flourishing or *eudaimonia*. Although my argument does not rely on this particular theory of values, I construe values as (often) tacit norms for selectivity in a context. Our talk of values betokens especially central, perduring, and well-reinforced clusters of beliefs and desires in one's psychological economy. Throughout this chapter I have (in the tradition of epistemology) artificially abstracted beliefs from the desires with which they intertwine. Reasons and cognitive coherence pertain to desires and interrelated networks of beliefs and desires as well as simply to beliefs. That values comprise both beliefs and desires explains two phenomena. First, values motivate (i.e. enable selection). Motivation requires both beliefs and desires. Lacking either, paralysis results. Desires remain impotent without beliefs to guide one in their satisfaction and beliefs leave one inert without desires which apply them. Second, values appear Janus-faced. Sometimes they are best discussed in the idiom of beliefs and other times in that of desires.

Despite the numerous attempts, one cannot reduce epistemic values to ethical values. Epistemic and ethical values pertain to different contexts of selectivity (i.e. clusters of beliefs and desires). Unless one could reduce one context to another, we must consider epistemic and ethical values as different species of values. Diverse cultures and historical epochs, however, do carve contexts of selectivity into categorial domains differently. The moral sphere, for instance, represents a recent (Enlightenment) category which includes a domain of selectivity distinguished from the theological and the legal. In light of the numerous possible ways to individuate species of values, we should expect some taxonomic relativity.

Beliefs and values interrelate in fundamental ways. First, epistemic values comprise objectivity. The fact that we maintain that universally held beliefs can yet be wrong (i.e. that a *consensus gentium* argument is by no means invulnerable) points to the role epistemic values play. They represent the backdrop against which we hold beliefs. Without values, we would have no "world" at all because our values, as action-guiding norms for selectivity, contribute to the discernment of facts. They pass sentence on potential beliefs. The factual proves, at bottom, inseparable from the normative. Yet, secondly, because beliefs in part comprise values, knowledge can impugn or justify values. Various species of values can bear on one another as well.[47] Our ethical values and knowledge, for instance, can influence our epistemic values. Ideals of human flourishing evolve and are capable of reform. Cognitive life resembles a feedback loop or hermeneutic circle whereby our values inform our epistemic judgments and our consequent factual knowledge influences our values. Importantly, therefore, we must recognize the necessity of a certain vagueness in discussing epistemic issues. Justification does not reduce to criteria or an algorithm. At its deepest level it includes argument and change. To socially justify a belief one must offer good reasons contributing to the best explanatory account of the phenomena in question. The goodness of the reasons obtains relative to the values and explanatory commitments embraced in a culture's ideal of human flourishing.

---

[47] William James distinguished four aspects of rationality that correspond to our different areas of concern and vie simultaneously for satisfaction. A rational conception will strike a compromise between our intellectual, aesthetical, moral and practical interests. *A Pluralistic Universe* (New York: Longmans, Green, and Co., 1909), pp. 112–113.

CHAPTER 4

Perennialism revisited

In chapter 2 I rehearsed, through a discussion of James, the common thesis that context mediates experience. This view, like any other, generates detractors. Recently Robert K. C. Forman has attempted to muster support for the existence of a form of experience peculiarly unaffected by prior beliefs, language or concepts. He takes the position that the specifically mystical experiences reported in the literature of many different religious traditions include an unmediated, and therefore non-context-relative or qualitatively identical, core. In this chapter I consider this challenge. To reopen the debate he has solicited essays from like-minded scholars for his book, *The Problem of Pure Consciousness*. Predictably, the focus of the volume rests on the refutation of the position most notably expounded in Steven Katz's influential article of 1978, "Language, Epistemology, and Mysticism."

In that work Katz adopts a polemical tone to criticize a prevalent tendency in studies of mysticism. Many prominent works in the field embrace the mystics' claims about mystical experience which they assert provides some form of direct epistemological access to reality. Katz links this uncritical stance to ecumenically or dogmatically inspired attempts to conflate the cross-cultural varieties of mystical experience to one or a few general types. He refers to this method as "essentialist reductionism." In its place Katz offers the thesis that "linguistic, social, historical, and conceptual contextuality" affects the mystic before, during and after the event to color or shape his experience.[1] Context provides the basis for the mystic to

---

[1] Steven T. Katz, "Language, Epistemology, and Mysticism," *Mysticism and Philosophical Analysis* (New York: Oxford University Press, 1978), p. 29.

interpret his experience through his expectations and explanations which affect the nature of the experience as it occurs. Katz maintains that context conditions the mystical experience and Forman labels this widely hailed formulation "constructivism."

Of the contributors to his volume, Forman most fully articulates an alternative to constructivism. He inaugurates this collective attempt to rehabilitate the essentialist position with his keynote essay entitled "Introduction: Mysticism, Constructivism, and Forgetting." Here Forman undertakes to outline briefly the history of the study of mysticism and explain the rationale for the present dominance of the constructivist paradigm, undermine Katz's position and that of constructivism in general, and proffer a substitute methodology to replace the constructivist paradigm he finds so unsatisfactory. Unfortunately, Forman, in his exposition of the constructivist position, muddies its logic.

His most damning omission consists in a failure to distinguish adequately between the event we designate a mystical experience (which one can specify under any number of descriptions) and the mystic's experience of the event (in which one must privilege the mystic's description). He commits something like an inverted version of the "psychologist's fallacy." The psychologist's fallacy occurs when the psychologist imputes his knowledge to the mental state of his subject. Conversely, Forman grants the mystic's description of the experience priority in characterizing the event. Many of the other authors in *The Problem of Pure Consciousness* share this same confusion, which, in the service of apologetic aims, amounts to a "protective strategy" blocking explanations incompatible with those implicitly embedded in the mystics' descriptions. Barricaded behind this redoubt, Forman, in his own theory of mystical experience, commits the very fallacies that he enumerates as having contributed to the justified rejection of the early essentialist models. In place of constructivism, Forman essentially advocates a regressive return to an uncritical literary approach.

At the very beginning of his article, Forman discusses the reasons that historically led to the rejection of the thesis that mysticism universally entails an identical (or a few general types

of) phenomenological experience colored *ex post facto* by interpretation. He outlines and endorses three major reproofs of the
early scholarship on mysticism. First, he points out that the first
scholars of mysticism made uncritical use of primary sources.
They took portions of documents out of context and relied on
particularly tendentious translations and interpretations of
texts, all of which allowed for facile cross-cultural comparisons
of mysticism. Generally, the scholars made "naive and methodologically unsound use of primary texts."[2] Second, later
researchers came to recognize that the claims for the cross-
cultural homogeneity of mysticism had as their foundation only
the earlier scholars' assumption of their homogeneity. The early
works carefully catalogued apparent similarities between instances or schools of mysticism, but never entertained the
suggestion that the differences might preclude assimilation.
Third, in comparing texts from different cultures and attempting to demonstrate their essential similarity, the earlier scholars
adopted a "hermeneutically naive" methodology because they
claimed the ability to recognize the experience behind the
foreign linguistic description. The later researchers came to
view this tendency to bifurcate the experience and the description as illicit. Eventually, Forman suggests, these criticisms
prompted the application, which he rejects, of the widely
accepted constructivist epistemological theory to mystical experience.

   Unfortunately, however, Forman, in concert with his contributors, misinterprets the structure of Katz's seminal article.
Sharing a common misreading of "Language, Epistemology,
and Mysticism," Forman, Stephen Bernhardt, Philip Almond
and Anthony Perovich all assume that Katz's "single epistemological assumption" that "exercised" his thinking and "forced"
him to undertake this investigation provides the first premise in
an *a priori* deductive proof.[3] Perovich and Franklin both go so
far as to supply a shorthand syllogism of the argument. Perovich
invokes *modus ponens* and Franklin *modus tollens*, but both

[2] Robert K. C. Forman, "Introduction: Mysticism, Constructivism, and Forgetting,"
The Problem of Pure Consciousness (New York: Oxford University Press, 1990), p. 4.
[3] Katz, "Language," p. 26.

condemn the argument for begging the question. Bernhardt also insists that: "Instead of addressing the issues, Katz simply begs it [the question of pure, unmediated consciousness] by assuming the very thesis in question to illustrate his point. The obvious possible counterinstance, pure consciousness, has been excluded outright on *a priori* principles."[4] Nevertheless, Bernhardt notes that Katz does consider the putative pure consciousness achieved through religious practice and rejects it not on *a priori* principles, but because "there is no substantive evidence to suggest that there is any pure consciousness *per se* achieved by these various, common mystical practices, e.g. fasting, yoga, and the like."[5] Throughout his paper, Katz tries to present evidence to support his *intuition* that "*There are* NO *pure (i.e. unmediated) experiences.*"[6] He does not employ his "assumption" in the strong logical and deductive sense. In mentioning this "assumption" he simply makes reference to the hypothesis he hopes to support adequately with documentary and cultural evidence. To view him as mounting a blatantly circular deductive, *a priori* argument uncharitably misreads his article. One might, of course, object that Katz fails to supply adequate evidence to confirm his hypothesis. Indeed the structure of Katz's piece, that he tries to corroborate his hypothesis using at least three different traditions in the space of one article (admittedly of considerable length), invites the objection that he has left his claims undersupported. Katz's difficulties on this score reinforce one of my central theses in this book: philosophers can no longer continue to write about mysticism without detailed study and documentation of specific mystics and traditions.

Despite his intentions, Forman's own indictment of Katz's alleged circularity correctly assesses the structure and weight of the argument. "All he [Katz] offers are summaries of religious doctrines and restatements of the original assumption. These are *instances* of an assumed claim, not arguments."[7] Forman,

---

[4] Stephen Bernhardt, "Are Pure Consciousness Events Unmediated?," *The Problem of Pure Consciousness* (New York: Oxford University Press, 1990), p. 227.
[5] Katz, "Language," p. 56.   [6] Ibid., p. 26.
[7] Forman, "Introduction," p. 16.

while assailing Katz, accurately characterizes the *a posteriori* nature of his argument. Katz presents a wealth of evidence and "instances" to support an "assumption" or hypothesis. The length of Katz's documentation alone should signal that his emphasis lies not with *a priori* argumentation, but rather inductive evidence. Katz also states that the mediation of experience represents an "epistemological fact" which, invoking Hume's fork, indicates that it does not involve logical necessity.[8] The unanimity and vehemence with which the contributors to Forman's volume condemn Katz for harboring something so intrusive as an "assumption" suggests that these scholars intend to develop what Wayne Proudfoot has labeled a "protective strategy." In demanding an unattainable, absolute impartiality on the part of the scholar investigating mystical claims, they handicap the scholar's ability to explain mysticism in terms and theories other than those employed by the mystics themselves. By denouncing the legitimacy of the scholar's theoretical commitments, they implicitly privilege the mystical explanation and include it in their allegedly neutral description of the experience *and* the event. I intend to explore this issue more deeply when I address the alternative methodology advocated by Forman *et al.*

Franklin provides the most sophisticated discussion of Katz's argument and therefore his failure on this point proves most frustrating. He initially recognizes that Katz takes the weak rather than the strong position in regard to the possibility of unmediated experience. The stronger premise holds that context "must" mediate experience and the weaker premise that it simply "does" mediate all experience. Franklin rightly observes that Katz denies that unmediated experience entails a self-contradiction, but falsely supposes that Katz must adopt this strong position. Franklin drops the weak premise because he finds it insufficient to Katz's aim of demonstrating that context mediates mystical experience as well as ordinary experience. Franklin tries to argue that mysticism diverges in structure from ordinary experience, but the weight of Katz's evidence aims to show that it does not. Clearly, Katz marshals the kind of

---

[8] Katz, "Language," p. 26.

evidence he does because he intends to defend the weaker premise. When Franklin inadvisedly embraces the stronger reading of Katz, he invites the same trouble that plagues the other accounts; he objects to the supposed *a priori* deduction and consequent *petitio principis*. Similarly, Almond encounters difficulties in Katz's argument because he reads him as supporting the stronger premise. Almond erroneously believes that Katz lays the force of his "rhetoric" on the premise that "all experience is *by definition* mediated."[9] The value of Franklin's contribution rests in unwittingly drawing attention to the specific shortcoming in the interpretations of Katz offered in Forman's volume.

In his own exposition of Katz's article, Forman imagines three possible applications of the constructivist thesis to mysticism. Each remains true to the general intention of constructivism to include, as Katz summarizes it, the "linguistic, social, historical and conceptual context" in the understanding of a mystical experience. Forman's first interpretation he calls "complete constructivism." On this view, he claims, the constructivist believes that the mystic's social beliefs and linguistic framework solely cause the experience. " . . . the experience is one hundred percent shaped, determined, and provided by the set."[10] Forman believes that this construal accounts for hallucinations where no sensory input influences the experience. Forman labels his second interpretation of the constructivist model "incomplete constructivism." On this view, which he describes as "more plausible," the mystic's epistemological framework causes part of the mystical experience and the sensory input causes part. Forman feels the incomplete constructivist interpretation weakens the constructivist claims against the perennial philosophers because the incomplete constructivist model allows for similarity between experiences because of the possibility of similar sensory input. The third interpretation of the constructivist model that Forman considers he labels "catalytic constructivism." He gleans this construal from passages in

---

[9] Philip Almond, "Mysticism and Its Contexts," *The Problem of Pure Consciousness* (New York: Oxford University Press, 1990), p. 216.

[10] Forman, "Introduction," p. 13.

"Language, Epistemology, and Mysticism" where Katz claims the social context of the mystic includes a religious tradition which provides the individual with a psychic map which corresponds to the particular problems the religion attempts to address. Forman interprets Katz to mean that these problems initiate a series of reactions in the individual which leads to the production of a mystical experience. "It is that the adept's generating problems leads him or her to hold to beliefs and perform practices which themselves act as catalysts for mystical experiences."[11] Forman also alludes to his belief that Katz holds a thesis whereby a mystic's conceptual set necessarily causes his mysticism.

This proliferation of interpretations derives from Forman's misunderstanding of the basic constructivist contention. This misapprehension also contributes to his heavily psychological (as opposed to logical) rendering of the constructivist model: the set of beliefs *cause* the mysticism. Indeed, at the end of this section of the article, Forman asks: "Everybody has models, and thus everyone has similar 'causes.' Why do so few have mystical experiences?"[12] As I have already suggested, the unnecessary difficulty introduced by Forman in this discussion derives from his failure to distinguish in the constructivist argument between the event designated a mystical experience and the mystic's experience. Forman seems to believe erroneously that Katz employs the terms "event" and "experience" interchangeably although, ironically, in his own work he clearly recognizes the difference. In choosing to designate the type of mysticism on which he focuses his study a Pure Consciousness *Event* (italics added), Forman signals his awareness of the semantic disparity between an event and an experience. Whereas the grammar of the term "event" places no constraints on the vocabulary employed to describe one, an experience must be specified by its intentional object, the description the subject gives of what the experience is *of*. Forman trades on this distinction because the description of the "Event" as he fashions it includes the mystic's explanation that it is free of conceptual or cognitive

---

[11] Ibid., p. 14.   [12] Ibid., p. 15.

conditioning. While missing the profound implications of the distinction between an event and an experience, Forman exploits the grammar to mask the explanatory commitments of his theory. The confusion which Forman brings to the constructivist position disappears with the understanding that the constructivists do not make the strong claim that the conceptual set *causes* any event. Rather they insist that the conceptual set *conditions* the mystical experience because the mystic interprets an event mystically. The mystic's experience draws on the concepts.

Katz takes great care in his article to bracket questions concerning the validity of the ontological or existential claims mystics make for the objects of their experiences. He leaves the cause of the event unquestioned, and simply wants to show "that there is a clear causal connection between the religious and social structure one brings to experience and the nature of one's actual religious experience."[13] As Proudfoot notes, the relationship between concepts and experience is really logical or grammatical rather than causal and so the phrase "clear causal connection" misleads.[14] Nevertheless, the inaptly phrased "connection" does not obtain between the epistemological framework and the event, but rather between the framework and the experience. He does not claim it causes the event, only that it gives the experience its character. Additionally, Katz does not claim that because the "causes" of the experiences vary cross-culturally, the causes of the events must differ cross-culturally as well. He leaves that question for theology, physiology, or neurology and only insists that philosophically the mystical data can reveal no answer. Fundamentally, his contention centers on the conceptual nature of experiences and the consequent differences between them.

With this clarification in mind, the distinction between complete, incomplete, and catalytic constructivism is barren. The experience draws on the contextual conceptual set regardless of the corresponding presence or absence of sensory input. For Forman to allow this distinction in the first place appears

[13] Katz, "Language," p. 40.
[14] Wayne Proudfoot, *Religious Experience* (Berkeley: University of California Press, 1985), p. 123.

somewhat ill-considered because he does not deny the constructivist model for ordinary experience and he must realize (as
does James) that one cannot separate sensory input from the
conditioned reception of it without creating abstractions. (Even
he admits that an epistemological framework mediates sensory
input, yet does this presence of sensory input purport to
distinguish two constructivist models?) The constructivist does
not address the question as to whether some exterior reality
exists. She observes the difference between, for example,
Titian's (had he viewed it) and Monet's experiences of Notre
Dame and leaves the "real" cathedral out of the inquiry. She
simply maintains that different individuals have different
experiences and the presence or absence of necessarily
mediated sensory input does not bear on this issue.

As for catalytic constructivism, Forman fails to recognize that
the generating problems simply form part of the cultural
context in which an individual has experiences. Katz does not
indicate that he thinks these cultural generating problems cause
some event for an individual (although religious traditions often
supply a method to cultivate certain physical states for which
they provide a religious interpretation). Rather, they, as part of
the conceptual background inculcated by the mystic, cause the
nature of the experience. Generating problems form the terms in
which the mystic experiences the event. When Forman questions how a conceptual framework can cause mysticism, he
most clearly demonstrates his confusion about the constructivist
position. The constructivists do not try to account for the
existence of mysticism. They do, however, make suggestions
about the mystical experience.

Before addressing Forman's suggested substitute for the constructivist model, I would like to discuss briefly *some* of his
objections to the constructivist thesis. One of these arguments
concerns the relationship between concepts and experiences.
Forman holds that not all concepts bear directly on every
experience, because in that case one changed concept, however
minor, would change all of an individual's experiences. James,
for one, would certainly not view this consequence with much
dismay. He explicitly and plausibly argued that we never have

the same experience twice. Forman further holds that the constructivist could not account for learning on such a view because learning presupposes a stable set of background experiences. This argument seems reversed to me because one might describe the object of education as changing how one views the background experiences themselves. If however we grant Forman these points and allow that only some concepts affect experience, he makes the further claim that, "If differences in some concepts do not imply changes in mystical experiences, then the perennialist might argue that concepts like *shunyata* and *samadhi* are 'close enough' to claim a parallelism of experience."[15] This conclusion proves unwarranted because only differences in concepts completely irrelevant to mystical experience would allow an assimilation of different mystical experiences. If any concepts could effectively differentiate mystical experiences, these complex, culture-specific, religious concepts would clearly qualify as the most likely candidates. Needless to say, *shunyata* and *samadhi* do resemble each other at some level of generality. The relative similarity of the two concepts should not surprise, however, when we consider that both derive from Indian philosophy and yoga. *Shunyata* and *samadhi* have no greater similarity than, say, Buddhism and Hinduism, and we lump those two under the rubric religion without conflating or reducing their very real differences. In other words, *shunyata* and *samadhi* do exhibit a *general* level of similarity, but the perennialist asks if they denote the *same* experience.

Forman raises a similar objection relating to identity and multiple denotations by invoking Frege's famous distinction between sense and reference. Frege reminded the philosophical community that one reference can support two terms with entirely different senses or meanings. As an example Frege adduced the two terms with different semantic senses, Pole Star and North Star, which refer to the identical celestial body.

---

[15] Forman, "Introduction," p. 17. Simply for the sake of continuity and argumentation, I will disregard here the apparent misuse of these terms in this context. Matthew Kapstein has pointed out to me that *samadhi* is a term used by Hindus and Buddhists alike for a mystical state whose object or property is *shunyata*. My discussion will perpetuate the misleading use in which the terms seem to refer to different experiences in different religions.

Forman suggests that *samadhi* and *shunyata* function in semantically distinct senses, but refer to the identical experience. Forman neglects, however, to notice the equivocation in regard to "identical" in this response. He hopes to support the contention that the Buddhist's experience of *shunyata* is qualitatively identical to the Hindu's experience of *samadhi* whereas Frege's argument holds for cases of quantitative identity. Forman's shift from quantitative identity to qualitative identity sneaks in unobtrusively.

There can be as many terms for such a nonlinguistic event as there can be terms for, say, the North Star, for the relationship between language and that to which it refers is contingent. Thus, logically, it is plausible that there can be many different terms, significances, and so on, *offered for a single mystical experience or experience type.*[16]

Forman's confusion on this point bears on his failure to make the necessary distinction between an event and an experience. If we could discuss the single cause (in theological or religious terms) of the different events, then we would have a case of one reference supporting different senses in different traditions. Instead, however, we have as the object of inquiry a manifold of descriptions of experiences like, for instance, "seeing the Pole Star" and "seeing the North Star" which clearly do not have the same reference.

Forman's crucial failure surfaces again when he considers another objection to constructivism. He borrows Wainwright's example of the Eskimo and the Frenchman who endure different gastrointestinal experiences because of their different cultures. Armed with this analogy, Forman ponders Katz's claims about causation and experience and accuses him of committing the fallacy of *post hoc, ergo propter hoc.* "But that [the fact of different gastrointestinal experiences] does not mean that either their culture or their expectations *caused* those experiences. The relationship between experience and expectation may be contingent, not necessary."[17] Once again Forman fails to distinguish between the event and the experience. The conceptual set of the Eskimo did not, to be sure, necessarily cause any gastro-

---

[16] Ibid., p. 42. Italics added.   [17] Ibid., p. 19.

intestinal events. The conceptual set, however, may well have influenced the particular nature of the experience for the Eskimo. Forman's confusion of the event with the simultaneous experience of the event again leads him to picture constructivism in an absurd manner.

The definition of mysticism adhered to in Forman's volume narrows the discussion greatly. He hopes for the sake of his argument to limit the discussion to what he calls "Pure Consciousness Events" which he, largely informed by personal experience, defines as "wakeful though contentless (nonintentional) consciousness."[18] As indicated above, Forman employs the word "event" (rather than "experience") here to create the illusion of a neutral and objective descriptive term, but his characterization illicitly includes the explanatory commitments of the experiencing mystic (i.e. the possibility of unmediated experience). Forman's use of the term "event" reintroduces the same ambiguity he manifests in his misunderstanding of the term "experience" as Katz and others use it. His definition of mysticism purports to derive solely from description, but implicitly includes explanatory elements. Following Proudfoot and James, I argued in chapter 2 that phenomenological descriptions necessarily always include explanatory commitments.

The first section of *The Problem of Pure Consciousness* attempts to establish conclusively the existence of PCEs by the empirical study of specific religious traditions. Forman accepts this evidence and in his essay attempts to demonstrate that an epistemological framework could not mediate contentless consciousness. He considers the ways that a framework can mediate experience: by imposing form, by providing content, and by continuous, moment-by-moment shaping. With considerable care, he concludes that in the absence of conscious content, the framework cannot determine consciousness (Bernhardt concurs with Forman on this point).[19]

---

[18] Ibid., p. 8.

[19] In perhaps the least convincing article of the volume, Perovich presumes that Katz's position relies on a Kantian foundation. He then delineates the differences between the constructivist position and Kant and finally concludes that because of the variation from Kant's original work constructivism rests on a mistake. Essentially, Perovich, contrary to his presumption, proves Katz isn't Kantian, then uses Katz's

Before considering this conclusion and his further claims in light of Katz's original article, I would like to make three simple observations of my own. First, if the Pure Consciousness Event contains absolutely no conscious content, I fail to see how the mystic could possibly remember anything about the experience. The often vivid recollection of the PCE impugns its contentless nature.[20] Memory of a PCE also threatens the claim that concepts do not mediate the experience of it. To later describe a prior experience means that consciousness assimilated it. To remember an experience an individual must experience it *as* something. The fact that the mystic recalls the experience demonstrates that consciousness catalogued the experience. Even if it catalogued it *as* contentless, consciousness still mediated the experience (which adumbrates my next consideration). Second, Forman fails to consider the possibility that the linguistic framework (including our expectations) conforms so closely to our mental processes and consciousness that even in the event of contentless consciousness the linguistic framework continues to operate and shape experience at a subconscious level. This suggestion seems plausible because of the observable power of the subconscious when we learn from the environment without conscious formulations. James explained such common phenomena through the mechanism of habit. Usually, when we see the sun and identify it as such, we do not make any conscious inference. Our language and belief systems function at a level more fundamental than consciousness. James seeks to convince of at least this much. Third, even if we grant the existence of the PCE, while that would have great repercussions on epistemological or cognitive theory, I see little real advance in the study or practice of religion. The PCE would demonstrate the possibility of a peculiar mental state in humans qualitatively unlike any we currently accept, but what information could it yield about ultimate reality, religious

departures from Kant as grounds for dismissing constructivism. Perovich fails to consider that constructivism can stand independently from Kant.

[20] Correspondence with Jonathan Shear has reminded me to leave this question to psychology.

truths, or, for that matter, mysticism? The religious meaning
of the PCE comes with the religious interpretation of the
PCE. In the end the PCE does little to undermine the
constructivist position.

Forman's approach in substantiating the PCE subjects him to
the very criticisms levied at the early and unsophisticated
scholars of mystical data. His peculiarly limited definition of
mysticism smacks of an illicit move to homogenize diverse data
(in addition to concealing his theoretical commitments). By
designating as mysticism only those experiences which advert to
contentless consciousness, Forman has implicitly made mysticism appear very similar cross-culturally. He has selected particular strains from a vast wealth of differences to create the
appearance of great cross-cultural agreement. Katz addressed
this tendency directly:

The fact is that these lists of supposedly common elements not only
always *reduce* the actual variety of disparate experiences to fit a specific
theory (in each case the context for the terms used being the specific
investigator's own system which varies the lists accordingly and which
demonstrates, if nothing else, that the material can be arranged in
different ways according to alternative ulterior purposes) . . .[21]

By narrowing the field of experiences legitimately labeled
mystical, Forman has artificially strengthened his claim for the
similarity of mystical experiences.

Once Forman has attacked the constructivist position and
delimited the scope of his interests, he explicates his own
methodology for interpreting mystical claims. Unfortunately,
this theory also strongly recalls the early fallacies. He begins this
section of the article with a deceptive procedural claim.
"Rather than beginning with *a priori* epistemological or ontological assumptions, I propose looking at mystical texts."[22] As I
indicated earlier this avowed impartiality masks an implicit
protective strategy designed to preserve the claims of mystics
from explanatory reduction. His pretensions to unbiased study
while obviously quixotic also serve to eliminate the possibility of
explaining the experiences in terms other than those expressed

[21] Katz, "Language," p. 47. Italics original.   [22] Forman, "Introduction," p. 30.

in the texts. Forman may privilege the first-person perspective because of his trust in a simple sort of phenomenology. He asserts that, "In ordinary experiences it is possible (at least in phenomenological theory) to trace out the succession of epistemological processes involved during any period of time. Through introspection one should be able to specify just which connections led from this thought to that one, from this sensation to that perception, and so on."[23] It is rare any longer to find even phenomenologists who believe our epistemic processes so transparent.

Forman and his colleagues also neglect to distinguish fully between explanatory and descriptive reduction.[24] Explanatory reduction is a perfectly legitimate intellectual enterprise which explains an emotion, practice or experience in terms different from those employed by the subject in describing it. Descriptive reduction, by contrast, is the illegitimate identification of an emotion, practice or experience in terms other than those employed by the subject. Forman, in his cross-cultural category of the PCE, has removed experiences from the particular contexts which invest the subjects' reports with meaning while asserting that he preserves their validity. He, in effect, descriptively reduces the experiences while protecting them from explanatory reduction.

Rothberg, likewise, claims, "Katz prejudges ... the question of validity, rejecting implicitly the epistemological frameworks in which many mystical claims find meaning, without making it clear how mystical claims might possibly be valid."[25] In this passage, he clearly misses the point that Katz's "plea for the recognition of differences" and call for "further careful, expert, study of specific mystical traditions ... to uncover what their characteristics are and especially how they relate to the larger theological milieu out of which they emerge ... " more thoroughly preserves the semantic contexts of mystical claims and more vigilantly defends them against descriptive reduction than does the project of assimilating mystical claims to one mystical

---

[23] Ibid., p. 24.   [24] See Proudfoot, *Religious Experience*, ch. VI for this distinction.

[25] Donald Rothberg, "Contemporary Epistemology and the Study of Mysticism," *The Problem of Pure Consciousness* (New York: Oxford University Press, 1990), p. 181.

model (which Rothberg does implicitly by equating claims from different contexts).[26] Rothberg conflates descriptive reduction with explanatory reduction and illicitly charges Katz with inconsistency. "Katz's use of these tools [of Western scholarship] may thus be viewed as, in part, an imposition of recent Western cultural assumptions upon those of other cultures and other epochs, violating Katz's own stricture to respect the inherent differences contained within each tradition."[27] Rothberg fails to distinguish completely explanatory and descriptive reduction and therefore cannot fathom the sympathy to the text that constructivism entails. Intent on protecting what *they* conceive as the central or most significant claims of mystics throughout all times, the scholars in Forman's coterie actually considerably damage the mystics' reports by their inattention to the subtle and culture-relative nature of mystical reports.

In this same vein the authors in Forman's volume defend the primary texts inconsistently. The primary texts often do not impute relativity to ordinary mediated experience (i.e. although the Indian tradition differs, many primary mystical texts don't discuss the epistemological mediation involved in ordinary experience), yet careful to preserve the descriptive, cultural tenor of the text, we overlook this omission and nonetheless treat the text as context relative. In fact, in our "postmodern" age and its quest for universal tolerance we quickly note contextuality. These authors, however, grant mystical experience impunity and insist that even with care to use the descriptive lexicon of the mystic, we cannot "argue against the text" to explain the experience in terms unavailable to the mystic.[28] This prohibition reveals the protective strategy designed to prevent non-mystical explanation.

At the very least Forman's assumption that the mystical texts refer to the same process and experience of contentless consciousness clearly belies his statement that he begins with no "epistemological or ontological assumptions." Again, he mentions this fallacy in his introduction to the history of the topic.

---

[26] Katz, "Language," p. 66.
[27] Rothberg, "Contemporary Epistemology," p. 180.
[28] Bernhardt, "Pure Consciousness Events," p. 228.

Forman then advocates a study of texts to compare the experiences described. The *a priori* supposition that through some hermeneutic the interpreter can reach the experience behind the linguistic and cultural context represents precisely the unsophistication that the consensus of contemporary scholars (including Forman, judging from his introductory historical remarks) has roundly condemned. Forman has simply reintroduced the discarded hermeneutic principle that impelled the entire debate.

Before considering the actual comparisons Forman makes between texts of vastly different cultures, we should note that even the agreement between representatives of different mystical traditions on exactly the same words does not necessarily mean that they refer to the same experience. The fact that an ecumenical colloquy between mystics could agree on the description of the mystical experience as, say, a Pure Consciousness Event, for instance, does not guarantee qualitative identity. Katz comments in "Language, Epistemology, and Mysticism":

> That is to say, what appear to be similar-sounding descriptions are not similar descriptions and do not indicate the same experience. They do not because language is itself contextual and words "mean" only in contexts. The same words ... can apply and have been applied to more than one object. Their mere presence alone does not guarantee anything; neither the nature of the experience nor the nature of the referent nor the comparability of narrow claims is assured by this seemingly verbal presence alone.[29]

Another culture with another whole linguistic and cultural understanding of the words "contentless" and "consciousness," for example, could have a different experience to match the same description. This is not to say that a cross-cultural technical vocabulary of extraordinary experience could not be developed, but only that prior to the development of this lexicon agreement upon the use of similar words in different contexts proves nothing.

With that in mind, Forman's actual textual comparisons appear very weak. He urges a theoretical understanding of mysticism in terms of forgetting and quotes from Eckhart to

[29] Katz, "Language," p. 46.

substantiate his approach. Soon he tries to apply this theoretical framework to another tradition. He chooses Buddhism and quotes at length from Buddhaghosa who writes of a series of "spheres" or steps that the mystic must "transcend." At the end of the quotation, Forman writes: "Here, spelled out in formulaic detail, we have how the practitioner is to successively eliminate, or 'forget,' the defining features of each preceding stage."[30] Without even the slightest explanation, Forman equates "forgetting" with "transcending." Do these terms really mean the same thing or suggest the same process? I submit that even in English they do not, let alone in the different social, linguistic, and historical contexts. For the Neo-platonic Eckhart, we must understand forgetting in the light of successive emanations from the Godhead. Forgetting, in this context, means reversing the direction of emanations to a rebirth in the Godhead. For the Theravadin Buddhaghosa, we must understand transcending in the light of the insubstantiality of conditioned things. Transcending, in this context, means recognizing the insubstantiality of everything. Forgetting refers to pure undivided being and transcending refers to the absence of being. The purported objects of the two experiences preclude a *close* similarity of experience. Surely we cannot assimilate the experiences recommended by these two texts by the nearness in English of two words.

By advocating such a view, Forman entertains the very same errors that he enumerates at the beginning of his article. He makes "naive and methodologically unsound use of primary texts," implicitly claims the ability to "divine" the experience behind the text, and makes an *a priori* assumption about the homogeneity of mystical experiences. Short of refuting Katz's argument as he set out to do, Forman ends as a paradigmatic example of what Katz refers to as the least sophisticated form of the essentialist thesis. "(1) All mystical experiences are the same; even their descriptions reflect an underlying similarity which transcends cultural or religious diversity."[31] The compulsion these authors feel to defend mysticism against a theory that they

---

[30] Forman, "Introduction," p. 33.   [31] Katz, "Language," p. 23.

generally accept for non-mystical experience forces them to embrace a position that entails weaknesses that they often recognize in earlier scholarship. While framed as an advance in the theoretical discussion of mysticism, the view espoused by Forman and his colleagues employs a protective strategy and reverts to an earlier and rightly surpassed stage of the scholarly discussion.

We can hardly view them, therefore, as having seriously endangered the view of experience adopted in chapter 2, that experience always includes mediating explanatory commitments. In the next chapter I examine the views of William Alston who argues that perceptions of God justify beliefs about God. I will object to his account of experience and to his account of justification. They both slight the importance of explanation.

CHAPTER 5

The miracle of minimal foundationalism

Once we accept anyone's postulates he becomes our professor and our god: for his foundations he will grab territory so ample and so easy that, if he so wishes, he will drag us up to the clouds.

Montaigne (1580)[1]

Whereas the balance of this book argues for my preferred view of experience and justification, in this chapter I will survey and evaluate the line of thought which motivates the topic. During the last fifteen years, some philosophers have again enlisted religious experience to justify theism. Two parallel, and until quite recently, largely discrete discussions have appeared in the literature. One exchange centers on Richard Swinburne's discussion of the topic in *The Existence of God*.[2] Both Caroline Franks Davis, a student of Swinburne's at Oxford, and Jerome Gellman have since given Swinburne's approach a fuller and more extensive treatment in book-length studies.[3] The other debate stems from the work of Alvin Plantinga and the Reformed Epistemologists. Whereas Reformed Epistemology generally points to experience as proper justification,[4] William Alston in a series of articles, and, recently, a full-length

---

[1] Michel de Montaigne, *An Apology For Raymond Sebond*, M. A. Screech, tr. (London: Penguin Books, 1987), p. 115.
[2] Richard Swinburne, *The Existence of God* (Oxford: Oxford University Press, 1979), ch. 13 ("The Argument From Religious Experience").
[3] Caroline Franks Davis, *The Evidential Force of Religious Experience* (Oxford: Clarendon Press, 1989); Jerome I. Gellman, *Experience of God and the Rationality of Theistic Belief* (Ithaca: Cornell University Press, 1997).
[4] See Alvin Plantinga, "Reason and Belief in God," *Faith and Rationality*, A. Plantinga and N. Wolterstorff, eds. (Notre Dame: University of Notre Dame Press, 1983), p. 80.

monograph has most explicitly given religious experience consideration as a source of justification for theism.[5]

Initially the uses to which these two camps put religious experience substantially differed. On the one hand, Swinburne, Franks Davis, and Gellman seek evidence with which to bolster an argument for the existence of God. The Reformed Epistemologists, on the other hand, repudiate evidentialism (that rationality requires one to have evidence in support of religious belief) as the legacy of an abandoned classical foundationalist epistemology. Rather than attempting to demonstrate even the probability of God's existence, Alston, in his early essays on this subject, employs religious experience with the more modest intention of defending the rationality of religious belief, that "one's experience can provide justification sufficient for rational acceptance."[6]

Alston's position, however, has increasingly converged with Swinburne's. For instance, on the apparently disputed point about arguments for the existence of God, Alston has lately noted the resemblance between his program and that of Swinburne (*PG*, p. 3n). He specifies that he objects to arguments for the existence of God that appeal to God as the best explanation, rather than allowing for the direct experience of God which both Swinburne and he posit. Interestingly, in the final chapter of *Perceiving God*, Alston also endorses a "cumulative case" approach, Swinburne and Franks Davis's preferred mode of argument, to promote the claim, "we have sufficient reason to take the beliefs [of the Christian tradition] to be *true*" (*PG*, p. 306, italics mine). Ironically and significantly, inference to the best explanation figures prominently here as the other

---

[5] William Alston, "Religious Experience and Religious Belief," *Nous* 16 (1982), pp. 3–12; "Christian Experience and Christian Belief," *Faith and Rationality*, pp. 103–134; "Perceiving God," *Journal of Philosophy* 83 (1986), pp. 655–665; "Religious Diversity and Perceptual Knowledge of God," *Faith and Philosophy* 5 (1988), pp. 433–448; *Perceiving God* (Ithaca: Cornell University Press, 1991).

[6] Alston, "Christian Experience," p. 111. Swinburne champions the rationality of religious belief in *The Coherence of Theism* (Oxford: Oxford University Press, 1987), the companion book to *The Existence of God*. He intended the latter effort to argue positively for the truth of theistic claims, a tactic which the Reformed Epistemologists perceive as epistemologically anachronistic and which they believe unnecessarily commits theism to a defensive posture.

major source of grounds for theism. Alston bears out this increasing interest in providing positive considerations in favor of theism when he comments in his latest work about the limits of Plantinga's "internal" defense and "negative critiques" (*PG*, p. 197).

While the ends to which Alston dedicates his efforts increasingly resemble those of Swinburne, Franks Davis and Gellman, they have all long championed virtually interchangeable epistemologies and strategies. Both Swinburne and Alston approach religious experience as a form of perception similar in certain respects to ordinary sensory perception and conclude that we must respect the mechanism for belief formation in both these instances by granting their deliverances *prima facie* acceptance. Although Alston more pointedly than Swinburne, Franks Davis or Gellman opposes his epistemology to strong or classical foundationalism, all four want to establish basic or fundamental, but yet defeasible principles of belief formation. That is to say, they employ the sort of regulative particularist principles I discussed in chapter 3. Alston generally refers to epistemic "practices," while Swinburne, Franks Davis and Gellman consider epistemic "principles." This difference presents no objection to my claim about the practical indistinguishability of their respective epistemologies because Alston allows for the interchangeability of the terms. He believes that epistemic principles lie embedded but generally unformulated within epistemic practices.[7] Furthermore, in *Perceiving God* he directly addresses the relation of his practices to Swinburne's principle and contends that the active, socially established character of practices bestows additional confirming support to what he correctly interprets as a construal of our epistemological foundations that he largely shares with Swinburne (*PG*, p. 195).

They all openly concede that these basic principles or practices admit of no non-circular justification. Swinburne insists that we must "rely" on "a basic principle not further justifiable" or an "ultimate principle of rationality."[8] Similarly, Franks

---

[7] Alston, "Religious Experience," p. 3n.
[8] Swinburne, *The Existence of God*, pp. 255, 256.

Davis invokes "fundamental principles of rationality."[9] Both view this tactic as necessary to skirt a "sceptical bog." Likewise, Alston posits socially conditioned, basic epistemic practices to evade the traditional epistemological impasses.[10] All commit the mistake reviewed in chapter 3: they embrace particularist principles in the face of a phantom skeptic. In other words, they all, in differing degrees of avowal, want to retain the means for a foundationalist epistemology while jettisoning the implications of a *strong* or *classical* foundationalism (i.e. one which defeats skepticism with justified and indubitable bases).[11] Having thereby undercut the notion of justifying a fundamental principle or practice of belief formation, they attempt to bring beliefs formed in connection with religious experience within the purview of a fundamental epistemic principle or practice.[12]

In this chapter I intend to focus primarily on Alston's work because he has presented a more detailed, thoughtful and stronger account than Swinburne, Franks Davis, or Gellman. Wherever possible within spatial constraints, I will, however, point to Alston's differences from and improvements on the Oxford gambit. After some brief exposition and critical assessment, I will offer my objection to the direction pursued by Swinburne, Alston, Franks Davis, and Gellman. While the types of objections hitherto appearing in the philosophical literature all attack the experiential justification of religious knowledge from within the same general epistemological theory as the proponents and, therefore, on their home turf so to speak, I will follow Montaigne's implied counsel and object to the very

---

[9]   Franks Davis, *Evidential Force*, p. 100.

[10] Alston, "Christian Experience," pp. 108–109.

[11] Gellman correctly observes that his fundamental principles are compatible with a coherentist epistemology. Although fundamental epistemic principles more naturally belong in a foundationalist epistemology, we noted in the second section of chapter 3 that they can appear in a coherentist epistemology unnecessarily influenced by skepticism. This point undermines nothing crucial, so I will continue to describe particularist principles as part of a foundationalist epistemology.

[12] Although less explicit about its foundational status, another American, Keith Yandell, also promotes "a unified *principle of experiential evidence*" to justify belief in "a numinous being." *The Epistemology of Religious Experience* (Cambridge: Cambridge University Press, 1993), pp. 37, 274. Italics original.

epistemology which Swinburne and Alston embrace before they "drag us up to the clouds." In fact, the epistemology they employ functions as a protective strategy. This conclusion accords with my claim in chapter 3 that particularist principles prove too conservative. Both camps have referred to the judicial model as ideal and wish to saddle the skeptic with the burden of proof. In other words, they propose we (including non-theists) consider perceptions of God innocent (veridical) until proven guilty (non-veridical). The epistemology to which they subscribe, "minimal foundationalism," enables their project. This result, that they can describe beliefs based on religious experience as the product of an unjustifiable yet fundamental principle of rationality or a basic epistemic practice on a par with others of uncontroversial and more mundane character, signals one very significant way in which minimal foundation-alism is not consequentially "indistinguishable" from anti-foundationalism as Jeffrey Stout suggests.[13] Finally, I hope to point to some well-known criticisms of foundationalism which impugn minimal foundationalism as well as strong foundationalism.

In his articles and book, Alston portrays religious experience as a type of non-sensory perception[14] and rejects non-circular means of justifying basic principles of rationality. In contrast to Swinburne, he allows for a variety of basic or fundamental principles of perceptual belief formation rather than just one (he calls them doxastic practices). At one point early in *Perceiving God*, Alston briefly proposes the broad sort of principle advo-cated by Swinburne and represented in his "Principle of Credulity." Compare Alston, "(II) If S's belief that X is Ø is based on an experience in which, so it seems to S, X is appearing to S as Ø, then that belief is prima facie justified" (*PG*, p. 100) to Swinburne, "(in the absence of special considera-

---

[13] Jeffrey Stout, *The Flight from Authority* (Notre Dame: University of Notre Dame Press, 1981), p. 36.

[14] In *Perceiving God* Alston changes his preferred term from "religious experience" to "mystical perception." His fundamental view remains unaltered despite the lexical shift. The ambiguities in "religious experience" motivate the change. Aware of similar difficulties with "mystical," Alston limits "mystical" to (especially non-sensory) experiences with God perceptibly present as the object of consciousness.

tions) if it seems (epistemically) to a person that X is present, then probably X is present; what one seems to perceive is probably so."[15] Immediately, however, Alston ruefully acknowledges the influence of background beliefs on the formation of perceptual beliefs and resorts to his depiction of myriad socially established practices of belief formation. This pluralism greatly enhances the facility with which Alston can dismiss most objections to his position. He believes that although religious experience represents a type of perception, it entails a different doxastic practice from sensory perception. No basic doxastic practice, however, can justify itself. Therefore, all basic doxastic practices share similar epistemic footing. Naturalistic explanations of religious experience or invidious comparisons of religious perception to sense perception represent from this perspective a mere epistemic chauvinism or imperialism because they arbitrarily employ one ungrounded practice to subvert another.[16]

Alston seems to view our epistemic situation in terms of alternatives explicitly drawn by Swinburne and Franks Davis. Ostensibly, we can either (1) employ the doxastic practice based on sensory perceptual experience but not the one based on religious perceptual experience, although we have no noncircular way to justify either practice. This alternative unenviably requires a non-circular reason for privileging sensory experience over other sorts of experience. Or, (2) employ neither practice, because we have no non-circular means of

---

[15] Swinburne, *The Existence of God*, p. 254. Swinburne invokes Chisholm's distinction between the epistemic and comparative use of words such as "seems." The epistemic use describes "what the subject is inclined to believe on the basis of his present sensory experience." The comparative use notes a similarity in "the way an object looks with the way other objects normally look" (p. 246). Although I will not draw further attention to it, the tremendous debt owed to Chisholm by Swinburne and Alston should become apparent throughout the course of this exposition.

[16] Peter Losin, "Experience of God and the Principle of Credulity: A Reply to Rowe," *Faith and Philosophy* 4 (1987), pp. 59–70, and Michael Levine, "Mystical Experience and Non-Basically Justified Belief," *Religious Studies* 25 (1990), pp. 335–345 echo Alston on this point. Both believe that the criteria for adjudicating claims based on religious experience must derive from the stock of accepted claims based on religious experience and the community who practice the belief-forming practice (although Levine does not regard beliefs resulting from religious experience as properly basic beliefs).

justifying them, and consequently landing in a "sceptical bog." In a passage on our inability to justify our doxastic practices, he writes,

[I]t would seem that we are confined to either taking all of them to be acceptable (i.e. regarding them as reliable) or taking all of them to be unacceptable. It would be arbitrary to distinguish between them. Clearly, abstention from all such practices is not a live option; therefore the only rational alternative open to us is to accord prima facie acceptance to all basic socially established practices (regard them as prima facie reliable), pending a demonstration of unreliability, or the invocation of any other disqualifying consideration.[17]

Alston pictures the choice as one between total skepticism on the one hand, and, on the other, accepting all basic doxastic practices, including those pertaining to perceptual beliefs derived from religious experience, unless they prove somehow unreliable.

Because we have no means of non-circularly justifying a doxastic practice, Alston claims that we cannot suppose any of them J_{ns} or "Justified in the normative sense on the stronger requirement."[18] By that he means that in fulfilling our intellectual obligations we cannot advance reasons to justify or support our practice if we deem practices guilty until proven innocent. In his early articles he maintains that we can, however, label our practices J_{nw} or justified in the normative sense on the weaker requirement, if we have no sufficient reasons to regard them as unreliable. In *Perceiving God* he modifies his conception of justification so as to preclude the justification of doxastic practices in any normative sense. This later understanding of justification he labels "nondeontological" because rather than settling for the fulfillment of epistemic obligations it requires for justification that a belief "be in a *strong position* for realizing the epistemic aim of getting the truth" (*PG*, p. 73). On this "truth-conducive" rendering of justification, we can no longer non-circularly demonstrate the justification of a doxastic practice. To restore the desideratum (the justification of beliefs based on doxastic practices), Alston

17 Alston, "Religious Diversity," p. 437.
18 Alston, "Religious Experience," p. 7.

relies on a complicated hierarchy of logical levels. He responds to the higher-level question about the reliability of a socially established doxastic practice in terms of practical rationality. He eschews the attempt to justify practices and instead demonstrates the rationality of assuming the reliability of those doxastic practices which do not demonstrate large scale discrepancies with the outputs of other doxastic practices. With this foundation Alston can maintain that on the lower level of individual beliefs, the level in which our interest lies, we can rationally suppose beliefs based on the doxastic practice *prima facie* justified. Alston performs this distinction employing the language and logic of adequacy assumptions (*PG*, p. 86). In order for a belief to be justified, we need not possess the means of justifying our further belief (assumption) that the basis of the belief in question proves sufficient (adequate); the assumption need only, in fact, obtain. Accordingly, if practical rationality suggests supposing the doxastic practice reliable, rationality prompts us to suppose the beliefs produced by that practice *prima facie* justified.

Doxastic practices differ according to the variety of experiences that serve as inputs, the variety of input-output functions – the particular mechanism by which we arrive at a judgment – and the variety of "checks and tests" employed to assess the resultant beliefs ("overrider system"). (Different doxastic practices also entail distinct means of "self-support." The output of doxastic practices can provide confirming evidence of their reliability. Sense perception, for instance, enables prediction and control. While undeniably circular, this phenomenon nonetheless indicates reliability because the practices simply of themselves don't necessitate such favorable results.) The thoroughly social character of doxastic practices leads to the recognition of a diversity of practices, including variations in doxastic practices concerning religious experience in different religions. Alston wants to defend the following doxastic practice within the Christian community: "P. The experience (or, as I prefer to say, the 'perception' of God) provides prima facie epistemic justification for beliefs about what God is doing or how God is 'situated' *vis-à-vis* one at the moment ('M-beliefs', 'M' for 'manifestation')."[19] He believes that the M-beliefs arrived at in the Christian community through the Christian doxastic practice exhibit *prima facie* justification. Importantly and perceptively, Alston notes that doxastic practices do not work in complete isolation from one another. They rely on each other for both input and information with which to override a belief.[20] People share certain doxastic practices across religions and, generally, doxastic practices interrelate in their functioning. He pictures the various outputs of epistemic mechanisms as reinforcing one another.

This phenomenon of "reciprocal support" appears according to Alston in both antifoundational epistemologies and his own "modest foundationalism" (*PG*, p. 300). Such an observation, however, delivers the requisite purchase to criticize Alston's epistemology. Certain shared doxastic practices which work in conjunction with the religious doxastic practices might not only reciprocally support one another, indeed they might also provide the necessary common ground to assess the individual outputs of religious doxastic practices. Teresa, as we shall see, freely relied on the judgments of sense perception and other "doxastic practices" when she evaluated her religious experiences. She lived in a cosmos permeated with the supernatural and had no reason to isolate protectively her spiritual faculties. Alston, however, must defensively and unrealistically partition religious perception from the remainder of our epistemic life. His account of doxastic practices pictures them as too unimpeachable and far too isolated from one another in our overall epistemological functioning. In fact, the complexity and interrelatedness of the epistemological elements involved in acquiring beliefs leads me to question the motivation for thinking in terms of basic principles or practices at all.

Unsurprisingly, Alston cites Wittgenstein's *On Certainty* as the inspiration for his doxastic practice conception. In this regard his interpretation of Wittgenstein resembles the regrettable

---

[19] Alston, "Religious Diversity," p. 434.
[20] Ibid., pp. 435–436.

alternate language-games approach championed by Malcolm[21] and Phillips.[22] Alston's effort to insulate religious belief-forming mechanisms as much as possible from their more mundane counterparts recalls Malcolm's desire to protect religious forms of life from external critique. Gary Gutting in rebutting Malcolm and Phillips reasonably concludes that "religions do not constitute our basic forms of life but rather criticize and transform them."[23] Similarly, I would, without taking the space to mount an argument, simply observe that the sorts of beliefs which emanate from Alston's religious doxastic practices don't much resemble the sorts of groundless beliefs that Wittgenstein viewed as encrusted in the bedrock girding our form of life. Finally, the alternate language-games approach does not pay sufficient heed to the holistic nature of language (the discovery of which, ironically, we often attribute to Wittgenstein). The meaning of the words in a language is a function of the beliefs they are used to express. Different doxastic practices, moreover, operate within a shared language. This fact suggests that doxastic practices cannot be strongly isolated because they work together to invest a language with meaning. That any sentence can only be uttered meaningfully in certain contexts does nothing to counter the fact that the meaning of a word is a function of beliefs and that most words appear, without change of meaning, in multiple doxastic practices. The nature of language itself undermines the segregation of doxastic practices.

Charles Larmore once remarked that everyone has his own Wittgenstein, but Bernard Williams, with equal truth, recently noted that most interpretations of Wittgenstein evince a decid-

---

[21] Norman Malcolm, "The Groundlessness of Belief," S. Brown, ed., *Reason and Religion* (Ithaca: Cornell University Press, 1977). Alston's early views on religion and language-games appear in "The Christian Language-Game," *The Autonomy of Religious Belief*, Frederick Crosson, ed. (Notre Dame: University of Notre Dame Press, 1981), pp. 128–162.

[22] D. Z. Phillips, *Faith and Philosophical Inquiry* (London: Routledge & Kegan Paul, 1970), ch. 5.

[23] Gary Gutting, *Religious Belief and Religious Skepticism* (Notre Dame: University of Notre Dame Press, 1982), p. 77. Nancy Frankenberry, *Religion and Radical Empiricism* (Albany: SUNY Press, 1987) and Proudfoot both condemn the alternate language-games approach for its excessively conservative stance. See also Richard Gale, *On the Nature and Existence of God* (Cambridge: Cambridge University Press, 1991), p. 296.

edly conservative bent. What he calls "Right Wittgenstein-ianism" emphasizes the ongoing, functioning character of culture and minimizes the opportunities for cultural critique.[24] Alston's "Wittgensteinian" effort to segregate and buttress areas of culture by highlighting ongoing, functioning practices of arriving at beliefs exemplifies "Right Wittgensteinianism." My approach to investigating or assessing culture or epistemology more resembles "Left Wittgensteinianism." Williams describes "Left Wittgensteinianism" as an historically self-conscious anti-foundationalism which leaves "room for a critique of what some of 'us' do in terms of our understanding of a wider 'we'."[25] Williams here endorses the sort of approach I under-take in this book, to critique the beliefs of some of "us" through historical understanding and values "we" share.

Although Swinburne does not avail himself of this "Right Wittgensteinian" strategy, he and Alston share a foundationalist epistemology while repudiating strong foundationalism. By employing a minimal foundationalism, they reap benefits in two ways. First, they can posit or formulate wholesale particularist principles which force those suspicious of religious experience to grant it at least initial respectability until somehow defeated. Second, they avoid the easy evidentialist condemnation of religious experience possible with strong foundationalist empirical epistemologies. The criticism of their work in the philosophical literature all implicitly (or sometimes explicitly) grants this foundationalist epistemology. Michael Martin[26] and William Rowe,[27] for instance, both propose restricting Swin-burne's Principle of Credulity. As it stands, they believe it vulnerable to what Martin calls the objection from gullibilism. It grants *prima facie* justification to beliefs about elves, demons, ghosts, etc. They suggest restrictions on the Principle that acknowledge the conditions under which experiences occur and

---

[24] Bernard Williams, "Left-Wing Wittgenstein, Right-Wing Marx," *Common Knowledge* 1 (1992), pp. 33–42.

[25] Ibid., p. 41.

[26] Michael Martin, "The Principle of Credulity and Religious Experience," *Religious Studies* 22 (1987), pp. 79–93.

[27] William Rowe, "Religious Experience and the Principle of Credulity," *International Journal for Philosophy of Religion* 16 (1984), pp. 189–202.

under which one could conclusively expect them not to occur. These additions qualify the Principle in a manner that leaves it intact for sensory experience, but removes religious experience from its protection. In a sense, Martin and Rowe simply isolate and challenge the idea behind the argument from experience. Swinburne and Alston posit an analogy between religious perception and sense perception, positioning the latter in the paradigmatic role. Martin and Rowe insist that religious perception exhibit features analogous to those of sense perception before granting it the epistemic approbation accorded to sense perception.

In essence, they highlight the significant disanalogies between sense perception and religious perception. Alston designed his pluralism to trump this "chauvinistic" expectation that all doxastic practices conform to one model. Richard Gale, however, alerts us to the seduction perpetrated by Alston here. Alston believes that if he can explain why doxastic practices differ, the disanalogy between them proves benign. Exasperated, Gale writes, "Again, we find Alston committing the fallacy of thinking that if he can give a categoreally based explanation for a disanalogy between the religious- and sense-experience doxastic practices, it renders the disanalogy harmless. This should be called the 'Alston fallacy'."[28] Alston wants it both ways. The similarities between religious perception and sense perception license the epistemic respectability of religious perception, while the differences, suitably explained by the nature of the faculty, remain innocuous. In rejoinder to Gale, he argues that only certain features of religious perception, like the fact that it is socially established, need resemble sense perception for religious perception to be rationally acceptable (*PG*, pp. 223–224). Gale's original observation, that this tactic reverts upon scrutiny to a reprehensible, anything-goes sort of language-game fideism, seems borne out here.

Although I find Gale's critique compelling, I wish to pursue a more radical approach. As Montaigne suggests, the most promising strategy for undermining Alston's conclusions concen-

---

[28] Gale, *Nature and Existence*, pp. 322–323.

trates on his premises. While I too reject strong foundationalism, I also believe that minimal foundationalism with its
particularist principles extends to whole classes of beliefs a *prima
facie* justification which a truly antifoundationalist epistemology
(i.e. one not shaped by skepticism) would not permit. For this
reason, I believe (as I intimate above) minimal foundationalism
results in an elaborate protective strategy. It protects beliefs
based on religious experiences from reduction, explanation,
and criticism.

The frequent references to the principle of jurisprudence,
"innocent until proven guilty," signal Alston and Swinburne's
protective intentions. In judicial reasoning we employ this tenet
in our system, not because of its *a priori* necessity, but because
we wish to *protect* the accused individual as much as feasible
from mistaken prosecution and punishment. As evidence from
other legal systems attests, our priorities could differ. Whereas
in our system we primarily aim to protect the innocent at the
expense of potentially permitting the guilty to go unpunished,
other systems could reverse these preferences. The scholars who
propose that we consider religious perception "innocent until
proven guilty" should explain why we should wish to protect
religious perception in this manner. (Ironically, Alston at one
point poses a rhetorical query similarly pertaining to the
relevance of political values to epistemological matters. He asks,
"Why this predilection for egalitarianism in the epistemic
sphere, where its credentials are much less impressive than in
the political sphere?" [*PG*, p. 169]Why indeed?)

A convincing argument in favor of minimal foundationalism
would obviate this requirement, but to date none appears in the
literature of religious experience. In *Perceiving God* Alston, while
for the most part "setting coherentism [what I often refer to in
this chapter as antifoundationalism] aside without a hearing"
(*PG*, p. 75), offers what we can formulate as two indirect
arguments for minimal foundationalism. Unfortunately, neither
successfully demonstrates the superiority of minimal foundationalism to antifoundationalism. One tack explains his dismissal of coherentism or holism in favor of his "linear"
epistemology. Coherentism or holism holds that any particular

belief finds its ground only from the subject's entire set or web of beliefs. A linear model, on the other hand, points to specific experiences or certain other relevant beliefs as a localized ground for a particular belief. The other tack arises in his defense of direct realism, a position I regard as integral, indeed fundamental, to his linear epistemology. Perceptual experience for a direct realist accounts for one of the possible grounds for a belief; one can on this view distinguish any conceptualization of experience from the direct givenness of the object.

In the first indirect argument Alston rejects coherentism on familiar grounds, because of the possibility of innumerable "mutually incompatible" but individually coherent sets of beliefs about the world. He demurs from expanding on this charge, however, because he believes we can justify religious beliefs more easily on a coherentist schema. He believes his linear epistemology toes the more difficult line. We should remember, however, his intentions in this project: he wishes to justify religious beliefs to the non-theist. Alston correctly surmises that justification of religious beliefs comes quite easily on a coherentist model, but I might add that this justification extends only to those who share the set of beliefs. In other words, on a coherentist epistemology, the theist cannot justify religious beliefs to the non-theist because they hold different standards of justification. The non-theist's set of beliefs won't allow justified beliefs about God. My views about justification in chapter 3, however, should indicate my hesitation to subordinate rational justification to the peculiar beliefs of an individual. I should here refer, therefore, to the more ingenuous argument I offered there.

Justification, I argued, necessitates the public exchange of explanatory reasons, the judgment of which relies on the ultimate values of human flourishing embraced by a community. This model includes an appeal to coherence, but repudiates any criterial conception of justification. Without delving further into issues elaborated earlier, I simply hope to demonstrate that on my model Alston cannot so blithely dismiss an antifoundationalist epistemology. To do so he would at least have to show the non-theist that the explanations informing perceptual experience of God potentially cohere with our deepest cultural values and assumptions. Ultimately, one's stance with regard to this last issue, yea or nay, will largely determine one's response to Swinburne and Alston's project. In chapter 7 I will strive to convince that the supernatural explanations covertly constituting mystical perception do not conform to our values. To accomplish his aim of justifying religious beliefs to the non-theist, therefore, Alston actually embraces the epistemology more conducive to his project, regardless of the type of coherence theory posed as opposition. This conclusion follows naturally from the consideration that any linear epistemology with its localized ground of justification isolates and thereby protects beliefs formed on one basis from those formed on another (within the limits established by potential overriders). Alston needs then, contrary to his assertion, to demonstrate more thoroughly why his linear, minimal foundationalist epistemology more plausibly obtains. Given the conclusions of chapter 3, he faces no easy task. His simple dismissal of coherentism proves insufficient.

Alston's defense of direct realism, the theory that perception entails direct awareness of and access to its objects, obviously has close affinities to his endorsement of a linear epistemology because perception of this sort would clearly provide probative grounds for beliefs based on it. In criticizing the opposition to direct realism, we might interpret Alston as indirectly arguing in favor of his linear epistemology. Unfortunately, he misapprehends the assertions of those who deny direct realism. Alston's conception of perception involves the presentation of an object to experience and his direct realism holds that "we mean what we assert to be true of realities that are what they are regardless of what we or other human beings believe of them" (*PG*, p. 4). This combination allows him to make the counter-intuitive and dubious point that we can be genuinely *aware* of God without necessarily understanding our experience this way (*PG*, p. 11). Wayne Proudfoot has rightly called attention to the imprecision of the term "experience" in philosophical parlance. "Experience" and by extension "awareness" harbor an ambiguity between a phenomenological sense and a causal sense. To distinguish, I reserve "experience" or "awareness" for a phenomenological description and employ "event" to refer to the physical cause of an experience. Non-veridical experiences produce awarenesses incompatible with the corresponding events. For instance, if I present you with a pen and you claim to perceive a pencil, I would not allow that you manifest awareness of a pen. Obviously, you manifest awareness of something, even something qualitatively quite close to a pen, but your experience doesn't warrant the ascription "awareness of a pen." On the contrary, you exhibit erroneous awareness of a pencil. I believe Alston's insistence on direct realism causes him to blur the distinction between the event of an object's presentation and the experience of the presentation. In other words, like Forman he commits the psychologist's fallacy. To review, it occurs when the psychologist allows her knowledge of a situation or her perspective on the situation to color her conclusions about her subject's experience of the situation. Many of Alston's central confusions pertain to forms of this fallacy. One manifestation of this carelessness with regard to presentations and experiences of presentations surfaces in Alston's misconstrual of his opponents' position.

Alston seems to believe that those who repudiate direct realism and believe that concepts or interpretation mediate all experience view experience as identical in structure to inferring the presence of something unobserved from other observed facts (e.g. like inferring unseen fire from visible smoke). In fact, he contrasts his notion of direct "appearance" to "judgment" (*PG*, p. 187). He charges that the pragmatists and recent scholars of religious experience confuse "direct awareness of an object, X and awareness of X *as* possessing some property, P (or the knowledge or justified belief, *that* the object has P)" (*PG*, p. 38). Alston maintains that direct awareness comprises some identifiable element of all perception because he believes that interpreted experience would lose its presented or given character and the subject could not in that case distinguish perception from imagination or abstract thought (*PG*, pp. 27, 38). Here Alston crucially fails to distinguish the event of presentation from the experience of the event. Those who deny direct realism do not deny the fact of the event which produces an experience, nor its presented character, but rather, claim that the experience of the event necessarily includes conceptualization. Steven Katz, for one, has referred to his view as "mediated immediacy" and urges that we not consider mediation the "obverse or disjunctive" of the phenomenological immediacy of experience.[29] All our experiences occur with non-inferential or non-deliberative immediacy to consciousness, but nonetheless involve a mediation of sorts in that concepts and beliefs condition the immediate experience.

Alston exhibits a similar misunderstanding of Wayne Proudfoot's position when he argues that Proudfoot errs in the claim that any identification of an experience as religious entails concepts like, for instance, a commitment to a theological explanation of the experience. In opposition to Proudfoot's position, Alston declares:

> From the fact that we use concepts to identify something as of a certain type (How else?!), it does *not* follow that *what* we are identifying "involves" concepts and judgements ... From the fact that we use a concept to pick out cabbages as vegetables, it does not follow that cabbages are, have, or use concepts or judgements. (*PG*, p. 41)

We could not ask for a clearer indication that Alston has neglected to distinguish between the event of a presentation to consciousness and the experience of this presentation. Proudfoot would not ludicrously insist that cabbages have concepts. Rather, he contends that our experience of a cabbage if so identified by us obviously and necessarily draws on the concept "cabbage."

Importantly, despite this flawed defense of direct realism, Alston concedes the most important point. "But I am acknowledging that X's looking (sounding ...) P to one *can be influenced* by S's knowledge, beliefs and conceptualizations, even though X's looking a certain way to S does not consist in S knowing or believing something about it or conceptualizing it in a certain

---

[29] Steven Katz, in a talk delivered at Columbia University, April 7, 1991. Ironically, Alston finds an unrelated use for the same phrase, "mediated immediacy." George Mavrodes includes in *Belief in God* (New York: Random House, 1981), p. 65, a clear discussion of the issues of phenomenological immediacy.

way" (*PG*, pp. 38–39). In the main I believe that those against whom Alston argues would acquiesce in this assertion and that Alston misunderstands his opponents (and sets up straw men) when he characterizes them as he does in the second clause of this passage. All would concur, for instance, that someone completely unfamiliar with either the concept "cabbage" or actual cabbages can nonetheless perceptually encounter an object we would call a cabbage. Proudfoot simply asserts that this culinary and agricultural naïf could not experience a cabbage *per se* with its various associations. Other concepts (an emphasis on form, color, texture or perhaps other associations) would "influence" both the experience and how the subject describes it.

Similarly, anyone might undergo the event which leads some, employing certain highly articulated concepts, to the experience of God's presence. Others might have an entirely unreligious experience in the same manner that the culinary and agricultural naïf can experience the "cabbage-event" as an experience unrelated to cabbages. Presumably, Alston's preference for the term "mystical perception" relates to the fact that it accentuates the parallel to the case of the cabbage where we unstintingly grant the existence of an object independent of our concepts and involved in the event producing the experience. The term "religious experience," conversely, does not immediately focus attention on an external object and leaves the nature of the event corresponding to the experience unspecified. Alston, trading on his failure adequately to distinguish events and experiences, wants to slip the complex concept, God, into a position analogous to the uncontroversial one occupied by the object sensed in ordinary perception. To say the least, therefore, we cannot deem Alston to have vindicated direct realism and therefore neither can we suppose that he has supplied positive reasons to prefer his minimal foundationalism to anti-foundationalism.

Conversely, we do possess positive reasons for rejecting minimal foundationalism, reasons related to the psychologist's fallacy and indicting direct realism. To its detriment minimal foundationalism extends over too wide a range of beliefs and traps us by forcing us to concede that certain beliefs gain credibility by their origin. "Thus a belief is justified because the circumstances of its formation are *of a certain kind* and are related in a certain way to the content of that belief."[30] Antifoundationalism, on the other hand, only allows a belief to gain support or justification from within the web of other beliefs *we actually hold*. It abjures epistemic principles in favor of an incessantly revised web of belief. Following the direction offered by Wilfrid Sellars and Richard Rorty in their critiques of strong foundationalism, I would argue that the minimal foundationalists in their direct realism continue to confuse the causal antecedents to knowledge with an attempt to justify knowledge. The non-cognitive objects and events in the world do not necessarily correspond in some metaphysically isomorphic way to our inherently linguistic assertions and beliefs. Objects and events can antecedently cause our beliefs through presentation, but the specific content and the justification of the beliefs derive completely from within sets of beliefs and languages.

Epistemological holism of the sort advocated by Rorty and Sellars recognizes that evidential force and justification pertain to languages and systems of beliefs (i.e. "the space of reasons"), not to the causal relations between human beliefs and events in the world. Rorty explains:

> The crucial premise of this argument is that there is no such thing as a justified belief which is non-propositional, and no such thing as justification which is not a relation between propositions. So to speak of our acquaintance with redness or with an instantiation of redness as "grounding" (as opposed to being a causal condition of) our knowledge that "this is a red object" or that "redness is a color" is always a mistake.[31]

The fact, then, that our present beliefs lead us to certain new beliefs in a perceptual situation does not give us warrant to suppose that the fact of perception itself confers any justification. The justification must come in weighing the new beliefs against other beliefs. Presentation, therefore, can cause a

---

[30] Alston, "Christian Experience," p. 110.
[31] Richard Rorty, *Philosophy and the Mirror of Nature* (Princeton: Princeton University Press, 1979), pp. 182–183.

belief, but it could never justify it. There exist no self-justifying experiences which require initial credulity; we have no reason to grant *prima facie* justification to any belief. While the minimal foundationalists evince varying degrees of awareness of the extent to which language pervades experience, they nonetheless want to offer the causal origin of a belief in perception as means of its justification. Rorty, of course, views this confusion as the source of the entire epistemological enterprise.

Sellars in "Empiricism and the Philosophy of Mind" arrives at this holist antifoundationalism by way of the position he labels "psychological nominalism." This "denial that there is any awareness of logical space prior to, or independent of, the acquisition of a language" constitutes the recognition that the foundationalist epistemology of direct realism involves the error for which I have borrowed James's term, the psychologist's fallacy.[32] Sellars observes that:

> [W]hen we picture a child – or a carrier of slabs – learning his *first* language, *we*, of course, locate the language learner in a structural logical space in which we are at home. Thus, we conceive of him as a person (or, at least, a potential person) in a world of physical objects, coloured, producing sounds, existing, in Space and Time. But though it is *we* who are familiar with this logical space, we run the danger, if we are not careful, of picturing the language learner as having *ab initio* some degree of awareness – "pre-analytic," limited and fragmentary though it may be – of this same logical space.[33]

We attribute our linguistically structured experiences to the prelinguistic child and suppose that this common "pre-analytic" experience provides a ground or base for justification. Sellars's psychological nominalism, in rejoinder, pays heed to the extensive stage setting (to maintain the Wittgensteinian motif) involved in the epistemic awareness of properties or objects. For someone to achieve sapient awareness (as opposed to mere sentient awareness) of a property or object, he must of necessity invoke the mastery of both the concept of the property or object noticed and other concepts by which to properly

---

[32] Wilfrid Sellars, "Empiricism and the Philosophy of Mind," *Science, Perception and Reality* (London: Routledge & Kegan Paul, 1963), p. 162.

[33] Ibid., p. 161.

discriminate the property or object. Sellars, thereby, undermines the direct realist notion of prelinguistic or unconceptua-
lized awareness of properties or objects because "*all* awareness
of *sorts, resemblances, facts* etc., in short all awareness of abstract
entities – indeed, all awareness even of particulars – is a
linguistic affair."[34]

Unfortunately, Alston tries to assimilate causal presentations
outside the normative space of reasons to *awarenesses* within the
logical space of facts and concepts. He wants to distinguish
direct awareness of objects and properties from inferential
awareness and claim that the direct awareness grounds knowledge. Direct awareness, however, if it is sapient awareness,
presupposes a whole battery of concepts inferentially related to
one another. Direct awareness of an object or property implicitly presupposes an endorsed claim about those inferential
implications. Such a claim transcends the range of causes and
enters the realm of reasons. In chapter 2 we explored how
William James dedicated himself to exploding the myth he saw
propagated by both empiricism and idealism that the presented
element of perception can be abstracted from the cognitive
element and used to ground knowledge. Alston succumbs to the
myth and claims that the presentation, abstracted from any
conceptualization, grounds the justification of perceptual
beliefs.

It regrettably complicates the issues that the passages in
Perceiving God where he describes his position appear inconsistent. At one point he claims his theory holds that "what
perception *is* is the awareness of something's appearing to one
as such-and-such, where this is a basic, unanalyzable relationship,
not reducible to conceptualizing an object as such-and-such, or
to judging or believing the object to be such-and-such" (*PG*,
p. 5). At another he distinguishes "direct awareness of an
object, X and awareness of X *as* possessing some property, P"
(*PG*, p. 38). Even if we reconcile these passages (as I believe we
should) to suggest that Alston views perception as non-
inferential awareness of an object or property, he nonetheless

[34] Ibid., p. 160.

conflates the causal presentation of an object to sense with awareness within the normative space of reasons. He commits the psychologist's fallacy and supposes that the event of sensory stimulation provides justification for beliefs based on the experience. Gellman makes this move in even clearer fashion. While acknowledging that, in addition to instinctive brain processing, perceptual recognition exhibits the features of a human practice, he nonetheless goes so far as to claim that in virtue of the instinctive process "[an organism] is *justified* in taking what it experiences as the object it is."[35] The ambiguity cited above between phenomenological and epistemological immediacy contributes to the difficulty here because the causal presentation, while not producing epistemological immediacy, clearly leads to a phenomenologically immediate experience. Nevertheless, we must insist with Sellars and Rorty that any justification of beliefs formed in perceptual situations occurs not because of the experience of causal presentation, but because of the belief's normative relation to other facts and beliefs within the space of reasons.

One indication of the centrality of direct realism to both Alston's and Swinburne's endeavor lies in their careful treatment of explanation. They each feel they must distinguish experiential evidence or justification for theistic belief from the other sorts of evidence or justification which all involve an inference to the best explanation.[36] Alston claims that we can reduce the major sources of grounds for theism to two main categories: religious perception and inference to the best explanation (including forms of revelation and all the arguments of natural theology except the ontological). Despite an offhand remark adverting to the underestimated strength of natural theology, Alston generally admits that the support for theistic claims generated by explanation remains weak and looks to the welcome and significant corroboration lent by direct perception of God.

If one is confined to what we might call these external sources of belief

[35] Gellman, *Experience of God*, p. 37. Italics added.
[36] Gutting joins them in both this assessment and the use of putative religious perception as a justification of theism.

(external to the experience of a contemporary person), a reflective intelligent individual, alive to various critical questions that have been aired concerning the Christian tradition and its traditional supports, may well feel uncertain about its credentials. (*PG*, p. 302)

An "actual encounter," however, can completely countervail such "questionable inferences from questionable data" to provide an "assurance not subject to doubts about the cogency of explanation and other influences" (*PG*, p. 303). Swinburne similarly emphasizes the explanatory element of the traditional arguments and construes the probabilities in the case for theism so as to give the argument from religious experience the decisive weight. He believes that the combined evidence from the other arguments for the existence of God must comprise a probability "very low indeed" if the testimony of those who have perceived God cannot push the probability beyond one half.[37]

The reluctant admission by both Swinburne and Alston that the explanatory power of theism remains insufficient for justification renders comprehensible the strong attachment to direct realism and minimal foundationalism. They gladly harness explanation when convenient, but their project turns on their ability to vindicate the perception of God and elevate it above the status of an explanatory claim. Alston, therefore, explicitly denies that perception involves an embedded causal explanation. In several places he distances his direct realism from theories of perception that call attention to the resemblance between a perceptual belief and an explanans. "From this standpoint the support given by a perceptual experience of X as Ø to the belief that X is Ø stands in sharp contrast to the support provided by explanatory considerations" (*PG*, p. 288). O'Hear and Proudfoot both urge, and I would concur, that we should view any perceptual belief as an endorsed proposition within the space of reasons (as Sellars would say) with an embedded causal claim (as Proudfoot would say) and subject to justification in terms of explanatory value. We evaluate a belief's implicit claim as the best explanation from the standpoint of our ultimate cultural values. Rather than two

---

[37] Swinburne, *The Existence of God*, p. 274.

categories of grounds – experience *and* explanation – perhaps we should register only one.

Alston's ambition to exploit inference to the best explanation while simultaneously propounding the heterogeneousness of direct perception produces a profound tension in *Perceiving God*. As noted above he declares his dissatisfaction with "arguments from religious experience" which rely on inference to the best explanation rather than allowing for direct perception of God. In several places, however, he must employ the inference to bridge the gap from justified beliefs about God to the very possibility of direct perception of God. For example, he writes:

It strains credulity to suppose that an entire sphere of putatively perceptual experience could be a source of justification for perceptual beliefs, while there is no, or virtually no, genuine perception of the objects involved. Therefore, if putative experience of God provides justification for beliefs about God, that provides very strong support for supposing that such experiences are, at least frequently, genuine perceptions of God. (*PG*, pp. 68–69)

Compare that inference to this earlier passage.

The thesis defended here is not that the existence of God provides the best explanation for facts about religious experience or that it is possible to *argue* in any way from the latter to the former. It is rather that people sometimes do perceive God and thereby acquire justified beliefs about God. (*PG*, p. 3)

Alston seems condemned to the inference he would avoid. This conclusion receives confirming support when his argument defending his "Wittgensteinian" epistemology against the position taken here – that inference to the best explanation underwrites all our major habits of belief formation – fails to alleviate this tension. Unhappily, his defense answers the wrong charge. He insists that we cannot, for example, non-circularly justify our sense-perceptual doxastic practice with an inference to the best explanation. This notion seems right to me. I want to assert, however, that inference to the best explanation functions to some degree in all of our belief-forming mechanisms, not that we can use it to non-circularly justify them. As I have argued, moreover, his advocacy of direct realism also disappoints as a bulwark against the ubiquity of inference to the best explanation.

Accordingly, I find the alternatives posed by Swinburne, Franks Davis and Alston too severe. I see no reason to believe that we cannot navigate a course between the horns of the dilemma. Rather than the extremes of epistemic circularity or skepticism, we can reject Swinburne's Principle of Credulity or Alston's wholesale epistemic practices and embrace an anti-foundationalist epistemology (a true particularism) which commits us to far less. I believe that although Gutting and Clark,[38] who both adduce exceptions to the Principle of Credulity, articulate their objections to Swinburne from within the foundationalist framework, they recognize that the Principle obligates us to extend credibility to outrageous beliefs, beliefs which might find no support from the web of our actual beliefs. They therefore aim to restrict the universal applicability of the Principle. They rightly see that we would reject such beliefs out of hand as improbable explanations. We cannot treat all beliefs derived from such mechanisms equally. To do so masks the processes we use to justify beliefs; we justify beliefs only by their forensic position with regard to other beliefs. Similarly, Alston's recognition that doxastic practices function together and assess each other represents an unacknowledged admission that our beliefs achieve justification through their interrelations and tensions. Once we recognize *prima facie* justification accorded to classes of beliefs as a vestige of an unnecessary foundationalism, the coercive force of the arguments that Swinburne, Franks Davis, Gellman and Alston present withers.

Neither does a more adequate model of the relationship between beliefs and justification save the minimal foundationalists. If we, for instance, follow Alston's pluralism to its logical conclusion – that justification occurs at the level of socially influenced beliefs rather than practices – but allow Swinburne his ultimate, foundational principle of rationality, the Principle of Credulity devolves into the assertion that "what one *believes* to be so, probably is so." While this reformulation might seem

---

[38] Ralph Clark, "The Evidential Value of Religious Experiences," *International Journal for Philosophy of Religion* 16 (1984), pp. 189–202.

innocuous, the protective intentions with which Swinburne invokes his principle nonetheless render it objectionable. Just such an implicit principle serving to justify beliefs based on religious perception (conjoined to his conviction about its potential for socially pernicious effects) motivated Locke, three hundred years ago, to resort to evidentialism. Enthusiasts, he wrote, "are sure, because they are sure: and their persuasions are right, because they are strong in them. For, when what they say is stripped of the metaphor of seeing and feeling, this is all it amounts to."[39] Despite his untenable strong foundationalism, Locke correctly rejects this principle. To employ such a dictum in an area of manifest controversy lends an unfair advantage to what the believer in fact believes. As we all know too well, what we believe often turns out false, especially in controversial instances. In cases of widespread disagreement, therefore, we should (and usually do) promote investigation rather than attempt to preclude inquiry by privileging one possible explanation. The Principle of Credulity in its essence attempts, on the other hand, to stifle inquiry. Gellman's version of the Principle, which explicitly invokes inference to the best explanation only to domesticate it, illustrates this fact clearly. In advance of any inquiry, it stipulates, everything else being equal, the best explanation of any experience. Viewed in this light, the Oxford strategy appears even more baldly protective and illegitimate, hardly a principle of rationality. But lacking their buoying foundations, the epistemic claims for religious perception founder. Without their foundational particularist principles and in the absence of demonstrations of the superiority of the religious explanation of religious experience to its competitors, Swinburne, Franks Davis and Alston can no longer compel the non-theist to accept beliefs based on religious experience as rationally justified.

---

[39] John Locke, *An Essay Concerning Human Understanding*, bk. IV, Chapter XIX, section 9.

CHAPTER 6

Loves noble Historie: Teresa of Avila's mystical theology

> Those *rare workes* where thou shalt leave writ,
> *Loves* noble *Historie*, with wit
> Taught thee by none but him, while here
> They feed our *soules*, shall cloath thine there.
> Each heav'nly word, by whose hid flame
> Our hard hearts shall strike fire, the same
> Shall flourish on thy browes, and be
> Both *fire* to us, and flame to thee;
> Whose light shall live bright, in thy Face
> By *glorie*, in our Hearts by *grace*.
>   Richard Crashaw, *Hymn to Sainte Teresa* (1648)[1]

In this chapter I undertake a detailed study of the entire spiritual path which Teresa promotes. By contrast, many contemporary thinkers excise limited passages from Teresa to lend their own agenda some historical weight. Both Forman and Alston, for example, employ short excerpts from Teresa to give their own favored experiences the heft of tradition. By culling from Teresa's vast corpus the particular experiences that most resemble those they wish to defend, they add gravity to their positions. Of all the different sorts of spiritual favors which Teresa relates, Alston singles out the intellectual vision as an exemplar of the particular experience he wishes to use to justify beliefs about God. He ignores all the other experiences and excerpts a passage from Teresa where she recounts an intellectual vision. He selects her famous vision of Christ at her side. He believes that her experience instantiates his model of the

---

[1] Helen Gardner, ed., *The Metaphysical Poets* (Baltimore: Penguin Books, 1957), pp. 206–211.

non-sensory perception of God.[2] To recall the point I emphasized with regard to Forman's work, to retain, in defense of
one's philosophical position, one peculiar sort of experience
from the myriad Teresa discusses without properly viewing it in
relation to the rest invites the danger of misunderstanding.

In most of the contemporary apologetic work on mysticism,
one never hears mention of the visions of demons and the
deceased. Teresa's experiences that either simply differ from the
apologists' favored ones or those that to modern eyes would
lessen her credibility end up on the cutting room floor. Teresa's
visions of a little snarling negro, for instance, never survive the
first cut. These experiences offend modern sensibilities and so
we rarely see reference to them even though they are integral to
an understanding of her mystical theology. Instead, we hear
about the suspension of the faculties and intellectual visions (of
God; the Devil has fallen vastly out of favor as a putative object
of experience), neither of which contain anything sensory and,
therefore, testable by empirical means. These latter experiences
gain prominence because of their more ethereal character. I,
however, wish to give a more complete and balanced picture of
Teresa's spiritual life and have tried to include mention of all
the major types of spiritual experience she reports.

Additionally, I examine the mystical testimonies of St. Teresa
of Avila in light of the setting in which they occurred. I hope to
include enough information on the religious culture in which
Teresa flourished to render her experiences comprehensible on
her own terms. My approach to Teresa contrasts with that of
Nelson Pike in his recent *Mystic Union*.[3] We both maintain that
the message of the primary mystical literature "should be
accurately and sympathetically represented in the contemporary philosophical dialogue," but pursue that desideratum by
drastically different methods.

He aims to provide a "phenomenography" ("the study of
phenomena by way of *reports* thereof" or the "hermeneutics of

---

[2] In E. Allison Peers's translation of the *Life* (New York: Image Books, 1960) it appears
on page 249. Alston quotes J. M. Cohen's translation (London: Penguin Books, 1957).

[3] *Mystic Union: An Essay in the Phenomenology of Mysticism* (Ithaca: Cornell University Press,
1992).

experiential biography"[4]) of Christian union experiences. From a multitude of textual sources, he assembles a hierarchically ordered, tri-partite typology – the Prayer of Quiet, the Prayer of Union, and Rapture – but lends Teresa special importance "because her portrayals are, for the most part, more precise than those provided by other mystics."[5] To gather data for his phenomenography, Pike examines three sets of metaphors the mystics use to depict the three types of union experience: metaphors expressing degrees of proximity between God and the soul, metaphors concerning spiritual senses, and metaphors describing God as either the soul's mother or lover. All three sets of metaphors, on Pike's reading, correlate; the sensory metaphors and maternal or bridal metaphors depend on the relative propinquity of the soul to God.

Unfortunately, in seeking to impose order on the mystics, Pike's typology appears ruthlessly Procrustean. Teresa, the source to which he makes greatest appeal, does not even seem to conform to his model. In fact, Pike often ignores Teresa's claims. In several places, for instance, she avers *contra* Pike, that Union and Rapture do not substantially differ. The Prayer of Union and Rapture, she claims, both represent subspecies of the suspension of the faculties, which occurs in a variety of union experiences. Additionally, Teresa reports that at the highest levels of mortal perfection, i.e. in Spiritual Marriage when the soul's will enjoys continual harmony with God's will for it, Raptures generally cease. That Pike should without real defense grant Rapture such importance and autonomy seems strange, especially when Evelyn Underhill, another dedicated student of the "classical primary literature of the Christian mystical tradition," deems Rapture no more than an "acci-dent" of the mystical path. Elsewhere he writes that Teresa considers the Prayer of Quiet the lowest form of supernatural prayer and portrays the Prayer of Recollection as a natural state achieved by one's own efforts, without noting that in at least two places Teresa describes a supernaturally inspired form of the Prayer of Recollection which ranks below the Prayer of

[4] Ibid., p. 168.   [5] Ibid., p. 1.

Quiet. Pike also leads the reader to believe that Teresa employs the terms "Rapture" and "transport" interchangeably,[6] whereas, although they both involve suspension of the faculties, she takes considerable pains to describe their felt differences.

These problems arise because his goal of producing "a single complex collage" from his various sources constrains the sensitivity to nuance necessary to render accurately the individual sources.[7] It also precludes the sort of hermeneutics which interprets philosophical and theological texts by looking carefully at the social, historical, and intellectual context in which their author composed them. (Perhaps intentionally, Pike echoes James who composed the *Varieties*, a book sharing these liabilities, to resemble a "composite photograph.") In light of the recent wealth of historical scholarship on Teresa and her times, *Mystic Union* seems willfully ahistorical. Pike has no interest in the historical factors shaping Teresa and her religiosity. His emphasis, moreover, on the phenomenology of discrete, datable mystical experiences neglects the weight Teresa placed on perfection, the gradual remaking of the will to conform to God's will for it. Only in the framework of this quest for perfection can we truly understand the experiential import of union and the other favors God bestowed on Teresa. Pike isolates descriptions of extraordinary union-with-God experiences and thereby ends up misrepresenting Teresa.

His explication of the bridal metaphor perfectly exemplifies the combined dangers of ahistorical analysis and a privileging of the explicitly mystical passages in texts. Pike attends to the use of the bridal metaphor in the union experiences only and concludes "that the bridal metaphor carries the pictorial implication of *equal* partners ..."[8] To support this analysis, he adduces passages from John of the Cross. Such a result, however, completely misses the import of the bridal metaphor for Teresa who conceives of Spiritual Marriage as a *subordination* of the mystic's will to God's will for it. Even John believes that God, in what we might call an act of supreme narcissism, makes the soul "equal" by consuming or transforming all in its will

---

[6] Ibid., p. 11.   [7] Ibid., p. xiii.   [8] Ibid., p. 81. Italics original.

that does not conform to his.[9] The bridal metaphor does not carry the late twentieth-century associations of a partnership between equals, but rather implies a profound inequality: the soul completely submits its will to God's will for it, just as the bride completely submits her will to the bridegroom's will for her. Teresa refers to both Spiritual Marriage and ordinary mundane marriage as "slavery." In a chapter on Spiritual Marriage, she writes, "Do you know when people really become spiritual? It is when they become slaves of God and are branded with His sign ... in token that they have given Him their freedom. Then He can sell them as slaves to the whole world ... "[10] Close attention to Teresa's entire corpus and some awareness of historical placement helps to prevent such misunderstandings.

In this chapter I try to avoid some of these shortcomings by exploring Teresa's mystical theology in conjunction with some consideration, however brief, of the context in which she lived and wrote. Throughout this book I have stressed that judicious philosophical discussion of mysticism requires careful historical study. I shall here attempt to heed my repeated admonition. The first section explores Teresa's religious and cultural milieu. The second describes Teresa's rationale for her texts and outlines the importance of the virtues for her. The lengthy final section provides a synoptic catalogue of Teresa's descriptions of the spiritual life. I intend the first two sections to illuminate the last. Throughout this chapter, furthermore, I will highlight the explanatory practices exhibited by Teresa and her contemporaries. Even this cursory look at sixteenth-century Spain indicates, I think, that Teresa had clear justifications for her beliefs. In the final chapter I will compare Teresa's context to our own and offer reasons to deny that the explanatory commitments implicit in extraordinary religious experience justify belief. In other words, the present chapter not only aims to demonstrate the cultural situatedness and complexity of Teresa's mystical theology, a corpus widely excerpted and

---

[9] See the *Spiritual Canticle*, E. Allison Peers, tr. (New York: Image Books, 1961), p. 213.

[10] *Interior Castle*, E. Allison Peers, tr. and ed. (New York: Image Books, 1961), p. 229.

misleadingly hitched to various philosophical wagons, but also represents spadework for my concluding chapter.

The life of St. Teresa of Avila (1515–1582) spanned a period of enormous religious change in Spain. The advent of a new religious sensibility in the sixteenth century conjoined with the Protestant schism to alter drastically the character of Spanish devotion. Certain basic elements of Spanish religiosity perdured, however, by undergoing a transmutation of sorts. This intersection of traditional Spanish cultic practice and the *devotio moderna* with the dual pressures of the Protestant Reformation and economic upheaval account for many of the salient features of Teresa's mystical theology. To fully comprehend her thought we must properly situate it in its context.

Traditional Spanish local religion evinces a remarkable degree of interaction between human and supernatural forces. Supernatural influence pervaded all aspects of mundane life.[11] The people expected God, the Devil, and any number of saints to intervene in their daily affairs. In fact, they believed their survival depended on it. Their precarious lease on life necessitated, in an era of plague, infestation, and famine, a close working relationship with the supernatural. To this end towns and villages supported shrines and undertook corporate vows to facilitate interaction. Saints also regularly appeared to individuals bearing messages of vital community import. William Christian rejects the usual distinction between high and low religion for sixteenth-century Spain because local religion bridged the classes. Aristocrats, town elders, clergy, and royalty all maintained certain allegiances to their local shrines and the vows undertaken by their communities. The vows, he insists, were orthodox. Furthermore, the orthodox clergy competed with all sorts of unorthodox necromancers, enpsalmers, and

---

[11] William Christian Jr. sees "the sense of divine participation in the landscape" common at this time as an "aspect of local religion that has largely disappeared." *Local Religion in Sixteenth-Century Spain* (Princeton: Princeton University Press, 1981), p. 208.

conjurers whom even the clergy considered effective, their efficacy deriving from the Devil. The clerical attitude toward the occult was complex: only those occult practices that relied on demonic powers were prohibited. In 1568, for instance, the Inquisition reprehended an overzealous inquisitor in Barcelona for fining a woman who had employed charms and incantations to cure the ill.[12]

Teresa narrates in her autobiography one memory which illustrates her own ambivalence about the occult. When she had become especially close to a confessor, she recounts, he divulged to her his sordid tale. He had disgraced himself with a local woman. Teresa continues:

I got to know more about this priest by making enquiries of members of his household. I then realized what great trouble the poor man had got himself into and found that it was not altogether his own fault. For the unhappy woman had cast a spell over him, giving him a little copper figure and begging, for love of her, to wear it round his neck, and no one had been able to persuade him to take it off. Now, with regard to this particular incident of the spell, I do not believe there is the least truth in it.[13]

This passage displays an intriguing inconsistency. Despite the rather direct disavowal of the spell culminating it, Teresa absolves the priest of some responsibility for his plight because of the spell. Teresa's course of action to save the priest may also indicate more credence in the effects of the spell than she admits. She labored to garner the priest's affections and, successful, she asked for the talisman. "[I]n order to please me, he gave me the little figure, which I at once got someone to throw into a river. When he had done this, he became like a man awakening from a deep sleep and he began to recall everything that he had been doing during those years. He was amazed at himself and grieved at his lost condition and he began to hate the woman who had led him to it" (*L*, p. 87). Of course, she could have described the events this way because

[12] David Goodman, *Power and Penury: Government, technology and science in Philip II's Spain* (Cambridge: Cambridge University Press, 1988), p. 19. See chapter one for a discussion of the occult in sixteenth-century Spain.

[13] *The Life of Teresa of Jesus*, E. Allison Peers, tr. and ed. (New York: Image Books, 1960), p. 86.

the priest believed in the spell, but Teresa's focus on the copper figure suggests a conviction in the efficacy of the occult which she does not feel the liberty to acknowledge in a book written for her ecclesiastical superiors. Such a reluctance could result from a number of factors including a fear of unorthodoxy or a fear of ridicule (although Teresa often counsels against this latter servile fear).

All sorts of partisans of various superstitions claimed efficacy for their techniques and the clergy, for their part, had an arsenal of prayers and exorcisms to disperse storm clouds and a procedure for excommunications with which to chase away pests. The orthodoxy of these latter trials, however, was under dispute. Christian cites one trial which occurred only after two years had elapsed in which exorcisms, holy water, processions, novenas, and "the reform of public sinners" had failed.[14] Villagers also usually tried other supernatural entreaties before undertaking vows to saints. Christian explains that "the first response would be the conjuring of the danger by the priest with a cross, on the supposition that storms and locusts were works of the devil and could be reversed by divine power. If the conjuring failed, one conclusion might be that the trouble was a punishment sent by God, and religious remedies would be of the petitionary or placatory variety."[15] The Dominican Friars of Santo Tomás in Avila, for instance, performed penitential processions in 1518–1519 to alleviate a plague.

Anomaly represents the hallmark of the commerce between supernatural figures and communities at this time. Supernatural agents communicated their requests for vows to a community through signs. Signs, however, bore the marks of the strange or uncanny. Any occurrence which in relation to a religious time, place, or object seemed extraordinary could inspire a vow. Christian lists natural disasters, the butchering of a bloodless ram, a pillar of flame in a river, the inopportune breaking of a hunter's bowstring, and the falling of a church door. Depending on the circumstances the saint indicated could be the one on whose day the unusual event occurred or the patron saint of the

---

[14] Christian, *Local Religion*, p. 30.   [15] Ibid., p. 63.

activity in which it happened, etc. "[T]he sign was an anomalous event, invested with meaning by its occurrence in relation to the annual calendar and the way it 'fit' with the village's devotional history."[16] One sort of sign presented little difficulty in interpretation. Often a vision of a saint would appear to a layperson in the community, demand worship and specify the details of the vow he or she wanted undertaken.

If no sign immediately presented itself by which to divine the supernatural agent, the villagers contrived to induce a sign. The town authorities would organize a lottery to discern whose supernatural aid to seek. Christian points out, incidentally, that this lottery procedure had complete orthodox acceptance. Aquinas himself gives qualified sanction to geomancy in the *Summa Theologiae* (2–2.95.8). One lottery technique consisted in writing various saints' names on pieces of paper, crumpling them, dipping them in wax, mixing them up in a receptacle, then drawing one. Another technique assigned one saint's name to each of twelve exactly similar candles. The last candle burning bore the name of the saint to whom the community must vow.

As elsewhere in Catholic Europe, holy relics housed in shrines healed miraculously. The Council of Trent in 1563 condemned the views of those who rejected the efficacy of relics. For the most part the shrines provided the venue for personal petitions, although some relics protected communities against storms or, when petitioned, brought rain. The mania for relics at all levels of society continued unabated throughout the sixteenth century. Historians have well documented, for instance, King Philip II's enthusiasm for relics. In 1598 he had several crates of relics imported from Germany and upon their arrival had some of them applied to his body to relieve his gout. Many years earlier when his son lay irretrievably unconscious after a fall, Philip had the body of Fray Diego de Alcalá, a fifteenth-century holy man, brought in a procession and placed above the prince. The friar then appeared to the unconscious prince in a vision and the prince subsequently regained

[16] Ibid., p. 39.

consciousness. Philip considered the recovery a miracle and recommended canonization for the friar.[17] Teresa's story, in fact, bears out this fascination with relics. Months after her death, when Teresa's body was exhumed and found to have the odor of sanctity, relic-seekers dismembered her remains. Fray Jerónimo de la Madre de Dios Gracián, Teresa's confessor, colleague, and confidant kept her little finger with him for the rest of his life.[18] At the proceedings for her beatification, testimony attributed healings to her relics and miracles to her books.

Anomaly governed the activity of shrines. They developed around the occurrence of miraculous events and grew with further reports of divine activity. The shrines each had a saint from whose intercession the miraculous activity stemmed. Individuals made vows and pleaded for intercession at shrines. Shrines, for the purpose of curing ailments, also provided special candles, small crucifixes, medals, ribbons, or replicas of the shrine's images. In fairness, Christian notes that at the end of the sixteenth century credulity about the miracles alleged at these shrines was far from universal. He adds that incredulity was no more prevalent in cities than in villages. To combat the skeptics, shrines posted testimonies swearing to the miracles occurring there. "By the end of the sixteenth century," he claims, "most printed books containing miracles also carried careful explanations of how miracles were verified, openly admitting that many people in Spain did not believe in miracles at all."[19] Nonetheless, devotion to saints associated with the local shrine exerted a great influence in the religious life and thought of the sixteenth-century Spaniard.

In understanding the role of anomaly in sixteenth-century Spanish religiosity, one must avoid an easy misapprehension. Accustomed to widespread skepticism about God's existence, we naturally assume that these supernatural signs (when accepted as such) provided the villagers with evidence about God's existence. We see the signs confirming for the townsfolk

---

[17] Goodman, *Power and Penury*, pp. 16–17.

[18] Deirdre Green, *Gold in the Crucible* (Longmeadow: Element Books, 1989).

[19] Christian, *Local Religion*, p. 103.

the presence of the divine. Such a reading of the historical record would be terribly anachronistic. To them the signs merely indicated the saint to whom they should turn. The presence of divine activity in the world required no substantiating support. "The occurrence of a cloudburst during a petitionary ceremony was not interpreted – as it would be today[20] – as confirmation of the existence of divine power. Rather, it showed just whom to turn to in the future in such matters, who was helping out the town in such heavenly matters."[21] The work of Tycho Brahe illustrates that the sixteenth-century interpretive question was not *whether* an anomaly could substantiate the supernatural, but rather *what* was the meaning of the supernatural sign and by *whom* was the sign sent. Brahe, whose revolutionary theories threatened the medieval view of the cosmos, unself-consciously read the anomalous as a supernatural sign. Brahe demonstrated that the comet of 1577 was a celestial body beyond the moon. This discovery disturbed the Aristotelean conception of the cosmos, but left the supernatural import of the anomalous event unimpugned. Brahe believed God had formed the comet to signal the impending death of Philip and religious civil war in Spain.[22]

The incidents of Teresa's life provide us with further examples of how the anomalous bore meaning of supernatural significance in sixteenth-century Spain. In fact, she even warns against this tendency to freight the unusual with supernatural meaning: "For human nature is such that we scarcely notice what we see frequently but are astounded at what we see seldom or hardly at all."[23] The danger this inclination incites derives from the Devil who uses the astonishment to his own ends. Teresa herself, however, interpreted the oddities she witnessed as messages from God addressed specifically to her. She did not interpret them as information pertaining to the larger community. Perhaps the most striking instance she recounts in the *Life* occurs in the telling of an early, unprofitable

[20] I think we would here want to add to Christian's clause "by some people."
[21] Christian, *Local Religion*, p. 65.   [22] Goodman, *Power and Penury*, p. 29.
[23] *The Way of Perfection*, E. Allison Peers, tr. and ed. (New York: Image Books, 1964), p. 260.

affection. Upon witnessing a natural oddity, she makes a remarkable inference.

> On another occasion, when I was with that same person, we saw coming towards us – and others who were there saw this too – something like a great toad, but crawling much more quickly than toads are wont to do. I cannot imagine how such a reptile could have come from the place in question in broad daylight; it had never happened before, and the incident made such an impression on me that I think it must have had a hidden meaning, and I have never forgotten this either. O greatness of God! With what care and compassion didst Thou warn me in every way and how little did I profit by Thy warnings. (*L*, p. 100)

The sheer unusualness of this toad's behavior led Teresa to suppose that God sent her a warning. God so inhabited the natural order for Teresa that an event which baffled her expectations and understanding invited a supernatural explanation. In her eyes the best explanation for this anomaly reached outside the natural order. The best explanation invoked God and invested him with the intention to provide a sign.

Despite her affinities with the common religiosity, Teresa sought successfully to reform the Carmelites. The convergence of new religious ideas sweeping through Spain with felicitous economic trends in Avila contributed to her foundation. Teresa's first momentous and identifiable exposure to the *devotio moderna* occurred when her uncle provided her with a copy of Francisco de Osuna's *Third Spiritual Alphabet*. This book introduced her to the fundamentals of mental prayer or meditation, provided her with vocabulary for her own later works, and would encourage her interest in reform.[24] Teresa, from early on, also encountered and respected many Jesuits, some of whom became her confessors. Their revolutionary ideas about piety, social relations, and worship influenced her greatly. Proponents and effects of the *devotio moderna* surrounded Teresa, however, far more completely than these influences would indicate.

---

[24] Osuna shares with Teresa a concern with demonic experiences, an affinity for martial metaphors, and much mystical vocabulary (e.g. vocal prayer, mental prayer, meditation, Recollection, Quiet, and Union). Along with most other spiritual books in the vernacular, the *Third Spiritual Alphabet* was placed on the index in 1559.

Teresa's Avila numbered among its inhabitants prominent exponents of the *devotio moderna*. Juan de Avila, one of Erasmus's well-known followers, for instance, emphasized charity, education, and the imitation of Christ. He favored mental prayer and piety over external observance and disparaged hereditary lineages in the clergy. Ignatius Loyola, the founder of the Society of Jesus, corresponded with Juan and adopted many of his views and practices. The so-called Jesuits undertook in Avila to mediate conflicts and made a name for themselves as accomplished confessors. Furthermore, they endeavored to hear confession from the ordinary as well as the socially important. One of Juan's followers, Gaspar Daza, had a hand in nearly all of the reforms occurring in Avila at this time. A holy charismatic named Mari Diaz, a woman "better known than Teresa of Jesus during Teresa's lifetime" illustrates the degree of influence *beatas*, or holy women, wielded in late medieval Spain.[25] This holy woman achieved renown for her devotion, piety, and wisdom. Although they often remained outside the church hierarchy, *beatas* often best captured the spirit of the sixteenth-century religious impulse. The new religious ideals promoted a more egalitarian religious vision with social welfare prominently figuring. This reformism, similarly to Protestantism, stresses the individual's unmediated access to the divine.

A change in attitude about visions of saints accompanied the reformist sensibility. Public apparitions or visions apprehended by lay seers received far greater critical scrutiny as the sixteenth century wore on. What had represented a prevalent, established, and approved manner of divine contact rather rapidly fell into disrepute. Clearly, the crisis provoked by the Reformation had an impact on the initiative allowed the Catholic laity in matters of religion. The repressive Church authorities worked in concert, however, with an independent and autonomous trend characterizing the religious life and thought of the time.[26] Whether stifled by the Inquisition or naturally ex-

---

[25] Jodi Bilinkoff, *The Avila of Saint Teresa* (Ithaca: Cornell University Press, 1989), p. 97.

[26] Christian writes in *Apparitions in Late Medieval and Renaissance Spain* (Princeton: Princeton University Press, 1981), "In the early sixteenth century, the cultural form

hausted, this form of direct contact with the supernatural assumed less and less importance in the general religious life of Spain. Direct personal contact with the divine did not disappear altogether, however. The contact occurred in a revised form and played a far less central social role. Supernatural communication used mental prayer as the medium. The visionary now, however, achieved insights into personal rather than social or communal matters. That these messages from beyond spoke to the occasional and isolated concerns of individuals mitigated their danger to the institutional church.

These new developments in the spirituality of the age reflected an evolving social and economic landscape and also exacerbated the tensions produced by it. Historically, Avila's social and economic power resided in an hereditary aristocracy. The landed expressed their piety through endowments given to found chaplaincies and monasteries. The clergy, monks, or nuns, predominantly of aristocratic heritage and financially beholden to the aristocracy, would continuously chant or vocally pray seeking intercession on behalf of the benefactor. Advocates of reform threatened this arrangement. Their emphasis on poverty, service to the poor, and personal, internal, spiritual development clashed with the interests of the traditional elite. A religious institution that practices strict poverty cannot accept beneficences and therefore has no reason to cater to the wealthy. Similarly, a foundation dedicated to alleviating the plight of the poor cannot dedicate itself to the soteriological welfare of the landed without also endangering the economic and social status quo. The aristocracy, moreover, has no tangible evidence of intercessory prayers if an order practices mental prayer. Although Teresa, in the constitution of her order, drew on various strands of the *devotio moderna* including the Jesuits, she admonishes her nuns to pray continually for those who give alms (*WP*, p. 44). God desires that nuns pray on behalf of almsgivers. The prayer, she claims, might free the donor from hell.

of public, lay visions itself may have worn out. This particular way of connecting with God was no longer believable enough ... Perhaps by 1523 the Inquisition was ratifying and enforcing a point of view that was more general in the society" (p. 184).

Sixteenth-century Avila underwent a vast demographic and economic expansion which enabled this clash of religious sensibilities. A burgeoning textile industry attracted rural populations, which circumstance in turn spurred construction growth. Eventually, these developments served both to impinge on the poor's quality of life and to elevate the economic influence and prestige of a class of non-noble families. Many of this class of "new men" came from *converso* stock. *Conversos* belonged to families which had converted to Christianity from Judaism rather than leave Spain in the Expulsion of 1492. Prejudice against and suspicion of the "new Christians" ran wide and deep. Until fairly late the office of the Inquisition virtually solely concerned the discovery and reform of Judaizers. *Conversos* became scapegoats for the religious crises and impediments to imperial ambition facing the Spanish monarchy. In 1556 King Philip II even attributed the Protestant Reformation to the subversive activities of *conversos:* "All the heresies which have occurred in Germany and France have been sown by the descendants of Jews, as we have seen and still see daily in Spain."[27] These "new men" exerted a great deal of pressure on the aristocracy. The parvenus and the poor found themselves in a tactical alliance against the hereditary oligarchy, the obstacle to change. Along with other attempted inroads to social and political power, the "new men" "channeled their energies into supporting religious movements and institutions that reflected the changing conditions of urban life in sixteenth-century Avila, including the monastic reform of Teresa of Jesus."[28] Significantly, many exponents of the new forms of spirituality counted *conversos* among their ancestors, including Juan de Avila, probably Gaspar Daza, Saint John of the Cross, and even Teresa herself.[29] The Jewish origins of many promoters of reform lent the authorities an additional reason to suspect it.

---

[27] Quoted by Carole Slade, *St. Teresa of Avila, Author of a Heroic Life* (Berkeley: University of California Press, 1995), p. 20.

[28] Bilinkoff, *Avila,* p. 77.

[29] A spate of recent works explore the fact that Teresa's grandfather (and maybe even her father) went before the Inquisition for Judaizing and received punishment. Much of this scholarship is fanciful, finding Jewish influence on features of Teresa's work which Christian influence could as easily explain. See Gareth Alban Davies,

In 1559 the discovery of "Lutheran"[30] heretics in Spain itself underscored the importance of doctrinal purity. Any area where heterodoxy might develop or flourish demanded careful attention. Accordingly, after this time the Inquisition especially scrutinized mental prayer, meditation, and contemplation even within the Church hierarchy. The possibility of heresy arising from a claim to supernatural communication worried the authorities. The Church hierarchy evinced particular concern with ecstatic experience and contemplation because of the high proportion of women and "new Christians" who practiced mental prayer. The correlation between women and visionary experience gave reason for pause because of women's generally acknowledged weakness. Their feeble constitutions and intellects enable the Devil more easily to lead women into heterodoxy through counterfeit experiences. Indeed, Teresa herself seems to have subscribed to this view (*L*, p. 137).[31] Ironically, that women comprised the majority of these visionaries may have equally contributed to a leniency toward visionary experience because that fact assured that seers occupied subordinate positions within the Church hierarchy.

Similarly, the authorities believed "new Christians" susceptible to demonic experience because of vestigial allegiances and propensities. Diabolical experience could lead to the sorts of heresy exemplified by "Lutherans" or *alumbrados* (Illuminati). These latter, a pietistic sect (repressed after 1525) which believed in the humanity of Christ, "advocated direct, ecstatic, personal contact with God for lay people, and rejected many of the

"Saint Teresa and the Jewish Question," Margaret A. Rees, ed., *Teresa de Jesús and Her World* (Leeds: Trinity and All Saints' College, 1981), pp. 51–73. The best discussion of the manifest similarities between Teresa's mystical theology and Jewish Zoharic Cabala appears in Catherine Swietlicki's *Spanish Christian Cabala* (Columbia: University of Missouri Press, 1986), ch. 3. Without making unproven claims about influence, she points to shared metaphors (palaces, mirrors, silkworms, doves, nuts, trees, etc.) and even to similarly mixed metaphors. Green includes a discussion of this topic as well.

[30] The term "Lutheran" served widely at this time to refer either to any unorthodox doctrines which overlapped with those of the Protestant reformers or to those who held such beliefs.

[31] Alison Weber in *Teresa of Avila and the Rhetoric of Femininity* (Princeton: Princeton University Press, 1990) argues that Teresa employed disparaging remarks about women strategically to empower herself.

tenets of outward popular devotion: for example, they held that it was unnecessary or even idolatrous to venerate images, and that fasts and similar outward practices were useless in the quest for salvation."[32] Additionally, a prurient intimation common in this era linked demonic experience to sexual license. Satan fosters the heresy that at a certain exalted level of spiritual development no behavior qualifies as sin. Teresa's life bears out this Reformation preoccupation as well. A disgruntled novice once complained about Teresa's order to the Inquisition, alleging lurid sexual improprieties initiated and orchestrated by Teresa herself (Teresa always raised suspicions because in founding the various chapters of her order, she continually broke her own rule of strict enclosure). The Inquisition finally exonerated her.

At the Council of Trent the Church hierarchy coopted the forces of reform. In substance it approved many of the institutional reforms and social objectives of the *devotio moderna*. (Despite the Council of Trent, Teresa encountered fierce opposition to her conception of poverty. She intended to found her order without any fixed income.) That the new arena of divine contact found in mental prayer would escape complete repression from the Inquisition quite possibly owes to this cooption. In a monastic setting these experiences occurred within the jurisdiction and control of the Church authorities. Contact with the divine within the Church's sanctioned precincts presents a far less threatening danger than lay apparitions at large. In a sense the newer visionaries became professional. They cultivated their communication with the divine and to the best of their ability sought to make it an habitual component of orthodox practice.

Within a Church now dedicated to reform a clear division sedimented around these issues.

Sides now formed in an ongoing, although not always explicitly defined, debate between *letrados*, "learned men" with academic training in theology, and *espirituales* or *experimentados*, spiritual people who exalted the knowledge gained through direct religious experience and prayer. The dominant letrado faction mistrusted any form of

[32] Green, *Gold*, p. 17.

spirituality not grounded in a firm understanding of dogma, convinced that the espirituales' emphasis on private mental prayer served as a screen for Protestant pietism and other forms of heterodox belief, and as a means of avoiding the control of the Church hierarchy. They stressed the outward ceremonies and duties of the Church and, for members of the religious orders, vocal choral prayer as the appropriate and traditional manner of praising God.[33]

In this factional divide between *letrados* and *espirituales*, Teresa obviously falls in with the *espirituales* and she had no doubts about it. Although, as her writing makes abundantly clear, defending the Church against the encroaching Reformation was one of her primary motivations, she trod a very fine line with a skeptical and threatened Church hierarchy. She, whom we now view as a major heroine of the Counter-Reformation, found herself delated to the Inquisition on two separate occasions and opponents delated her writings three times. M. E. Williams summarizes the objections to her writings which resulted in their delation:

She maintained, like the alumbrados, that all Christians were called to a high state of perfection;

Her way of speaking of the union of the soul with God led to pantheism;

She despised vocal prayer and external acts and rites;

She insisted too much on her own experiences and neglected scripture and Church authority;

She has [sic] erroneous ideas about human liberty;

In the prayer of Quiet, she maintained that the soul was purely passive.[34]

Regardless of the veracity of these charges, they read like a textbook of the concerns vexing the Catholic Church at this crucial moment in its history.

The worry that the Devil used Teresa as an instrument arose early in her career as a contemplative. From her very first supernatural experiences Teresa herself worried about their cause. She spent years trying to find confessors with sufficient experience to pronounce authoritatively on her spiritual con-

---

[33] Bilinkoff, *Avila*, p. 142.

[34] M. E. Williams, "St. Teresa, Doctor of the Church (Orthodoxy and Public Opinion)" in Rees, *Teresa de Jesús*.

dition. We owe all Teresa's major literary endeavors to the commands of the confessors she eventually found. They wanted full accounts of her spiritual and interior life by which to judge the orthodoxy of her beliefs.[35] To best determine the divine or demonic origin of her extraordinary experiences and favors, they needed detailed and thorough descriptions of the experiences themselves and their influence on her disposition and behavior. Once convinced of the divine provenance of her favors, her confessors ordered her to compose treatises on mental prayer for her nuns' benefit. In her texts Teresa amply displays her reformist zeal and concern for the forces of orthodoxy and, importantly, maintains unquestioned the traditional liaison between anomaly and supernatural explanations.

VIRTUES AND THE REFORMATION

I have described how Teresa's own anxiety, shared by the Church authorities, about her orthodoxy resulted in the bountiful library of her work which we have today. Teresa's fear of heterodoxy and of the possibility of demonic influence mirrored the larger Church's fear of heterodoxy. Faced with tremendous upheaval in Northern Europe, the Catholic Church took great pains to prevent the spread of heresy and Protestantism into Southern Europe's more secure regions. Although the reforms taking place in Spain at this time have an earlier and deeper lineage than a simple response to "Lutheranism," they received a focus and additional impetus from the Reformation. Teresa leaves no doubt about this urgency when she explains the rationale for her monastic reform.

She most fully relays this information in *The Way of Perfection*, where she wishes to instill in her young nuns a sense of the gravity of their purpose. At the beginning of the first chapter, Teresa describes the sentiment that caused her to found the reform. I will quote liberally the next few passages to impart a sense of Teresa's style.

---

[35] *The Foundations* must be exempted from this generalization. It chronicles the historical establishment of her order, rather than her personal development.

At about this time there came to my notice the harm and havoc that were being wrought in France by these Lutherans and the way in which their unhappy sect was increasing. This troubled me very much, and, as though I could do anything, or be of any help in the matter, I wept before the Lord and entreated Him to remedy this great evil. I felt that I would have laid down a thousand lives to save a single one of all the souls that were being lost there. And, seeing that I was a woman, and a sinner, and incapable of doing all I should like in the Lord's service, and as my whole yearning was, and still is, that, as He has so many enemies and so few friends, these last should be trusty ones, I determined to do the little that was in me – namely, to follow the evangelical counsels as perfectly as I could, and to see that these few nuns who are here should do the same ... I hoped ... I should thus be able to give the Lord some pleasure ... (*WP*, pp. 36–37)

Here we see clearly the Reformation's effect on Teresa. Most generally, her reform intends to requite God's goodness with love and devotion at a time when the Protestants so defiantly spurn his concern and offer of eternal salvation. A few pages later she dramatically outlines the extent of the cosmic crisis. "The world is on fire. Men try to condemn Christ once again, as it were, for they bring a thousand false witnesses against Him. They would raze His Church to the ground" (*WP*, p. 38). In the "Spiritual Relations," she echoes this gravity and declares that any other distress appears "ridiculous" in comparison to distress caused by the plight of the Church.[36] At the beginning of the third chapter she picks up this theme again and maintains the martial imagery (possibly imbibed from the chivalric romances she reports having loved as a child[37]). She paints an alarmingly pessimistic picture.

Seeing how great are the evils of the present day and how no human strength will suffice to quench the fire kindled by these heretics (though attempts have been made to organize opposition to them, as though such a great and rapidly spreading evil could be remedied by force of arms), it seems to me that it is like a war in which the enemy

[36] "Spiritual Relations Addressed By Saint Teresa Of Jesus To Her Confessors," *Complete Works of St. Teresa*, vol. 1, E. Allison Peers, tr. and ed. (New York: Sheed and Ward, 1957), p. 317.
[37] Joseph F. Chorpenning, *The Divine Romance: Teresa of Avila's Narrative Theology* (Chicago: Loyola University Press, 1992).

has overrun the whole country, and the Lord of the country, hard pressed, retires into a city... (*WP,* p. 45)

Teresa depicts the forces of orthodoxy, truth, and God as retreating before the onslaughts of an unrighteous army. She locates the religious lives of her nuns against the backdrop of a frightening cosmic tumult.

Having portrayed the climate of crisis, Teresa then offers the "principal reason" for the founding of her order. She gives their cloistered devotions a universal importance. Rather than an irrelevance to the battle, Teresa's reform serves as a sort of rear-guard bulwark supporting the front-line warriors. Teresa sees preachers and theologians as the actual combatants and the convent's task lies in protecting and fortifying these "perfect" or "picked" men. Here she concisely relates what she expects from her nuns in this regard.

I beg you to try to live in such a way as to be worthy to obtain two things from God. First, that there may be many of these very learned and religious men who have the qualifications for their task which I have described; and that the Lord may prepare those who are not completely prepared already and who lack anything, for a single one who is perfect will do more than many who are not. Secondly, that after they have entered upon this struggle, which, as I say, is not light, but a very heavy one, the Lord may have them in His hand so that they may be delivered from all the dangers that are in the world, and, while sailing on this perilous sea, may shut their ears to the song of the sirens. If we can prevail with God in the smallest degree about this, we shall be fighting His battle even while living a cloistered life and I shall consider as well spent all the trouble to which I have gone in founding this retreat ... (*WP,* pp. 47–48)

Teresa explains that her order primarily functions to petition God on behalf of the representatives of his orthodoxy. She replaces the continual prayers said for the souls of benefactors with virtuous lives and mental prayer dedicated to the intellectual forces of the Catholic establishment. The nuns' cloister permits them to concentrate without distraction on petitioning God to cloister his surrogates spiritually.

By living exemplary lives the nuns may secure a position from which to importune God for outcomes favorable to God's forces. When Teresa mentions following the evangelical counsels in the

Lord's service, she means renouncing all worldly goods and one's individual will for God's sake. For this reason she finds the strict Primitive Rule so attractive. The Primitive Rule more effectively guides the individual to a complete submission to God's will. The importance of Mental Prayer and Contemplation fits squarely into her concern with an evangelical dedication to God. Human virtues, the interior life, and conformity to God's will form an intricate relationship in Teresa's thought, one often overlooked by contemporary readers interested mainly in the extraordinary states of consciousness described by Teresa. They usually ignore the moral, historical, and theological issues which invest the mystical states with meaning. The unusual experiences bestowed on Teresa only make sense within this larger framework. In fact the "favors" we commonly associate with Teresa comprise only some of the supernatural favors she describes. She regularly characterizes increases in her devotion or virtues as favors imparted by God.

Human perfection (the scriptural basis for which is Matthew 5:48) represents the overarching desideratum for Teresa and her order. One pursues perfection through the cultivation of the virtues and perfection results in a soul entirely pleasing to God. The metaphors she employs (especially in the *Interior Castle*) concerning the spiritual courtship, betrothal and marriage all refer to this objective. Human perfection or spiritual marriage to the Bridegroom consists in the complete conformity of the Bride's will to God's will for her. This metaphor relies on the simple three-faculty psychology to which Teresa subscribes: the soul comprises the will, the understanding, and the imagination/memory. In medieval psychology the action of the will is love; the proper action of the virtuous will is love of God. "Love (amor) . . . is an arrow shot by the will, . . . directed towards God alone . . . ," explains Teresa.[38] The increase of perfection, therefore, is "the increase of love" (*IC*, p. 67). The union of love represented by the metaphor of Spiritual Marriage signifies a will subordinated to God's will.

Teresa's views accord well with other medieval explanations

---

[38] "Conceptions of the Love of God," *Complete Works of St. Teresa*, vol. II, E. Allison Peers, tr. and ed. (New York: Sheed and Ward, 1957), p. 392.

of human perfection and virtue. Aquinas, for instance, who predates late medieval voluntarism and its exaltation of the will as the noblest faculty, nonetheless offers an account resembling Teresa's. In the *Summa Theologiae* he argues that although humans cannot know God perfectly, they can love God perfectly (2–1.27.2.2). Union, furthermore, is an effect of love for Aquinas (2–1.28.1). The virtue he calls charity – participation in God's self-love, a sharing of love for God for God's sake (not ours) – is the chief and most excellent of the virtues (2–2.23.6). Human perfection consists in charity which unites humans to God (2–2.23.3). Charity amounts to a sharing of desires or a common goal with God. Aquinas (borrowing from Aristotle) calls this love "friendship" and cites John 15:15: "No longer do I call you servants ... but I have called you friends" (2–2.23.1). In light of this background Teresa can with perfect consistency therefore describe the soul as bride, friend, and servant to God. Perfection entails total self-renunciation. "The aim of all my advice to you in this book," she summarizes in *The Way of Perfection*, "is that we should surrender ourselves wholly to the Creator, place our will in His hands and detach ourselves from the creatures" (*WP*, p. 214). Continual practice of the virtues, striving to make them habits (*WP*, p. 270) improves us and moves us up the path to perfection and Spiritual Marriage.

The Union states of infused contemplation which she describes in such outstanding detail only make sense within an understanding of this ambition to unify one's will with God's will for one. The relationship between the perpetual union of Spiritual Marriage and the discrete, isolated experience of the Prayer of Union illustrates this dependence.

To return to union: I understood that the spirit in union is pure and lifted up above everything earthly, and that there is nothing remaining in it that will depart from the will of God, but that the spirit and the will are in conformity with His will, and detached from everything, and occupied in God so as to leave no recollection of love of self or of any created thing. I thought that, if this is union, we can say at once that a soul which always adheres to that resolution is always in the Prayer of Union; yet it is true that the union itself can last only for a very short time. It occurs to me that, so far as walking in righteousness, winning merits and gaining benefits are concerned, it will be so, but it cannot be said that the soul is united as it is in contemplation.[39]

Teresa explains that the extraordinary state of infused contemplation cannot last long. Human perfection consists in perpetually maintaining the more prosaic sort of union characterized by humility and righteousness. In the paragraph immediately prior to the one just cited, Teresa recounts a locution in which God declares that Union states do not necessarily mean that a soul exists in union with God. The soul in right relation to God, not spiritual favors, signifies true conformity to the will of God. Humans cannot fathom the rationale behind God's gratuitous gifts. The extraordinary experiences represent but one inessential element of "loves noble historie."

Teresa often reminds her nuns that God ordains different paths for everyone and not to expect everyone to receive states of contemplation. While undoubtedly a consolation, divinely inspired contemplation need not attend perfection.

[I]t is very important for us to realize that God does not lead us all by the same road, and perhaps she who believes herself to be going along the lowest of roads is the highest in the Lord's eyes. So it does not follow that, because all of us in this house practice prayer, we are all *perforce* to be contemplative. That is impossible; and those of us who are not would be greatly discouraged if we did not grasp the truth that contemplation is something given by God, and, as it is not necessary for salvation and God does not ask it of us before He gives us our reward, we must not suppose that anyone else will require it of us. We shall not fail to attain perfection if we do what has been said here; we may, in fact, gain much more merit, because what we do will cost us more labor; the Lord will be treating us like those who are strong and will be laying up for us all that we cannot enjoy in this life. (*WP*, p. 124)

Teresa insists that many nuns never achieve contemplative states and perfection does not directly correlate with the profundity of mystical consciousness experienced. God directs spiritual growth according to the capacities and necessities of individuals. For this reason one cannot measure perfection in

---

[39] Teresa, "Relations," p. 348.

terms of experiences reported. Only consistent practice of the virtues insures spiritual progress.

Progress has nothing to do with enjoying the greatest number of consolations in prayer, or with raptures, visions or favours given by the Lord, the value of which we cannot estimate until we reach the world to come. The other things I have been describing are current coin, an unfailing source of revenue and a perpetual inheritance – not payments liable at any time to cease, like those favours which are given us and then come to an end. (*WP*, pp. 131–132)

Teresa's message here and elsewhere cautions against the allure of a sort of antinomianism. Only by practice of the virtues can we have the security of God's favor. We have not the compass to fathom God's reason for sending favors and we have no reason then to suppose those favors infallibly indicate spiritual growth. She also, however, wants to skirt any Pelagian view and insists that God makes possible our successful practice of the virtues.

Teresa interprets communion in light of her concern for spiritual perfection. In *The Way of Perfection* she explains the significance of the sacrament. As Jesus taught the apostles to recite the Lord's Prayer and included the phrase, "And thy will be done," he offered our individual wills to God. Jesus realized, however, the strength of base human impulses. The Lord's Supper, then, represents Jesus's sacrifice, his offering of himself, to fortify our weakness. Jesus imparts his will to us through the transubstantiated bread and wine. He helps us to fulfill the pledge he made to God on our behalf. Communion itself represents a union of wills. This fact explains both Teresa's exhorting her nuns to exercise piety during the period in which they digest the communion meal and her autobiographical preoccupation with the size of the host. She recommends that her daughters practice recollection after receiving communion. Naturally, the topic of communion invites comment on the Reformation and Teresa claims that receiving communion in a proper spirit also works in defense of the Church.

Since His Holy Son has given us this excellent way in which we can offer Him up frequently as a sacrifice, let us make use of this precious gift so that it may stay the advance of such terrible evil and irreverence as in many places is paid to this Most Holy Sacrament. For these

Lutherans seem to want to drive Him out of the world again: they destroy churches, cause the loss of many priests and abolish the sacraments. (*WP*, pp. 234–235)

Again we see the notion that leading a life directed at human perfection has an historical impact. Teresa and her nuns, using communion to conform their wills to God, affect the larger, international disputes.

In *The Way of Perfection* Teresa reminds her "daughters" that their rule requires constant prayer. When she does not specify, she generally means mental prayer because in the *Interior Castle* as well as *The Way of Perfection* she adjures her nuns that meditation must accompany either vocal or mental prayer. "I do not say mental prayer rather than vocal, for, if it is prayer at all, it must be accompanied by meditation. If a person does not think Whom he is addressing, and what he is asking for, and who it is that is asking and of Whom he is asking it, I do not consider that he is praying at all even though he be constantly moving his lips" (*IC*, pp. 31–32). Meditation must invest prayer with meaning. Meditation makes mental prayer mental and makes vocal prayer mental. She explains, "If, while I am speaking with God, I have a clear realization and full consciousness that I am doing so, and if this is more real to me than the words I am uttering, then I am combining mental and vocal prayer" (*WP*, p. 156).

Authentic prayer, she further instructs, necessitates the practice of the other elements of the Rule. Mortifications properly accompany prayer. "Our Primitive Rule tells us to pray without ceasing. Provided we do this with all possible care (and it is the most important thing of all) we shall not fail to observe the fasts, disciplines and periods of silence which the Order commands; for, as you know, if prayer is to be genuine it must be reinforced with these things – prayer cannot be accompanied by self-indulgence" (*WP*, p. 52). The burden of the following fifteen chapters of *The Way of Perfection* demonstrates that Teresa does not have in mind here a legalistic conformity to the Rule. She lists three virtues which she considers indispensable for inward and outward peace, mental prayer, and contemplation: spiritual love, detachment from everything save God, and humility.

Teresa contrasts a purely spiritual love with the love which entertains sensuality. She admonishes her daughters to cultivate a moderate and spiritual love toward each other and their confessors, a friendship in service to God. She cites the dangers posed by an immoderate concern for another nun or an inappropriate affection for a confessor. Natural familial affection also endangers purely spiritual love. Teresa counsels the nuns to "shun" their relatives. The major distinction between approved, purely spiritual love and earthly love regards the degree of self-interest informing the affection. "This [purely spiritual love] ...," Teresa explains, "is love without any degree whatsoever of self-interest; all that this soul wishes and desires is to see the soul [it loves] enriched with blessings from heaven. This is love, quite unlike our ill-starred earthly affections – to say nothing of illicit affections, from which may God keep us free" (*WP*, p. 73). Spiritual love, as expounded in this passage, explains how Teresa can define human perfection as both the increase of love for God and as the conformity of the will to God. A love for God without self-interest will naturally subordinate the individual's will to God's will. With this equivalence in view, we can understand how Teresa believes that the proper practice of this virtue "would take us a long way towards the keeping of the rest" (*WP*, p. 54).

The remaining two virtues, detachment and humility, overlap considerably as well. A complete detachment includes one's own goals and comforts and a thoroughly humble person could not have any autonomy to harbor self-interested attachments. Detachment is mortification or dying for Christ. Teresa notes that detachment from self always accompanies true humility. Humility, the opposite of pride or self-love, is self-hatred. As for detachment, Teresa claims that if achieved it includes the other two virtues. Similarly, she insists (in keeping with Osuna who, in the *Third Spiritual Alphabet*, labeled humility the "sovereign virtue") that humility ranks as the "principal virtue" and "embraces all the rest." We must take as our guides to humility and detachment the gospel accounts of the extreme humility displayed by both Mary and Jesus. These last two virtues display an interesting logical and practical conundrum. Our attribution of them to ourselves entails a self-referential inconsistency.

These virtues, it is true, have the property of hiding themselves from one who possesses them, in such a way that he never sees them nor can believe that he has any of them, even if he be told so. But he esteems them so much that he is forever trying to obtain them, and thus he perfects them in himself more and more. And those who possess them soon make the fact clear, even against their will, to any with whom they have intercourse. (*WP*, p. 90)

Anyone who genuinely possesses these virtues could never esteem herself highly enough to consider describing herself as possessing them. Alison Weber regards this feature of humility, that to attribute it to oneself is to indicate its absence, as constituting Teresa's rhetorical "double bind" in the *Life*: how to demonstrate her humility and thereby authenticate her experiences without fostering the contrary appearance.[40] In the advice she gives, Teresa suggests that we can only accurately assess these virtues in others. As for ourselves we can only continue to strive after improvement, although she does make some remarks concerning the assessment of our own humility.

Even the belief in our own wickedness and worthlessness cannot infallibly signal humility because sometimes temptation comes packaged in such a belief. The assessment of these beliefs hinges on the feelings they inspire. A belief in one's wickedness that does not overly disturb the soul points toward humility and, conversely, an especially disturbing belief in one's wickedness signals temptation.

Humility, however deep it be, neither disquiets nor troubles nor disturbs the soul; it is accompanied by peace, joy and tranquillity. Although, on realizing how wicked we are, we can see clearly that we deserve to be in hell, and are distressed by our sinfulness, and rightly think that everyone should hate us, yet, if our humility is true, this distress is accompanied by an interior peace and joy of which we should not like to be deprived. Far from disturbing or depressing the soul, it enlarges it and makes it fit to serve God better. The other kind of distress only disturbs and upsets the mind and troubles the soul, so grievous is it. I think the devil is anxious for us to believe that we are humble, and, if he can, to lead us to distrust God. (*WP*, p. 257)

---

[40] Weber, *Rhetoric*, p. 48.

If the distressful recognition of our sinfulness does not disguise a temptation, it brings a peace and joy which enable better practice of the virtues. Beliefs and feelings which inhibit spiritual growth derive from the Devil. Later when we examine Teresa's counsels on the discernment of spirits, we will find a very similar formula: effects produced by God bring spiritual growth whilst effects produced by the Devil bring spiritual aridities. As another test of true humility, Teresa claims that when aware of one's wretchedness, if one cannot turn one's attention to God's mercy, the humility masks a temptation.[41]

To avoid the Devil's snares surrounding these virtues, Teresa urges a continual effort both to love and to fear God. As she puts it, "love will make us quicken our steps, while fear will make us look where we are setting our feet so that we shall not fall on a road where there are so many obstacles" (*WP*, p. 261). In both *The Way of Perfection* and the *Interior Castle* she repeatedly emphasizes the importance of filial fear in the spiritual life.[42] We make progress as long as we grow in love and fear of God. Fear of God or lack of confidence in our own abilities signals humility. How do we recognize these virtues? We can never attain certainty, she admits, but as for love, "Those who really love God love all good, seek all good, help forward all good, praise all good, and invariably join forces with good men and help and defend them. They love only truth and things worthy

[41] Teresa combines both tests in this passage from the *Life*: "For, though the soul is conscious of its own wretchedness and it distresses us to see what we are and our wickedness seems to us to be of the worst possible kind ... and we feel it very deeply, yet genuine humility does not produce inward turmoil, nor does it cause unrest in the soul, or bring it darkness or aridity: on the contrary, it cheers it and produces in it the opposite effects – quietness, sweetness and light. Though it causes us distress, we are comforted to see what a great favor God is granting us by sending us that distress and how well the soul is occupied. Grieved as it is at having offended God, it is also encouraged by His mercy. It is sufficiently enlightened to feel ashamed, but it praises His Majesty, Who for so long has borne with it. In that other humility, which is the work of the devil, the soul has not light enough to do anything good and thinks of God as of one who is always wielding fire and sword. It pictures God's righteousness, and, although it has faith in His mercy, for the devil is not powerful enough to make it lose its faith, yet this is not such as to bring me consolation, for, when my soul considers God's mercy, this only increases its torment, since I realize that it involves me in greater obligations" (*L*, pp. 280–281).

[42] Augustine and Aquinas likewise extol fear of God. Augustine considers it the first of the seven gifts of the Spirit.

of love" (*WP*, p. 262). As for fear, the virtuous "forsake sin, occasions of sin, and bad company…" (*WP*, p. 267).

These virtues, love, detachment, and humility, comprise the key to spiritual progress. We increase in human perfection through the cultivation of these virtues. In varying degrees they represent necessary but not sufficient conditions for peace, mental prayer, and contemplation. And these desiderata all relate to the nuns' grand purpose, the union of wills. Mental prayer and contemplation help the soul achieve perfection, and in the *Conceptions* Teresa links peace with perfection. She describes the nine kinds of false peace and contrasts them with the true peace found in devotion to God. In Augustinean fashion, perfection brings in its trail true peace. Some minimal attainment of the virtues significantly abets one's ability to engage in mental prayer or meditation. Teresa claims that we must exert tremendous labor to pray mentally, if we do not possess the virtues to some small degree. Conversely, we cannot achieve states of infused contemplation through our own efforts and they require a high degree of human perfection.[43]

Teresa's central rationale for urging continual prayer lies in the capacity of prayer to develop the virtues. Meditation "is the first step to be taken toward the acquisition of the virtues and the very life of all Christians depends upon their beginning it" (*WP*, p. 117). This extreme importance rests on a set of equivalencies Teresa establishes, all commencing with meditation or mental prayer. The practice of meditation functions as an exercise in self-knowledge. Teresa continually refers to the *Interior Castle* as a guide to self-knowledge. She labels the entry to the castle or first mansion the room of self-knowledge. Furthermore, she insists that self-knowledge remains of paramount concern. "However high a state the soul may have

---

[43] In *The Way of Perfection* Teresa reasons that God will grant visions and other favors to the unvirtuous as a spur, but could not take pleasure in union with a defiled soul and, therefore, cannot induce contemplation (*WP*, p. 119). Within one page, however, she has contradicted herself and stated that God for motivational purposes will even grant contemplation to the undeserving, "though rarely and not for long at a time" (*WP*, p. 120). In the earlier *Life* she contends that God only gives consolations to those who pray because God must have the soul alone, pure and desirous in order "to take His delight in it" (*L*, p. 113).

attained, self-knowledge is incumbent upon it, and this it will never be able to neglect even should it so desire" (*IC*, p. 37). Self-knowledge remains crucial throughout the path of perfection or Spiritual Marriage. In *The Way of Perfection* Teresa suggests her daughters perform a spiritual self-examination before and after every period of prayer (*WP*, p. 259).

Self-knowledge holds such importance for Teresa because it is tantamount to humility. In the "Conceptions" Teresa notes that one can usually only attain true self-knowledge in a community where one must submit to the will of a superior and remain under the constant scrutiny of peers. Outside a community one can too easily fool oneself about one's humility. Spiritual exercises represent one route to humility. By meditating on or praying mentally to God, we naturally realize our own humble station. In the *Interior Castle* she gives two reasons for meditating on God in order to attain self-knowledge. First, we learn more about ourselves through the contrast with God. Second, even by entertaining thoughts of God, we become nobler (*IC*, p. 38). In the *Life* Teresa also points out that by meditating on God we reform more quickly because we become conscious of the attention he pays to us (*L*, p. 109). By constantly mentally conjuring God, the nun gains virtue (humility and love) through the recognition of her lowliness before God and, therefore, a profound degree of self-knowledge. Teresa also, incidentally, refers to this humble self-knowledge as truth because "to be humble is to walk in truth, for it is absolutely true to say that we have absolutely no good thing in ourselves, but only misery and nothingness; and anyone who fails to understand this is walking in falsehood" (*IC*, p. 196). Mental prayer or meditation underwrites the whole Christian mission for Teresa because it promotes self-knowledge which increases the virtues and provides a source of truth. Practice of mental prayer, as we have seen, both leads to individual perfection and defends Christ's Church on earth.

THE FAVORS OF MENTAL PRAYER

In her works Teresa employs several metaphors for the spiritual life (to which I have occasionally made reference). Her two most celebrated metaphors each contain an enumeration which contributes to the sense that a hierarchy informs prayer. A deep tension runs through Teresa's works because, on the one hand, she insists that one cannot measure spiritual progress by the consolations one receives from God. Only continual pursuit of the virtues insures spiritual progress. Yet, on the other hand, her writings rely on hierarchically structured metaphors illustrating the soul's progress through the various degrees of prayer. Over the course of eleven chapters the *Life* (completed in 1566) employs the conceit of watering a garden. The resulting metaphor of the "four waters" has had an enormous influence over the subsequent centuries. The imagery probably derives from Paul's analogy to the laborer who waters God's field (1 Corinthians 3:6–9), but also resembles the tree of life which grows in God's garden, sustained by God's flowing waters, and whose fruit are the virtues (Genesis 2:9–10, Psalm 1, Matthew 7:16–20), a Christian symbol of the religious life common since, at the latest, Bonaventure's *Lignum Vitae*. The garden represents the soul. The plants of the garden represent the virtues and water represents prayer, so necessary for the growth of the virtues.

The beginner must think of himself as of one setting out to make a garden in which the Lord is to take his delight, yet in soil most unfruitful and full of weeds. His Majesty uproots the weeds and will set good plants in their stead. Let us suppose that this is already done – that a soul has resolved to practice prayer and has already begun to do so. We have now, by God's help, like good gardeners, to make these plants grow, and to water them carefully, so that they may not perish, but may produce flowers which shall send forth great fragrance to give refreshment to this Lord of ours, so that He may often come into the garden to take His pleasure and have His delight among the virtues. (*L*, p. 127)

God has planted in the beginner the virtues necessary for perfection and she must now pray to cultivate those virtues. God will only delight in the soul if the gardener can water the plants. Human perfection, in other words, depends on the cultivation of the virtues. The four waters or degrees of prayer metaphorically correspond to four different ways in which water reaches a garden.

It seems to me that the garden can be watered in four ways: by taking the water from a well, which costs us great labor; or by a water-wheel and buckets, when the water is drawn by a windlass (I have sometimes drawn it in this way: it is less laborious than the other and often gives more water); or by a stream or brook, which waters the ground much better, for it saturates it more thoroughly and there is less need to water it often, so that the gardener's labor is much less; or by heavy rain, when the Lord waters it with no labor of ours, a way incomparably better than any of those which have been described. (*L*, p. 128)

The four waters represent four levels of prayer. The levels ascend in value and, inversely, descend in labor required of the gardener. The later waters result from God's direct activity which requires no effort from the individual.

Teresa's later and more mature *Interior Castle* (1577) divides the spiritual path into seven stages. The guiding conceit here involves "a castle made of a single diamond or of very clear crystal" (*IC*, p. 28). The mansion contains seven sets of rooms, "some above, others below, others at each side; and in the centre and midst of them all is the chiefest mansion where the most secret things pass between God and the soul" (*IC*, p. 29). The metaphor of the soul as a castle comprising seven chambers appears prominently in *Zoharan* Cabala. More orthodox sources are easily found however. Proverbs 8:31 and John 14:2 taken together suggest that God takes his delight in us and that his house has many mansions. Aquinas's account of heaven fosters the idea of a hierarchy of mansions distinguished according to degrees of charity (*Summa Theologiae Sup.* 93.3). Augustine's influence, moreover, accounts for the number seven. Because of the seven days of creation and the seven spiritual gifts enumerated in the Vulgate translation of Isaiah 11:2–3, Augustine attributed perfection and sanctity to the number seven. "Scripture, therefore," he claims, "as the Church has recognized, extols the number seven and presents it as consecrated in a sense to the Holy Spirit."[44] Like the *Interior Castle* Augustine's protomystical passages (Bk. xxxiii, *De quantitate animae*; Bk. i, *De Genesi contra Manichaeos*; Bk. xxvi, *De uera religione*) often

---

[44] *The Literal Meaning of Genesis*, John Hammond Taylor, SJ, tr. (New York: Newman Press, 1982), vol. i, p. 155.

consist of a hierarchy of seven stages, culminating in stasis or rest. The thirteenth- and fourteenth-century Christian mystics Hadewijch of Brabant, Beatrijs of Nazareth, and Marguerite Porete all follow Augustine and use the number seven enumeratively.

Teresa explains that the soul must enter into its most secret recesses to meet God who resides in the innermost chamber. Teresa recognizes that the notion of the castle entering itself requires some explication.

I seem rather to be talking nonsense; for, if this castle is the soul, there can clearly be no question of our entering it. For we ourselves are the castle: and it would be absurd to tell someone to enter a room when he was in it already! But you must understand that there are many ways of "being" in a place. Many souls remain in the outer court of the castle, which is the place occupied by the guards; they are not interested in entering it, and have no idea what there is in that wonderful place, or who dwells in it, or even how many rooms it has. You will have to read certain books on prayer which advise the soul to enter within itself: and that is exactly what this means. (*IC*, p. 31)

Teresa's perplexity here recalls Augustine's puzzlement in *De Trinitate* (Bk. x) about how the mind can come into the mind. To make sense of Teresa's metaphor, Pike distinguishes carefully between the two uses of "soul": the soul as the castle and the soul as the explorer of the castle. His rendering of the imagery probably formalizes Teresa too much, but it serves to remind us of the ambiguity of Teresa's metaphor. Worldly inclinations besmirch the outer mansions and God's light shines from the innermost mansion. Various reptiles lurk near the entryway to the castle, waiting for the soul, in a moment of weakness, to drop its defenses and hoping to slip inside and defile the castle. The soul's entry into the seventh chamber represents the Spiritual Marriage. The practice of mental prayer, on the other hand, represents entry through the doorway of the castle.

Deft practice of mental prayer brings about a state of the soul which Teresa, following Osuna, labels Recollection. Teresa prescribes in *The Way of Perfection* a method for recollecting the faculties. One must begin with an examination of conscience, confession of sin and signing oneself with the cross. Next, one must take Christ as a companion and imagine him teaching one. Teresa felt very strongly about meditating on God in his human aspect. In chapter xxii of the *Life*, she challenges the prevalent view that in prayer one should try to rise above the corporeal. She risked censure and argued that this technique invites temptation and deception. Imagining Christ does not mean cogitating about him. Teresa simply wants her nuns to look with the mind's eye at (i.e. imagine) Christ's unsurpassable beauty. One can look at the passion and see the compassion and love in his suffering eyes. One may use an image of Christ to facilitate the imagination and devotional books in the vernacular help in recollecting oneself as well. Finally, one should reverentially and tenderly speak to Christ. This method of prayer requires constant practice and arduous perseverance, but the rewards of this prayer provide ample recompense.

The practice of this manner of prayer, whether vocal or purely mental, results in recollection. Recollection means that the soul occupies the faculties entirely with God and that the five outward senses remain largely unoccupied. The faculties focus on God while the outward senses languish. In fact, the experienced often find their eyes shutting involuntarily in recollection. Importantly, recollection does not mean a silence or sleep or suspension of the faculties. It simply refers to a shutting-up of the faculties within the soul itself. The practice of mental prayer, which when properly executed results in recollection, accelerates spiritual progress.

Those who are able to shut themselves up in this way within this little Heaven of the soul, wherein dwells the Maker of Heaven and earth, and who have formed the habit of looking at nothing and staying in no place which will distract these outward senses, may be sure that they are walking on an excellent road, and will come without fail to drink of the water of the fountain, for they will journey a long way in a short time. (*WP*, p. 185)

The fact that the individual can herself induce recollection distinguishes it from higher levels of prayer. Through effort and training she can teach herself to enter into herself and experience the various benefits of recollection. These experiential benefits include devotions, spiritual tendernesses or sweetnesses, and the gift of tears. Recollection and its consequent benefits all occur within Teresa's first water in the *Life* where the gardener waters the garden through his own considerable labor. The gardener is responsible for the water necessary for the growth of the virtues. Similarly, these exertions and benefits occur within the first three mansions of the *Interior Castle*, where, Weber observes, martial metaphors (*miles Christi*) predominate.[45]

Throughout her writings Teresa makes an important distinction between natural and supernatural prayer or natural and supernatural experiences. This distinction assumes particular importance at this juncture because she declares all of the experiences described above natural. The experiences she begins describing in the second water and the fourth mansion she labels supernatural. Upon even a careless reading of Teresa's works, the sense of the distinction comes across. Although ultimately the responsibility for any of our desires or intentions rests with God, through our God-given volition we can ourselves achieve natural experiences. Supernatural experiences, on the other hand, require the special intervention of God. We cannot effect them at will. They "cannot be acquired by industry or diligence, though we can certainly prepare for" them.[46] "If one were to die of longing for" them, "it would be of no help, for" they "will not come except when God bestows" them.[47] The phrase "supernatural experiences" is not synonymous with "God-given experiences," however. For Teresa and her contemporaries another supernatural being regularly intervenes in the affairs and experiences of humans.

The Devil causes counterfeit experiences in an effort to drive a wedge between the individual and God. Supernatural experiences, therefore, could derive from either of two sources. In consequence, the individual practicing prayer faces two tasks. On the one hand, she must determine if her experience had a natural or supernatural origin. On the other, she must determine whether her supernatural experiences came from God. Teresa illustrates this two-fold task in this passage from the *Life*.

[45] Weber, *Rhetoric*, p. 110.   [46] Teresa, "Relations," p. 327.   [47] Ibid., p. 331.

"When I found that my fear was getting such a hold over me, because I was progressing in the practice of prayer, it seemed to me that there must either be something very good about this or something terribly bad; for I was quite sure that my experiences were supernatural because sometimes I was unable to resist them, nor could I come by them whenever I wanted to" (*L*, p. 221). The natural experiences associated with the first water and the first three mansions all work as benefits to the soul. Not all natural experiences have such a salutary impact. Natural experiences can have a pathological influence on the spiritual life and the Devil can use them to sway the traveler. Accordingly, Teresa employs various techniques to discover the natural or supernatural origin of an experience. As we shall see, supernatural experiences appear more vividly than the natural and one cannot control them, "for clearly, if she could [recall it to the imagination], it would be a case of imagination and not of actual presence, to recapture which is not in her power; and so it is with all supernatural matters."[48]

In her early works, Teresa drew the line between natural and supernatural experiences cleanly, with recollection described as a natural experience and anything higher, beginning with the famous Prayer of Quiet, described as supernatural. In "Relations" v and the *Interior Castle* which she based on it, however, Teresa amends her tidy schema. In both she discusses a supernaturally inspired form of recollection. To confuse matters further, in the *Interior Castle* she begins to describe the Prayer of Quiet in mansion four when she remembers to include "this Prayer of Recollection which ought to have been described first, for it comes far below the consolations of God already mentioned ... " (*IC*, p. 90). She fails to mention in what mansion this supernatural recollection properly belongs. In any case, in this supernatural recollection, the individual feels her attention involuntarily turning in upon herself. Her eyes close and she effortlessly enters the sort of recollection usually only attainable through effort. Teresa tries to draw this distinction as best she can, although she remains puzzled by God's ways.

---

[48] Ibid., p. 326.

Do not suppose that the understanding can attain to Him, merely by trying to think of Him as within the soul, or the imagination, by picturing Him as there. This is a good habit and an excellent kind of meditation, for it is founded upon a truth – namely, that God is within us. But it is not the kind of prayer that I have in mind, for anyone (with the help of the Lord, you understand) can practice it for himself. What I am describing is quite different. These people are sometimes in the castle before they have begun to think about God at all. I cannot say where they entered it or how they heard their Shepherd's call: it was certainly not with their ears, for outwardly such a call is not audible. They become markedly conscious that they are gradually retiring within themselves. (*IC*, pp. 86–87)

Teresa points out that despite the supernatural origin of this recollection, the faculties assume the same role as in natural recollection. The recollection does not still or suspend the faculties, but leaves them fully active to concentrate on God. The will, imagination, and understanding can continue to profit from their exercise. In "Relations" v Teresa does, however, describe the senses in an unfamiliar manner. She notes that the soul seems to have a new set of interior senses corresponding to the exterior senses. The soul meanwhile pays no attention to the exterior senses. Unfortunately, she does not elaborate on these newly acquired interior senses. In both places she seems to indicate that the higher forms of prayer, like the Prayer of Quiet, either begin directly from this supernatural recollection or only commence after having undergone this experience.

The Prayer of Quiet represents the lowest state of infused contemplation. Teresa discusses it in the second water and the fourth mansion. In the *Interior Castle* she maintains the water metaphor, but with less emphasis on the human effort involved. The second water pictures the gardener employing a windlass to irrigate the garden. Correspondingly, Teresa in the *Life* says that the Prayer of Quiet "in which the soul begins to recollect itself, borders on the supernatural" and admits that the labor involved can weary the soul (*L*, p. 148). The metaphor in the *Interior Castle*, however, draws the contrast between recollection and the Prayer of Quiet more dramatically.

These two large basins can be filled with water in different ways: the water in the one comes from a long distance, by means of numerous conduits and through human skill; but the other has been constructed at the very source of the water and fills without making any noise . . . [The former] corresponds to the spiritual sweetness which, as I say, is produced by meditation. It reaches us by way of the thoughts; we meditate upon created things and fatigue the understanding; and when at last, by means of our own efforts, it comes, the satisfaction which it brings to the soul fills the basin, but in doing so makes a noise, as I have said.

To the other fountain the water comes direct from its source, which is God, and, when it is His majesty's will and He is pleased to grant us some supernatural favour, its coming is accompanied by the greatest peace and quietness and sweetness within ourselves – I cannot say where it arises or how. And that content and delight are not felt, as earthly delights are felt, in the heart – I mean not at the outset, for later the basin becomes completely filled, and then this water begins to overflow all the Mansions and faculties, until it reaches the body. (*IC*, p. 81)

Teresa here contrasts natural and supernatural sweetness, but without mentioning recollection. She also fails to call attention to any human effort involved in the Prayer of Quiet. Teresa in the *Interior Castle*, in effect, foreshortens from the perspective of the advanced stages the picture she provides of the spiritual life's early stages.[49] In the later work she offers more stark contrasts between the various early levels of prayer and dedicates more time to the advanced stages. It appears that she may not yet have experienced the final stages described in the *Interior Castle* at the time she wrote the *Life*.

Despite this augmented emphasis on the supernatural inspiration of the Prayer of Quiet, Teresa still does not consider it a union experience. "[I]t is not a thing that we can fancy, nor, however hard we strive, can we acquire it, and from that very fact it is clear that it is a thing made, not of human metal, but of the purest gold of Divine wisdom. In this state the faculties are not, I think, in union, but they become absorbed and are amazed as they consider what is happening to them" (*IC*, pp. 82–83). The involuntary character of the experience

---

[49] I recognize clearly the dangers of imposing too much order on Teresa's texts. Teresa did not place nearly the premium on consistency that many of her interpreters would like. One of my strongest objections to Pike's *Mystic Union* concerns the artificial order he constructs from her disorder.

vouches for its supernatural character, but God does not suspend the faculties. They do not fail. Instead, he stills or absorbs them. Teresa does indicate that God unites the will to his own, but leaves the understanding and imagination free to help the will love him. The other faculties may function, she advises, but not so laboriously as to interfere with the favor which God bestows. The soul feels quietude, joy, satisfaction, tranquility and sweetness, although a markedly different sweetness from that cultivated in recollection. In several places Teresa likens this prayer to an intense ambient perfume. The body experiences delight and would prefer not to move lest it disturb the soul's communication with God. In the Prayer of Quiet God communicates his presence and delight to the soul of the individual, but not in the same degree or manner that he does at higher levels of spiritual progress.

> This state of prayer is different from that in which the soul is wholly united with God, for in the latter state it does not even swallow its nourishment: the Lord places this within it, and it has no idea how. But in this state it even seems to be His will that the soul should work a little, though so quietly that it is hardly conscious of doing so. What disturbs it is the understanding, and this is not the case when there is union of all the three faculties, since He Who created them suspends them: He keeps them occupied with the enjoyment that He has given them, without their knowing, or being able to understand the reason. (*WP,* p. 206)

By thralling only the will God forces the understanding to exert some effort in receiving his message. In this water the soul must still perform some labor to irrigate the garden of the virtues. The understanding, faced with the Divine, works to learn the truth about the relative unimportance of the worldly.

Because the Prayer of Quiet admixes the natural and supernatural, Teresa believed that the Devil could cause the most harm in the fourth mansion. The Devil can tempt the soul with his own supernatural effects or can use natural states to his own advantage (in fact the Devil can even use divine supernatural consolations to his benefit, *L,* pp. 187–188). The soul must pay special heed to its self-examination to determine the nature of the favors it receives. One can recognize a pernicious natural state because it leaves one in a state of aridity. Natural states only sometimes result from our efforts. Teresa warns against mistaking a certain spiritual languor brought on by physical weakness for true, supernatural Quiet. Genuine Quiet does not overwhelm the body and lasts a relatively short time. Most importantly, "It must be understood that although, when this state is something that really comes from God, there may be languor, both interior and exterior, there will be none in the soul, which, when it finds itself near God, is moved with great joy" (*IC*, p. 93). Supernatural Quiet, as opposed to this form of natural weakness, betrays itself by the growth of love for God and attention to the divine. Similarly, divine Quiet distinguishes itself from demonic quiet by its residue of joy and the growth of humility and virtue it inspires. It builds confidence in the mercy of God, increases the desire for penance, counters the fear of trials, and augments the resolution to revile the merely mundane. Demonic quiet ends in disquiet and, "It leaves neither light in the understanding nor steadfastness in the will" (*L*, p. 159).

Whereas the Prayer of Quiet usually occurs to the sedate, Teresa reports one similar state where the individual can engage in any number of activities while remaining in contemplation. Unfortunately, Teresa classifies this experience in different ways in different works. In the *Life* (p. 170) she describes it in the third water, the experiences contained in which succumb completely to foreshortening in the *Interior Castle*. The third water expounds on several sorts of experiences which involve a not yet complete sleep of the faculties or union. The faculties, though united with God, can nonetheless with difficulty act. The soul gains wisdom through these supernatural states. In her seven mansions Teresa makes no mention of this stage of experiences. In the "Relations" she describes this state similarly to its description in the *Life*, but in *The Way of Perfection* (p. 203) she clearly considers it a variant of the Prayer of Quiet.[50] These classificatory variations arise from a discrepancy about whether or not the faculties sleep during this experience. In the *Life* and

---

[50] Teresa, "Relations," p. 328.

the "Relations" Teresa indicates that God suspends the faculties in union, but not deeply. In fact, she leads the reader to believe that of all the types of contemplation recounted in the third water, God leaves the faculties most free in this one.

In all three accounts Teresa claims that God unites only the will to himself and leaves the other two faculties available to work in God's service. She considers this favor an especial blessing because it enables an individual to simultaneously perform both manners of devotion. The individual can, in this state, fulfill the office of both the contemplative and the active. She can emulate the ways of both Martha and Mary (Luke 10:38–42).

In the fourth water and the fifth mansion Teresa describes and commends the Prayer of Union. Here God completely unites the faculties and senses to himself by bringing the soul yet closer to him. Teresa reports that in the Prayer of Union one appears to have fainted. The body does not move, nor even detectably breathe.

It gradually ceases to breathe and all its bodily strength begins to fail it: it cannot even move its hands without great pain; its eyes involuntarily close, or, if they remain open, they can hardly see. If a person in this state attempts to read, he is unable to spell out a single letter: it is as much as he can do to recognize one. He sees that letters are there, but, as the understanding gives him no help, he cannot read them even if he so wishes. He can hear, but he cannot understand what he hears. He can apprehend nothing with the senses, which only hinder his soul's joy and thus harm rather than help him. It is futile for him to attempt to speak: his mind cannot manage to form a single word, nor, if it could, would he have the strength to pronounce it. For in this condition all outward strength vanishes, while the strength of the soul increases so that it may the better have fruition of its bliss. (*L*, pp. 177–178)

Whereas in the Prayer of Quiet, Teresa uses olfactory imagery, here she often uses tactile and gustatory imagery.[51] God induces

---

[51] Pike dedicates a portion of *Mystic Union* to this and similar descriptions found in other Christian mystics. He examines the correspondences between the relative propinquity of the soul to God and the sensory metaphors employed. The deeper union states require metaphors expressing closer contact. The mystics use the senses, like taste and touch, for the deepest states, which require contact between God and the mystic.

a sleep of the faculties and suspends them from their wonted stations. Because of the body's stillness and the faculties' inattention to the world, Teresa calls the soul "dead." The soul has no memory and cannot imagine or think. The will loves, but the understanding does not know anything except that it remains in God's presence; "in some respects it is like a child receiving and delighting in this caress without having the intelligence to understand whence it comes."[52] In this, the final, water, the soul undertakes no labor at all in bringing the consolations. The effort is all God's. The water springs up from the center of the soul. No labor can induce this state. Nor can the soul make any sort of effort during the contemplation. That the suspended will can still love requires, therefore, some explanation. Teresa resorts to divine action to explain it.

The soul is not even sufficiently awake to love, but blessed is the sleep, and happy the inebriation, wherein the Spouse supplies what the soul cannot and bestows on it so marvelous an "order" that, though all the faculties are dead or asleep, love remains alive. The Lord ordains that it shall work, without knowing how, and that so marvelously that, in complete purity, the soul becomes one with the very Lord of love, Who is God. (*L*, pp. 391–392)

Love, the product of the will, retains its ardor in the complete sleep of the faculties because of God's provision. This intense contemplation lasts only a short while, but it does the soul tremendous good. The wisdom imparted and consolations offered to the soul occur without any effort on the part of the soul and the soul has no conception of how God brings these benefits to it. The soul also cannot understand how it could possibly deserve such favors.

In this mansion the virtues continue to grow apace. The soul still tries to suborn its will to God. Teresa explains that at the stage of the Prayer of Union the soul has not yet achieved Spiritual Marriage; nor has it achieved Spiritual Betrothal. Here the soul prepares itself for betrothal to God. The Prayer of Union represents a meeting of sorts, a negotiation and a rendezvous for further acquaintance.

[52] Teresa, "Conceptions," p. 385.

It seems to me that this union has not yet reached the point of spiritual betrothal, but is rather like what happens in our earthly life when two people are about to be betrothed. There is a discussion as to whether or no they are suited to each other and are both in love; and then they meet again so that they may learn to appreciate each other better. So it is here. The contract is already drawn up and the soul has been clearly given to understand the happiness of her lot and is determined to do all the will of her Spouse in every way in which she sees that she can give Him pleasure. His Majesty, Who will know quite well if this is the case, is pleased with the soul, so He grants her this mercy [the Prayer of Union], desiring that she get to know Him better, and that, as we may say, they shall meet together, and He shall unite her with Himself. We can compare this kind of union to a short meeting of that nature because it is over in the very shortest time. (*IC*, p. 119)

God, recognizing the virtue of the soul, bestows the Prayer of Union so that the soul can learn more about her intended mate. This grace, in turn, strengthens the virtues even more. The soul becomes worthier of the Spouse and inflamed with love. The soul must warily evade the wiles of the Devil who eagerly attempts to win back the soul before losing it completely. Teresa notes, however, that God sounds "a thousand interior warnings of many kinds" to prevent the soul's fall (*IC*, p. 122). Advance requires the soul's careful attention.

If the soul experiences the Prayer of Union "and not illusions, or the results of melancholia, or the workings of nature itself" or the temptations of the deceiver, "time reveals the fact" through the extraordinary virtue and love that the soul evinces.[53] In various places Teresa catalogues the qualities displayed by someone who genuinely experiences the Prayer of Union. She feels an extreme tenderness and her humility flows more deeply. She exhibits tremendous resolve and courage in the face of danger and even welcomes trials by which to demonstrate the sincerity of her love for God. In her intercourse with others, she practices charity and cheerfully forgives wrongs, and contact with her brings profit to others. Although Teresa has reservations about discerning the origin of other favors based on their interior marks or felt quality, as for the Prayer of Union, she declares that the decisive indication that it

[53] Ibid., p. 395.

comes from God lies in the extraordinary certainty that God implants in the soul. When the soul returns to itself after union, the soul "cannot possibly doubt" that God united himself with it. "This certainty of the soul is very material" (*IC*, p. 101). Even if the soul cannot doubt that God visited the soul, however, the Devil can use this experience to his advantage through temptation and the resultant erosion of the virtues (the onset of pride, for example).

We have not yet discussed some of Teresa's best known experiences. In the *Life* she includes a number in the fourth water. She discusses rapture (elevation) and what she would later call impulses. Here she seems to want to say that the terms elevation, rapture, transport, and flight of the spirit all refer to the same experience. In the "Relations" and the sixth mansion of the *Interior Castle*, she draws a clear distinction between raptures (ecstasies or trances) and transports, but may treat the terms "transport" and "flight of the spirit" synonymously. In all three works, lacking precise terminology, she gropes to express the view that all these various experiences do not differ in their mechanisms from the Prayer of Union or from each other. They differ in their felt quality: "even though they both may be the same, the Lord works differently in them" (*L*, p. 176). She claims that they do not differ in substance, but then proceeds to describe their phenomenological differences. While all include the suspension of the faculties, the qualitative experience of the suspension comes in different varieties.[54] Not only does their felt quality differ, the degree of benefit that the experiences confer differs as well. Impulses too appear to involve some form of supernatural suspension (although she does not make much of this comment), for, in impulses, she says, "a great part of the time during which it is in that state, the faculties are inactive: they are suspended by their distress, just as in union and rapture they are suspended by joy" (*L*, p. 195).

Rapture differs from the Prayer of Union primarily in four ways. Firstly, one cannot resist a rapture. With great exertion, on the other hand, one can resist Union. Secondly, the subject

---

[54] Teresa, "Relations," p. 328.

can feel the stages of development of a rapture; it has a cumulative quality and lasts longer. After a rapture the faculties may remain absorbed for days. Union has a consistency of feeling that rapture does not. Raptures build to a higher level than Union. Teresa also reports that over time quantitatively different raptures become successively stronger. Thirdly, raptures prove more beneficial than Union. Whereas the Prayer of Union functions as a courtship of sorts, God bestows raptures when he betroths the soul (this difference presumably explains why Teresa treats of rapture in a higher mansion than Union). God communicates to the soul more clearly in raptures. He grants both imaginary and intellectual visions in raptures.[55] The soul apprehends God's messages so easily that Teresa declares: "My own belief is that, if the soul to whom God has given these secrets in its raptures never understands any of them, they proceed, not from raptures at all, but from some natural weakness, which is apt to affect people of feeble constitution, such as women" (*IC*, p. 153). The clarity of insight in raptures becomes, for Teresa, a means of culling the false from the genuine experiences. Fourthly, whereas Union occurs interiorly, raptures display both interior and exterior effects. Sometimes, Teresa reports, she lost consciousness. The body grows cold and, remarkably, the head and sometimes the entire body arise with the elevated soul. Sheerly for interest's sake, I offer her description of one incident: "On other occasions, when I have felt that the Lord was going to enrapture me (once it happened during a sermon, on our patronal festival, when some great ladies were present), I have lain on the ground and the sisters have come and held me down, but none the less rapture has been observed" (*L*, p. 191). Teresa here reports levitating during raptures![56]

Raptures differ from transports or flights of the spirit because of their gradual character. Transports, conversely, occur with striking rapidity. God shines a bright light from the center of the

---

[55] See below for a discussion of the varieties of visions.

[56] Amy Hollywood has suggested to me that Teresa might engage here in a bit of self-hagiography based on the accounts of saints' lives which she devoured throughout her life.

soul and the higher part of the soul (elsewhere identified by Teresa as the will or, synonymously, the spirit) rises so quickly as to feel, in flight, like it leaves the body. Teresa stresses the great importance of courage when undergoing transport because the soul has no idea where or by whom it is being taken. The soul must have prepared itself to die for God. Teresa returns to the water metaphor when describing transports, but with a fury missing from the metaphor in the *Life*.

I think that basin of water, of which we spoke in (I believe) the fourth mansion (but I do not remember exactly where), was being filled at that stage gently and quietly – I mean without any movement. But now this great God, Who controls the sources of the waters and forbids the sea to move beyond its bounds, has loosed the sources whence water has been coming into this basin; and with tremendous force there rises up so powerful a wave that this little ship – our soul – is lifted up on high. And if a ship can do nothing, and neither the pilot nor any of the crew has any power over it, when the waves make a furious assault upon it and toss it about at their will, even less able is the interior part of the soul to stop where it likes, while its senses and faculties can do no more than has been commanded them ... (*IC*, p. 158)

The metaphor has evolved from the means of watering a garden, through the filling of a basin, to the plight of a ship on rough seas. This new form of the metaphor serves to highlight a transport's violence and the soul's fear while experiencing it. It also works well with the way Teresa describes the experience's culmination. After this rough sea passage, the transported soul finds itself as if in "another world," exposed to many truths through an elaborate vision composed of mental images.

He feels as if he has been in another world, very different from this in which we live, and has been shown a fresh light there, so much unlike any to be found in this life that, if he had been imagining it, and similar things, all his life long, it would have been impossible for him to obtain any idea of them. In a single instant he is taught so many things all at once that, if he were to labor for years on end in trying to fit them all into his imagination and thought, he could not succeed with a thousandth part of them. (*IC*, p. 160)

Although the transport culminates in mental images, the unaided imagination could never produce such an experience.

Teresa employs this conclusion to argue for the supernatural origin of transports. The peace, tranquility, and benefits which follow in the wake of the transport insure its divine origin. She enumerates three benefits in particular: knowledge of the greatness of God, extreme humility, and a disregard for the things of this world.

Impulses represent the other major favor which Teresa includes in the fourth water. She describes them as intense desires which come from outside the soul and enrapture it. They occur suddenly with the memory of a significant word or the recognition of God's absence and last for perhaps half an hour. Sometimes the soul loses consciousness. The acute distress caused by the desires causes the soul great hardship. It wishes to die and see God and, in fact, fears that it might not die. The soul burns so ardently that it almost consumes itself. Teresa nonetheless labels this "dying for death" a delectable martyrdom; it brings incomparable happiness. In the *Life* Teresa warns that in an impulse the lower part of the soul seeks human companionship to alleviate a fear of death, but in her later works, claims that the soul shuns all companionship but God's. Impulses take a physical toll on the body. The pulse slows. The hands stiffen, causing pain in the wrists. One's bones feel racked for days. The individual doesn't notice these symptoms until after the impulse subsides because: "The subject is given enough to do by the consciousness of what is happening within him: even were he being severely tortured I do not think he would feel it. He is in possession of all his senses: he can speak – he can even observe; walk about, however, he cannot, for the sudden assault of love would fling him to the ground."[57] Elsewhere, she explains that during an impulse the enormity of the spiritual pain completely obscures the physical pain which the soul only perceives later.

In the sixth mansion Teresa describes other favors God grants the soul to awaken it to him. Sometimes the soul

[57] Teresa, "Relations," p. 331. These symptoms do not seem to warrant a diagnosis of rapture. In the places Teresa uses the word in connection with impulses she probably speaks loosely. She does not generally include impulses in her lists of types of suspension of the faculties.

suddenly and very clearly feels itself called to God. Teresa had this experience before she ever had impulses or raptures. It involves the absorption of neither the faculties nor the senses. They both remain fully awake. It feels a delectable wound to the heart (which she often calls an impulse, albeit of a different species), caused it cannot say how or by whom. God, although present, beckons the soul to him. The soul, in turn, feels a joyous grief about its position before God. This pain can either last a long time or end after a short duration. The soul hears this spiritual call with none of the senses or faculties. Teresa describes the distress arising from this call vividly. "I know that this distress seems to penetrate to its very bowels; and that, when He that has wounded it draws out the arrow, the bowels seem to come with it, so deeply does it feel this love" (*IC*, p. 136). This imagery strongly recalls the transverberation which Bernini captured in his renowned sculpture. In the *Life* Teresa follows an account of these woundings with the famous report of the transverberation. One major aspect of her description of transverberation distinguishes it from these woundings. In the transverberation Teresa reports experiencing a sensory vision of the angel who impaled her. These woundings, on the other hand, occur without one knowing by whom or how.

Teresa defends the divine origin of these woundings in several ways. The fact that the faculties and senses remain awake increases her confidence in her ability to judge. The Devil, on the one hand, could never cause a wounding because he could never combine pain with joy and tranquility. The pain, moreover, arises from the depths of the soul, the seventh mansion, where the Devil has no jurisdiction. Finally, the virtues that grow in the soul from this experience rule out a demonic origin. The wounding, on the other hand, could not result from fancy because the imagination could never create anything so wonderful. Here Teresa seems to mean that because we cannot, through direct intention, ourselves induce such an experience, the cause lies beyond the ability of the fancy. Melancholy, furthermore, cannot cause the wounding because melancholy influences the imagination and this experience comes from the interior of the soul. In summary, she concludes that if the soul has any doubt about the authenticity of the wounding it experiences, then the wounding is not genuine. Such a claim indicates the clarity of the call felt in the soul.

Another method in which God awakens the soul consists in his speaking to it. Danger, she says, accompanies this favor. The soul must always attend to the possibility of deception. In discussing the best course of action to take with those who falsely claim to receive messages from God, Teresa demonstrates perspicuity and a subtle understanding of human psychology. She advises that one should not place any credence in the locutions reported by the melancholy or those with feeble imaginations. Furthermore, she suggests that one not try to convince them that their experiences have demonic origin. This tactic only upsets them and encourages them to adamantly defend the locutions. Instead, one should counsel them to ignore the locutions because the virtuous life does not consist in receiving locutions. Teresa also, at one point, recognizes the possibility of self-fulfilling locutions ("It may also happen that, when such a person asks something of Our Lord with a great love, he thinks that the voices are telling him what he wants to be told; this does in fact sometimes happen" *IC*, p. 144).

Genuine, God-given locutions occur in different kinds. One sometimes hears locutions from outside the soul, sometimes from above the soul and sometimes from within the innermost part of the soul. All three types can come from God; the first two types from God, the Devil, or the imagination. Receiving locutions from God, however, indicates nothing about the spiritual state of the recipient. God sometimes speaks to those in peril. Locutions heard through the bodily ears invite the most danger of deception because the Devil can most easily counterfeit them. Locutions heard through the ears of the soul prove more reliable and less likely to deceive, but intellectual locutions prove trustworthy and safe. The second type of locution involves the hearing of speech in the mind's ear, so to speak. One hears words interiorly as when imagining conversation. In this case, however, the will takes no part in creating the speech. Intellectual locutions involve a "celestial language" in which one hears no ordinary words at all. God tells one things without any use of conventional language. Teresa's tri-partite schema of types of locutions corresponds precisely to the three types of visions. In fact, Teresa considers intellectual locutions a species of intellectual visions.

Of the first two sorts of locutions, Teresa explains the signs by which one can identify divine locutions. She prefaces this discussion with the general reminder that one must disregard any locution that does not conform to the teachings of scripture because all divine locutions will so conform. If the locution diverges from scripture, "There is no need, in that case, to go in search of signs, or to ask from what spirit it comes; for this is so clear a sign that it is of the devil"[58] (*L*, p. 239). Elsewhere Teresa emphasizes this point with regard to any favor. It also explains, of course, much of her literary production. She recorded her spiritual experiences for the approval of her confessors and superiors. She wanted to confirm that her favors conformed to scripture and the teachings of the Catholic Church. Writing about herself in the third person, Teresa noted, "She used to say that, if any of these things led her into opposition to the Catholic Faith and the law of God, she would not need to go in search of proofs, for she would know at once that they came from the devil."[59] Early in her career as a mystic, Teresa worried terribly about her favors, despite the fact that her behavior improved after receiving them. That God sent them represented her best explanation of her experiences; "though from the effects produced and the great favours wrought in her she judged that some of these things must have been caused by a good spirit."[60] Yet, she still fretted about the possibility of deception. Eventually, an inquisitor visited Avila and Teresa managed to secure an interview. After meeting her, he corroborated her inference. "He told her that there was nothing in all that she had said which had to do with his office, because all that she saw and heard only confirmed her more in the Catholic

---

[58] In the *Interior Castle*, she allows that a locution that diverges from scripture could derive from the imagination as well as the Devil. Nonetheless, one must ignore the locution.

[59] Teresa, "Relations," p. 323.   [60] Ibid.

Faith."[61] The inquisitor based his belief on this same general principle. Divine favors cannot contradict the scriptures or the teachings of the Church.

The more specific signs which Teresa offers to help in identifying divine locutions pertain to their effects. First, a sense of power and authority attends divine locutions. They alleviate distress and instill confidence in a troubled soul. A single word can serve as the antidote to aridities and disturbances of the soul. A demonic locution, conversely, not only fails to assuage one's spiritual trials, but rather, can actually introduce trials. Second, divine locutions bring tranquility and peacefulness to the soul. Through the power of the divine words, it becomes recollected. Third, the memory of the words the soul hears in a divine locution remains etched permanently in one's memory. The divine locution also instills a deep certainty concerning the truth of the locution. Locutions deriving from the imagination do not manifest these three signs. The understanding, rather than listening, finds itself actively composing the message. The words it strings together do not have the clarity of a divine locution and one can divert one's attention from a natural locution. God compels one's attention, conversely, when he speaks to the soul. Lastly, the fact that one cannot induce a locution exhibiting the three signs demonstrates their supernatural origin. Demonic locutions, although more dangerous than those deriving from the imagination, prove more easy to recognize. They also do not display the three signs. Teresa insists that the three signs provide sufficient evidence of a divine locution, but nonetheless, for insurance suggests that one consult a confessor whenever the locution concerns a matter of great importance.

Teresa considers intellectual locutions both the safest and the most valuable of the types of locutions.[62] They occur rarely and do not last long. In this experience one learns in a manner which baffles the intellect. God does not employ human language and one hears nothing with the bodily ears or with the ears of the soul. Because these locutions do not agitate the

---

[61] Ibid., p. 321.   [62] She agrees with John of the Cross in this judgment.

senses or faculties at all, the Devil can gain no purchase and remains impotent. God imparts knowledge without the recipient engaging in any activity. Teresa explains that God wishes the soul to have a feel for heaven where no one communicates by speech. Although in the previous types of locution God forces one to attend to his speech, here:

... the soul does nothing, for even the mere insignificant ability to listen, which it has possessed until now, is taken from it. It finds all its food cooked and eaten: it has nothing to do but to enjoy it. It is like one who, without having learned anything, or having taken the slightest trouble in order to learn to read, or even having ever studied, finds himself in possession of all existing knowledge; he has no idea how or whence it has come, since he has never done any work, even so much as was necessary for the learning of the alphabet. (*L*, p. 252)

This divinely inspired knowledge attests to some sort of communication whereby God explains both the difficult and the mysterious to the mystic. Although these locutions do not involve any bodily or spiritual senses, they do involve a language of sorts. In describing them Teresa mentions both syllables and words. The depth in the soul at which this learning takes place, the clarity of the speech, the secrecy of the utterance, the manner in which the communication proceeds and the subsequent effects of the locutions all serve to convince one that they do not derive from the Devil.

Teresa additionally produces five criteria by which to distinguish a genuine intellectual locution from one produced by the imagination. First, a genuine locution has a clarity and distinctness unattainable in locutions suggested by the imagination. One hears every phoneme and the phraseology. Second, genuine locutions sometimes occur unexpectedly, whereas the imagination would, Teresa assumes, require conscious thought of a topic to produce a locution about it.

The second reason is that often the soul has not been thinking of what it hears – I mean that the voice comes unexpectedly, sometimes even during a conversation, although it frequently has reference to something that was passing quickly through the mind or to what one was previously thinking of. But often it refers to things which one never thought would or could happen, so that the imagination cannot possibly have invented them, and the soul cannot be deceived about things it has not desired or wished for or that have never been brought to its notice. (*IC*, p. 145)

Here again we see clearly the inference that Teresa makes concerning the best explanation of unexpected psychic events. An extraordinary state or occurrence must have a supernatural origin if one has not consciously and intentionally induced it. Third, the soul simply hears genuine locutions. In locutions caused by the imagination, on the other hand, "someone seems to be composing bit by bit what the soul wishes to hear" (*IC*, p. 145). This criterion obviously closely relates to the previous one. Fanciful locutions tip their hand by one's conscious awareness of creating them. Fourth, one word of this "celestial language" employed by God in intellectual locutions contains a vastness of meaning. The understanding could never put this much meaning into language so quickly. Once again, the limits of ordinary consciousness mark the boundary beyond which supernatural explanations commence. Fifth and finally, in genuine intellectual locutions the soul gains more understanding than the words themselves deliver. Teresa concludes by noting that the Devil sometimes tries to fool one with ersatz intellectual locutions. He speaks clearly and distinctly enough to mimic God, but he cannot produce the extraordinary effects of divine intellectual locutions, nor does he leave the soul peaceful and tranquil.

Teresa's discussion of the only other remaining major sort of favor in the sixth mansion, visions, closely parallels her account of locutions. She does not, however, treat visions as one of God's means for awakening the soul. God simply communicates his love through visions. Visions share the same categorization as locutions. Just as Teresa mentioned locutions heard with the bodily ears, she discusses visions with the bodily eyes. As she mentioned locutions heard with the ears of the soul, she also discusses visions seen with the eyes of the soul. Finally, Teresa considers intellectual locutions a type of intellectual visions. Visions also have the same hierarchy as locutions. Corporeal visions invite the greatest opportunity for deception while, conversely, the Devil cannot counterfeit intellectual visions because he can only see the images in our minds. Teresa mentions that she never experienced corporeal visions. While Teresa's discussion of visions corresponds quite closely to Augustine's views in Bk. xii of *De Genesi ad litteram libri duodecim*, her mistrust of corporeal visions also corroborates Christian's observation about the decline of apparitions in late sixteenth-century Spain. Apparitions simply lost their cultural approbation. While she denigrates corporeal visions, Teresa trumpets the benefits attending visions seen with the eyes of the soul, or imaginary visions as she calls them, and intellectual visions.

Intellectual visions appear without any imagery or use of interior or exterior senses. They can last for long periods, as long as a year. These visions cannot possibly derive from the imagination or the Devil because of the good effects they bring to the soul. They bring confusion and humility. One's inability to understand how one perceives these visions and one's inability to produce them on one's own, humbles one before "this Almighty Lord, Who can do what we on earth cannot even understand, for there are things to a knowledge of which no man, however learned, can attain."[63] One's ignorance and impotence before these extraordinary psychological events humbles one before God. Demonic visions bring the opposite effects.

Imaginary visions employ the eyes of the mind and last only a short while. God compels one to see something beneficial which teaches the soul more than it could have learned itself. God permanently imprints on the mind the image received in an imaginary vision. The image is not static like a picture, but rather alive and responsive. These two types of visions usually occur together and often shortly after the climax of a rapture or transport. Teresa had both imaginary and intellectual visions of Christ, saints, demons, and the dead. When God appears, he always manifests himself in his humanity, although imaginary visions provide a better forum for Christ to reveal his bodily aspect and intellectual visions better communicate his divinity. Visions contrast with states of contemplation where the

---

[63] Teresa, "Relations," p. 326.

Godhead influences the soul and suspends the faculties meditating on Christ.

When he appears in an intellectual vision, "He presents
Himself to the soul by a knowledge brighter than the sun. I do
not mean that any sun is seen, or any brightness is perceived,
but that there is a light which, though not seen, illumines the
understanding so that the soul may have fruition of so great a
blessing" (*L,* p. 250). Although intellectual visions occupy a
higher station than imaginary visions, the latter can prove more
beneficial because of their conformity with our human nature,

> ... for, though the former type of vision [intellectual] which, as I said,
> reveals God without presenting any image of Him, is of a higher kind,
> yet, if the memory of it is to last, despite our weakness, and if the
> thoughts are to be well occupied, it is a great thing that so Divine a
> Presence should be presented to the imagination and should remain
> within it. These two kinds of vision almost invariably occur simultane-
> ously, and, as they come in this way, the eyes of the soul see the
> excellence and the beauty and the glory of the most holy Humanity.
> And in the other way which has been described it is revealed to us
> how He is God, and that He is powerful, and can do all things, and
> commands all things, and rules all things, and fills all things with His
> love. (*L,* p. 263)

The radiance and beauty of imaginary visions of Christ wield a
tremendous influence over the visionary. Teresa claims that
they even improve the health! The Devil's counterfeit imaginary
visions, on the contrary, exhibit neither the splendor of genuine
visions, nor the spiritually and physically salutary effects. As for
the possibility that the imagination could create these favors,
once again Teresa insists on the supernatural origin of a
psychological event because of the impossibility of one's consciously bringing about that event.

> Of all impossibilities, the most impossible is that these true visions
> should be the work of the imagination ... In any case, there is no
> other way in which it would be possible for us to see in a moment
> things of which we have no recollection, which we have never thought
> of, and which, even in a long period of time, we could not invent with
> our imagination, because, as I have already said, they far transcend
> what we can comprehend on earth. (*L,* p. 264)

For Teresa the limits of the conscious mind circumscribe the natural. If one could recall one of these visions to mind afterward, "it would be a case of imagination and not of actual presence, to recapture which is not in her power; and so it is with all supernatural matters."[64] That which we cannot consciously bring to mind must have its origin in the supernatural. A vision of God which we can't consciously repeat signals God's actual presence.

Teresa recounts visions of her deceased confessors, nuns and celebrants as well as Saints Mary, Peter, Paul, Joseph, and Clare. In one vision Mary and Joseph clothed her in celestial raiment. In another, Jesus reached out and grasped her rosary and transmuted it into four large jewels of incomparable beauty. He told her that henceforth it would always look that way to her, but to no one else. Teresa reports that this pronouncement indeed proved true. Without a great deal of specificity, Teresa claims that she regularly received prognostications in her visions that eventually came true. Once in a vision God also plunged Teresa into hell so as to better educate her about the perils of an unvirtuous life. He also bestowed visions which show how all things subsist in God and visions which seem to reveal the Godhead. In the *Life*, Teresa describes these last as the sublimest and most profitable of all the visions she received. On other occasions, God allowed her to vividly see the havoc that the Devil wrought for souls in sin. In one such instance Teresa witnessed demons at a funeral for a man who had led a bad life.

While his body was being wrapped in its shroud, I saw a great many devils taking hold of it and apparently playing with it and treating it roughly. I was horrified at this: they were dragging it about in turn with large hooks ... After what I had seen I was half crazy. During the whole of the funeral office I saw no more devils; but afterwards, when the body was laid in the grave, there was such a crowd of them waiting there to take possession of it that I was beside myself at the sight and had need of no little courage to hide the fact. (*L*, p. 372)

Through visions like this one, God enabled Teresa to see the consequences of behavior which remain veiled to most others.

---

[64] Ibid., p. 326.

He imparted to Teresa an esoteric knowledge of both the fate of individuals and the ways of the spiritual world.

In addition to the favors God bestowed on her, the Devil also appeared to Teresa in imaginary visions. Of course, she avoids any intimation of an heretical dualism by explaining that the Devil can only interfere in one's life when God permits it. She freights her accounts of these visions with palpable drama. Sometimes the Devil appeared to her in order to frighten her. Here she tells of a particularly vivid experience.

Once, when I was in an oratory, he appeared on my left hand in an abominable form; as he spoke to me, I paid particular attention to his mouth, which was horrible. Out of his body there seemed to be coming a great flame, which was intensely bright and cast no shadow. He told me in a horrible way that I had indeed escaped out of his hands but he would get hold of me still. (*L*, p. 288)

In this vision the Devil directly addresses Teresa; in another he "alighted" on her office-book while she performed her devotional prayers. In other visions of demons, however, God enabled Teresa to perceive the demons, usually invisible, who harassed her. He wanted her to understand the source of her torment. Teresa once offered herself as a surrogate object of demonic abuse, in place of an acquaintance who was fighting temptation after two and a half years of mortal sin. Soon after, she experienced excruciating bodily suffering. God permitted Teresa to see the cause of her suffering. "The Lord evidently meant me to realize that this was the work of the devil, for I saw beside me a most hideous little negro, snarling as if in despair at having lost what he was trying to gain" (*L*, p. 288). These demons appeared to her many times and at least once left behind them the smell of brimstone, perceptible by the other nuns. Teresa mentions two antidotes for the trials inflicted by these demons. Making the sign of the cross causes them to retreat, but they quickly return. Holy water, the other remedy, proves far more efficacious. "One night, too, about this time, I thought the devils were stifling me; and when the nuns had sprinkled a great deal of holy water about I saw a huge crowd of them running away as quickly as though they were about to fling themselves down a steep place" (*L*, p. 291). Holy water not only chases away the Devil, but also refreshes and restores the body.

The penultimate mansion, the sixth, comprises approximately one third of the *Interior Castle*. The final mansion, the seventh, which represents the culminating state of Spiritual Marriage, takes far fewer pages to expound. In part this disparity may owe to Teresa's humility. She expresses reluctance to write very much about Spiritual Marriage because to do so might indicate a presumption on her part that she has achieved it.

And indeed I have been in a state of great confusion and have wondered if it will not be better for me in a few words to bring my account of this mansion to an end. I am so much afraid it will be thought that my knowledge of it comes from experience, and this makes me very much ashamed; for, knowing myself as I do for what I am, such a thought is terrible. On the other hand, whatever your judgment about it may be, it has seemed to me that this shame is due to temptation and weakness. (*IC*, p. 207)

Although writing about Spiritual Marriage might indicate a lack of humility, Teresa concludes that the scruples which would lead her to avoid the topic themselves disguise a temptation and so she chooses to write. Elsewhere Teresa explains the difficulty involved in recognizing the Spiritual Marriage. Only those in grace can achieve Spiritual Marriage and, further, only those in grace can know that they have attained Spiritual Marriage. In keeping with orthodoxy, however, she claims that no one can know whether she is in grace. Ultimately, therefore, one cannot know if one has attained Spiritual Marriage.

The brevity of the final mansion might also owe to the fact that the chastened soul no longer needs extraordinary states and favors to teach it. Teresa states that raptures generally abate in the seventh mansion which represents God's abode within the soul. Upon entering this mansion, however, God, to prepare the soul for Marriage, suspends the faculties in some way that Teresa leaves unclear except to indicate it is a more profound union experience. He then delivers an unusual intellectual vision of the Holy Trinity.

First of all the spirit becomes enkindled and is illumined, as it were, by a cloud of the greatest brightness. It sees these three Persons, individually, and yet, by a wonderful kind of knowledge which is given to it, the soul realizes that most certainly and truly all these three Persons are one substance and one Power and one Knowledge and one God alone; so that what we hold by faith the soul may be said here to grasp by sight, although nothing is seen by the eyes, either of the body or of the soul, for it is no imaginary vision. Here all three Persons communicate Themselves to the soul and speak to the soul and explain to it those words which the Gospel attributes to the Lord – namely, that He and the Father and the Holy Spirit will come to dwell with the soul which loves Him and keeps His commandments. (*IC*, pp. 209–210)

Here the Godhead appears to the soul and reveals the mysteries of the trinity, but also in the end, through the gospel message, reiterates the significance of Spiritual Marriage. If the soul loves God and keeps the commandments, or in other words, suborns her will, God will dwell in her or unite himself to her. After this vision, the bride continually feels the companionship of the three in her heart's interior, although the soul sometimes feels their presence more strongly than at other times. This constant companionship fortifies the soul to work in the Lord's service even more ardently than before. With this effort the soul pursues even greater perfection. Because of the ever present possibility of backsliding the soul cannot undergo perfect Spiritual Marriage on earth.

Although Teresa admits that when granting Spiritual Marriage, God will bestow different experiences on others, she attempts to describe her own experience. She underwent a vision in which God announced a mingling of their affairs.[65] In

---

[65] Peers suggests the following passage from "Relations" xxxv as a more precise description of the message here bestowed on Teresa: "Then He revealed Himself to me, in an imaginary vision, most interiorly, as on other occasions, and He gave me His right hand, saying to me: 'Behold this nail. It is a sign that from to-day onward thou shalt be My bride. Until now, thou hadst not merited this; but henceforward thou shalt regard My honour as not only that of thy Creator and King and God but as that of My very bride. My honour is thine, and thine, Mine.'"

Peers's hypothesis has some merit, but we should not place too much weight on it because in the seventh mansion Teresa notes that she had experienced visions with a similar message to that of the Spiritual Marriage in the earlier mansions. They simply didn't manifest the sublimity of the vision signaling the Spiritual Marriage. The fact that this vision resembles those of "other occasions" militates against Peers's suggestion.

grappling to portray this favor she contradicts herself. Initially, she states that Jesus appeared in an imaginary vision, but one unlike any other she had previously witnessed. Later, she denies that Jesus appeared in an imaginary vision and claims he appeared in an intellectual vision, but again, an intellectual vision more subtle than any previous. Regardless, Jesus appeared as he looked after the resurrection. This vision strains her categories for visions because of its extreme force and the fact that it appears in the deepest recess of the soul, farther away from the senses and faculties than the others.

This instantaneous communication of God to the soul is so great a secret and so sublime a favour, and such delight is felt by the soul, that I do not know with what to compare it, beyond saying that the Lord is pleased to manifest to the soul at that moment the glory that is in Heaven, in a sublimer manner than is possible through any vision or spiritual consolation. It is impossible to say more than that, as far as one can understand, the soul (I mean the spirit of this soul) is made one with God, Who, being likewise a Spirit, has been pleased to reveal the love that He has for us by showing to certain persons the extent of that love, so that we may praise His greatness. (*IC*, p. 214)

Not only does God appear in a new manner, the profundity of the union between God and the soul has increased. Teresa compares the previous degrees of union to the joining of two candle flames, which though indisputably fused one can nonetheless separate by pulling apart the candles. The union of Spiritual Marriage more resembles rain falling into a body of water, where no hope of segregation remains after the commingling.

The Spiritual Marriage endows the soul with "secret aspirations" which Teresa professes an inability to describe. It feels tremendous obligations which it strives to fulfill. The soul in Spiritual Marriage remains in safety as long as God permits and the soul does not offend. Accordingly, the soul takes every opportunity to improve. Throughout all trials, however, the soul feels an inner security and peace because she has tamed the passions and God resides within the soul's innermost chamber. Teresa highlights two effects of the Spiritual Marriage. One involves a total self-forgetfulness of the soul. The soul's concerns focus entirely on the honor of God. Teresa reminds her nuns that this self-forgetfulness pertains to interior matters, not to exterior. She follows the Jesuit ideal of moderate physical mortification. Her nuns must eat, sleep and carry out the obligations of their profession. The other effect introduces "a great desire to suffer" on behalf of the Lord. The soul rejoices in the opportunity to endure trials sent by God. It also no longer longs for spiritual favors or consolations. It would like only solitude in which to render praise or service to God. It enjoys great tranquility and does not experience the spiritual aridity encountered in earlier mansions. The soul has no fear of deception in this mansion. The soul makes no use of the senses or faculties at all, so the Devil cannot interfere. God does not permit the Devil entrance to this mansion. Occasionally, however, God lets the soul experience the temptations and aridities associated with the earlier mansions, but only for at most a day, to further strengthen the soul's resolve.

Teresa ends the *Interior Castle* by urging her nuns that spiritual progress always depends on the imitation of Christ. They must continually cultivate the virtues and demonstrate a willingness to suffer. Contemplation without the virtues yields no progress. Teresa commends the ways of both Martha and Mary. Even the contemplative must dedicate herself to a life of virtue and service. Human perfection does not consist in the isolable experience bestowed by God, but in the constraining of one's will so that it conforms entirely to God's will. Prayer and contemplation represent means of attaining the virtues necessary for perfection. "This, my sisters," Teresa declares, "I should like us to strive to attain: we should desire and engage in prayer, not for our enjoyment, but for the sake of acquiring this strength which fits us for service" (*IC*, p. 231). The unions, raptures, visions, and locutions only assume their rightful meaning within this larger call to virtue, service, and selflessness.

CHAPTER 7

Modernity and its discontents

Credulity is certainly a fault as well as infidelity.
Archbishop Tillotson ("A Discourse Against
Transubstantiation", 1679)[1]

I concluded chapter 5 by exploring Alston and Swinburne's ambivalent and ambiguous stance toward explanation. They insist that direct perception of God provides an immediate source of grounds not based on an inference to the best explanation. It transfers the existence of God from the status of an explanatory hypothesis in need of defense to the status of an immediately justified belief. An unacknowledged explanation returns again, however, to bridge the gap between justified beliefs about God (based on putative encounters) and genuine perceptions of God. That God actually appears to individuals in experience best explains the justified beliefs.

In this chapter I intend to trace out another aspect of this tension concerning explanation. We explored how Alston and Swinburne's direct realism and particularist principles downplay the explanatory commitments embedded in experience and relieve the theist of the burden of proof. We did not pay much attention, however, to the peculiar nature of the explanations they seek to suppress. The rhetorical force imbuing the assimilation of religious experience to perception derives from the manner in which such a move masks the supernaturalism of the former with the naturalism of sense perception. To liken God-experiences to sense perception

---

[1] *The Works of Dr. John Tillotson*, vol. II (London: 1820), p. 451.

obscures supernaturalism behind the cloak of uncontroversial good sense. Here I will bring to light the covert supernaturalism involved in mystical perception and again suggest that Alston misplaces the burden of proof. Despite its alleged directness, mystical perception requires a commitment to supernatural causation. In a context of such controversy about theism he must offer reasons in defense of supernatural explanations.

In the following section I will summarize my conclusions from the study of Teresa of Avila in chapter 6. I intend here to highlight the importance of context in studies of religious experience and justification. The historicist theory of justification I outlined in chapter 3 relativizes justification to a context. Although, I argue, one can always subject the justified beliefs of a context to a larger inclusive debate about justification, beliefs justified (or not requiring justification) in one context can prove unjustified in another. I hope to demonstrate that the explanatory logic embedded in Teresa's mystical testimonies conforms to the wider explanatory values of her time. Teresa, additionally, serves to illustrate how alien a culture which fully and consistently embraces supernatural explanations appears to modern eyes. In the remaining portion I, with no pretense of originality, attempt to portray briefly the assumptions entailed by the modern mode of life. I argue that the epistemic values shared by theist and non-theist alike militate against supernatural explanations of phenomena within the causal nexus. In other words I attempt to demonstrate why the explanatory logic of Teresa's era seems so foreign. The philosophical project called classical foundationalism, I claim, represents a side issue to the major impetus of modern approaches to life and its rejection offers no solace to those employing supernatural explanations. The modern ideal of a unified sphere of inquiry with no areas immune from naturalistic explanation renders supernatural explanations suspect and in need of defense. In the face of this ideal, the onus rests on the defender of supernatural explanations to convince that they indeed represent good explanations.

THE RETURN OF THE FINITE SUPERNATURAL:
SUPERNATURAL EXPLANATIONS IN ALSTON

Alston's strategy in *Perceiving God* focuses on the task of rendering mystical perception *prima facie* acceptable. A number of the stances he takes conduce to this effect. His "Right Wittgensteinianism," or doxastic practice approach, protects beliefs formed on the basis of putative mystical perception from critique by other, better established belief-forming mechanisms. Particularist principles also serve to protect beliefs. They explicitly grant *prima facie* acceptability. Finally, construing perception in a directly realist manner minimizes the cognitive activity contributing to experience and thereby permits beliefs foundationally based in this way an initial credibility. These positions result in shifting the burden of proof off the mystical perceiver and onto the skeptic. The skeptic must produce defeaters from within the doxastic practice of mystical perception or acquiesce in the claims of the mystic.

Alston contrasts his model of religious experience with those like the one I adopt here. Despite his somewhat idiosyncratic terminology, he makes it clear that he believes his approach frees the mystic from defending any causal explanations. While my model requires the mystic to defend her embedded supernatural explanation, Alston's model, he claims, doesn't involve any such requirement. He writes:

[I]f we adopt the most common alternative to the perceptual construal – that mystical experience is a purely subjective mode of consciousness that the subject interprets as being due to a transcendent cause – the epistemological question will be whether this *hypothesis* of a transcendent cause can be supported. This means that the subject must have sufficient *reasons* for this supposition if it is to be justified, whereas on the perceptual construal there is at least the possibility of a direct knowledge of God, not based on reasons ... [2]

Although I could only speculate about what he means by "subjective," Alston accurately captures the relevant features of the position I take. Experiential beliefs have the character of

---

[2] William Alston, *Perceiving God* (Ithaca: Cornell University Press, 1991), p. 66. Italics original.

hypotheses and require supporting reasons for justification. Shortly after this passage follows another of like importance:

[O]n the widespread view that mystical experience is to be construed as purely subjective feelings, sensations, and the like, to which supernaturalistic causal hypotheses are added, the issues ... will look very different ... For on this subjectivist construal, the subject is faced with the task of justifying a causal hypothesis before he can warrantedly claim to be perceiving God; whereas if the experience is given a perceptual construal from the start, we will at least have to take seriously the view that a claim to be perceiving God is prima facie acceptable just on its own merits ... (*PG*, pp. 66–67)

In these passages Alston writes as if his model did not require any causal hypotheses, much less supernatural causal hypotheses. He contrasts the view of religious experience which fully attends to the implicit explanatory commitments of the experiencer to his own and leads one to believe that his involves no controversial explanatory commitments. The picture these remarks paint, however, misleads considerably.

Alston himself, only pages earlier, discusses the external conditions involved in perception. He canvasses various theories of perception including his favored "Theory of Appearing" and two others which add an extra condition to the Theory of Appearing. He aims here to preclude objections raised against mystical perception on the grounds that God could not possibly fulfill the external conditions for perception. He argues that God could indeed possibly fulfill the conditions imposed by any of these theories. Each explication of the concept of perception that he describes, however, includes as an essential element that the object perceived both exists and appears to the perceiver. This fact alone indicates that Alston should allow that perception includes a commitment to a belief that the object appearing to one is, in fact, capable of appearing to one. If the very concept of perception includes the commitment that the object appears to one, then it seems dubious to claim that his perceptual model involves no explanatory commitments. In the very making of a perceptual claim, one implicitly commits to the belief that the situation is best explained by the presence of the object allegedly perceived. Even more to the point, the mystical perceiver in particular must have a commitment to the belief that God can and does appear to him in the midst of the natural world. In proving the possibility of God's appearing, furthermore, Alston offers scenarios including supernatural causation and supernatural explanations. To say that his model does not rely on supernatural hypotheses in need of support by reasons simply obscures the conceptual facts about perception.

Once we recognize that perception entails explanatory commitments, that is, commitments that enable one to believe that one is appeared to in a certain way, we must allow for the evaluation of those commitments. When one's commitments invite the sort of controversy which supernatural explanations occasion, it seems obvious that the ethics of belief require that one must submit reasons to justify the commitments. Faced with certain sorts of disagreement, one courts obscurantism in declining to offer reasons in one's own support. Admittedly, the account of justification I offered in chapter 3 acknowledges Peirce's insight that one needs a reason that appeals to one's other beliefs to arouse the genuine doubt that inspires inquiry, but, though others deny it, I believe that protracted disagreement among presumably rational parties provides sufficient reason (by appealing to our rational belief in our own fallibility) to provoke doubt. Perhaps other conditions (better left unformalized) than mere disagreement are necessary in conjunction with it to arouse genuine doubt, but surely any such conditions have been amply met in the case of supernatural explanations. For Peirce, in fact, widespread disagreement over religious or moral beliefs represents the archetypical reason for genuine doubt.

The issue then does not turn, as Alston supposes, on the possibility of supernatural appearances, or, as others like to pose it, on the right to hold supernaturalist beliefs, but rather, turns on the epistemic goodness of supernatural explanations. Does the supernatural explanation of the experience represent the best explanation of the experience? Rather than offer reasons to suppose it does, Alston insulates the mystical perceiver against this question with several layers of epistemological impedimenta. In the final section of this chapter, I give reasons for supposing the supernatural explanation of mystical perception does not represent the best explanation.

Ironically, the point at which Alston most fully owns up to his commitment to supernatural explanations coincides with the clearest example of his misplacing the burden of proof. When addressing naturalistic explanations of mystical perception he admits that it requires a commitment to a supernatural cause. He articulates the naturalist position thus:

> But if the occurrence of mystical experience can be adequately explained solely in terms of this-worldly factors, God need never be mentioned in an adequate explanation. Nous n'avons pas besoin de cette hypothèse. Hence we have no justification for supposing that God is causally involved in the generation of the experience and thus no justification for supposing that the experience is a perception of God. (*PG*, p. 228)

This quotation captures the insight behind the naturalist's challenge: the supernatural explanation is unnecessary and uneconomical. Ultimately, however, Alston argues that the naturalistic challenge only succeeds if it rules out the possibility of God's causal activity. This task, of course, proves impossible because God can work through natural mechanisms. Despite Alston's approach, the burden of proof actually rests on the mystical perceiver who must in the face of acceptable naturalistic explanations justify the appeal to another order of causation within the course of mundane affairs. As we shall see in the final section, the burden of proof rests on the mystical perceiver even in those cases where we don't have an acceptable naturalistic explanation available, because she must demonstrate that a naturalistic explanation is inadequate *in principle*.

The various elements of Alston's epistemology of mystical perception all serve to reduce the prominence of explanation. Direct realism, minimal foundationalism, and "Right Wittgensteinianism," for instance, cooperatively function to bestow *prima facie* acceptability on beliefs formed through mystical perception. This account removes the space for an evaluation of the explanatory commitments entailed by the causal condition of the concept of perception. When the explanatory commitments include a commitment to another order of causation affecting the natural order, this systematic project to avoid the evaluation of explanations makes sense. Alston wishes to avoid having to defend such commitments. He hopes to reverse the burden of proof, to treat mystical perception as "innocent until proven guilty." Seen in this light, the protective intentions apparent throughout *Perceiving God* give the strong impression that Alston has run athwart the ethics of belief. When we attend to the suppressed explanatory elements in mystical perception, it becomes clear that the epistemic goodness of the explanations should guide our reactions to mystical perception. We need not merely seek defeating or overriding considerations.

The remainder of this chapter undertakes the evaluation of supernatural explanations. In the next section I discuss a context which approved of such explanations and in the last I attempt to convey why I believe that we can no longer accept such explanations.

SUPERNATURAL EXPLANATIONS IN TERESA OF AVILA

Experience, I have argued, entails an embedded claim about the best explanation of an event presented to consciousness. I aim in this chapter to demonstrate that the sorts of explanations implicit in Teresa's experiences conformed to the epistemic values of her culture for justified beliefs, but that the mystical perceiver today employs explanations in her experiences that do not conform to our ideals of human epistemic flourishing. In pursuit of this conclusion, therefore, I have had (in chapter 6) both to provide enough background to give a sense of the socio-cultural climate in which Teresa experienced her favors and also to lay out enough of Teresa's own testimonies and exposi-tions to isolate the implicit explanations informing her experi-ences. Let me for my purposes here briefly summarize some of the inferences informing Teresa's experiences and her explana-tions of her experiences.

Repeatedly, Teresa makes manifestly clear that anomalous or seemingly impossible events require a supernatural explana-tion. She recounts, for instance, an unusually large toad she came across whose presence Teresa attributed to God, and believed a warning to her about her wickedness. This sort of explanatory inference, that the best explanation of the unusual draws on the supernatural, enjoyed considerable cultural approbation, even from the social and educational elite. Political leaders and clergy both read the anomalous as a signifier and conducted public affairs in accordance with their interpretations of the sign. Teresa also regularly employs this inference in the interior sphere. Experiences or virtues which one has not brought about through one's own abilities and which one cannot explain otherwise must have a supernatural (*sobrenatural*) explanation. The best explanation of unaccountable interior change invokes the supernatural.

All the things I have described make me believe that these things come from God; for, when I remember what I was and how I was on the road to perdition and should soon have arrived there, my soul is truly amazed at these things, I cannot think whence these virtues have come to me. Without understanding myself, I have realized that they are things that have been bestowed on me and not gained by labor.[3]

Psychological change that one does not feel possible, one has not worked to fulfill, or that one cannot trace to physical illness or weakness has a supernatural origin. The discernment of spirits depends on precisely this principle. The best explanation for experiences which we could not consciously and intentionally induce or explain through infirmity invokes the supernatural.

Within the category of supernatural favors, furthermore, inference to the best explanation determines the divine or demonic origin of experiences and characteristics. In an unusually obvious example of her inferential logic, Teresa reasons:

I cannot believe that the devil has sought out all these means by which my soul has benefited, if they are eventually to be the means of his losing it: I do not take him to be so foolish as that. Nor can I believe it of God that, although I may have deserved to be deluded because of my sins, He has disregarded so many prayers offered by so many good

---

[3] "Spiritual Relations Addressed By Saint Teresa of Jesus To Her Confessors," *Complete Works of St. Teresa*, vol. 1, E. Allison Peers, tr. and ed. (New York: Sheed and Ward, 1957), p. 312.

people for two years past, for I do nothing but beg everybody to pray for me ... I do not think His Divine Majesty would allow these things to be so continually happening if they did not come from Him.[4]

Teresa begins with her beliefs about God and his powers and intentions, the Devil and his wiles, and the virtues she attained and infers their divine origin as the best explanation.

Conformity to scripture functions as one prominent element in this inference. Any experience which contradicts the orthodox and authoritative interpretation of the Bible, no matter what its *felt* qualities, cannot have divine origin. This premise provides a crystalline example of a mystic's beliefs overriding the phenomenological features of an experience. No matter how completely genuine and convincing an experience felt, if the knowledge imparted contradicts scripture, the best explanation of the experience cannot invoke God as the cause. Even the mystics themselves knew that what seems phenomenologically to be the case in mystical experience need not be taken as what is really happening. Nelson Pike draws attention to another example which does not readily apply to Teresa, but he claims appears in other major Christian mystics.[5] At the height of the Union experience, the mystic phenomenologically feels no distinction between the soul and God. Despite this felt quality, however, Christian mystics quickly insist that a distinction remains and that it only *feels* like union without distinctions. Why? Because the mystic knows that humans cannot become God. Despite how it feels, orthodoxy contributes to the best explanation of the experience. In this respect the classical mystics appear far more discerning than Forman who claims that Pure Consciousness Events are not mediated because they do not feel mediated. He gives too much privilege to the phenomenological report in inferring the best explanation of the mystical experience. Similarly, that we do not feel ourselves making inferences in perception does not mean that direct realism best explains perception.

The broad logic of the finite supernatural, that what one

---

[4] Ibid.
[5] Nelson Pike, *Mystic Union: An Essay in the Phenomenology of Mysticism* (Ithaca: Cornell University Press, 1992), pp. 31–40.

can't account for on natural principles must result from supernatural intervention, underlies Teresa and her contemporaries'
explication of the term "miracle." Interspersed throughout her
autobiography Teresa recounts miraculous events which involved the direct action of the deity. In one sterling example,
she begged God to restore an acquaintance's sight. God
appeared to her, tore a nail out of the flesh of his hand, and
assured her that having borne such trials for her, he would fulfill
her request. Within a week the person's sight returned. She
admits the possibility that her prayer may have had nothing to
do with the cure, but felt certain it did because of the vision.
Precisely what the term "miracle" means Teresa explains in the
"Relations." In an imaginary vision Jesus appeared to her and
declared that the founding of the convent at Medina had a
miraculous origin. Teresa says of this exchange, "He meant by
this that, when there had seemed no way of making the
foundation, He alone had done it" (p. 339). A miracle involves
the direct action of the supernatural and one identifies the
action of the supernatural, or a miracle, by the impossibility of a
natural explanation. Teresa draws attention to this connection
with the phrase "when there had seemed no way of making the
foundation." When the natural appears explanatorily bankrupt,
the supernatural assumes the explanatory weight. The same
inference lies behind the miracle of Teresa's uncorrupted
corpse and the supernatural effects attributed to Teresa's books.
One invokes supernatural explanations when known patterns of
natural causation seem explanatorily inadequate.

The symmetry in Teresa between the logic of miracles and
the discernment of spirits has important medieval precedents.
Aquinas, for instance, in the *Summa Theologiae* ruled out direct
experiential contact with the divine on earth, *unless* God performs a miracle and supplies the human with what he needs to
directly experience the divine. Mystical experience for Aquinas
literally takes the form of a miracle (1.12.11.2, 2–2.180.5). The
relation between supernatural experience and miracle will
figure prominently in my later discussion of the modern period.
I will argue that the epistemic values constitutive of modernity
have adverse consequences for supernatural explanations and,

by extension, miracles and the beliefs gained in supernaturally caused experience.

As for the mystical states which Teresa herself experienced, the books and treatises available to her provided much of the information on which she based her inferences. In her auto-biography she reports reading Osuna's *Third Spiritual Alphabet* which taught her about the virtues, prayer, and recollection. Soon after, she recalls, God granted her the Prayers of Quiet and Union before she knew anything about them. Later, she identified them in retrospect from passages she came across in Bernardino de Laredo's *Ascent of Mount Sion:*

> Looking through books to see if I could learn how to describe my method of prayer, I found in one, called *The Ascent of the Mount*, which describes the union of the soul with God, all the symptoms I had when I was unable to think of anything. It was exactly this that I was always saying – that when I was experiencing that type of prayer I could think of nothing. So I marked the relevant passages and gave him the book, in order that he and that other cleric to whom I have referred . . . should look at it and tell me what I ought to do.[6]

Teresa employed Laredo's treatise *ex post facto* to interpret her puzzling experiences. This book, by providing evidence, enabled her to infer that the strange prayer she experienced in which she "could think of nothing" actually accompanied a union of God with her soul. On reading his descriptions of union, she came to believe that divine union best explained her experiences. Laredo provided a template into which she could fit her experiences. After reading Laredo she had a richer context of beliefs about spiritual favors to bring to her future mystical states. The two superiors to whom Teresa gave both a marked copy of Osuna and an account of her life faced the same task with which she struggled. They had to infer the best explanation for the peculiarities of her interior life. To Teresa's dismay, they arrived at the conclusion that the Devil plagued her with these experiences. They also suggested that she confess to a Jesuit, as Jesuits made a vocation of spiritual guidance. The Jesuit, upon hearing her confession, concluded by inference to

---

[6] Teresa of Avila, *The Life of Teresa of Jesus*, E. Allison Peers, tr. and ed. (New York: Image Books, 1960), p. 225.

the best explanation that God led her spirit and gave her directions for self-improvement.

Throughout her corpus Teresa strongly underscores the importance of competent spiritual direction. She insists that a spiritual director himself practice contemplation. To make inferences most accurately about another's spiritual condition, the director must have a store of personal experience on which to draw. In the "Conceptions," a work which Teresa explicitly addresses to the contemplatives in her order, she confirms the role that a template plays in interpreting the inner life. There she claims that without some model, the soul has no understanding of its experiences and no security about their meaning. A text, for instance, can teach that "it is possible for a soul enamoured of her Spouse to experience all these joys and swoons and mortal agonies and afflictions and delights and rejoicings in Him, when she has left all worldly joys for love of Him and has placed herself and left herself wholly in his hands."[7] The text, in other words, provides a context for and explanation of the experiences. Of course, explanations inhere in the experiences as they occur, but a text can both retroactively provide a fuller meaning and, in advance of future experiences, increase the stock of beliefs. Teresa mentions someone she knows (in all likelihood herself) who found solace in the Song of Songs. It allayed her reservations about the favors she had received. It offered a consoling and approved explanation of her experiences. Scripture as we have seen represented an unassailable authority. Inferences based on scripture provided a special security.

All these inferences which Teresa made and which the authorities and texts seconded clearly did not have an unchallenged obviousness. When I argue that the sort of explanations on which Teresa relied conformed to the epistemic values of her era, I do not mean to imply that the explanations she specifically adopted were uncontroversial. In fact, her explanations of her experiences invited considerable controversy. The Inquisition's repeated interest in her writings and testimonies surely

---

[7] "Conceptions of the Love of God," *Complete Works of St. Teresa*, vol. II, E. Allison Peers, tr. and ed. (New York: Sheed and Ward, 1957), p. 361.

marks her explanations as questionable, judged by the standards of the day. The Inquisition's concerns, however, bolster my general case about the legitimacy of supernatural explanation in sixteenth-century Spain. Because it sought to expose the influence of the Devil in human life, the Inquisition demonstrates the centrality of supernatural explanations of mundane affairs. As Teresa's confessor, Domingo Báñez, put the point, "Paul would not have said that Satan transforms himself into an angel of light if that angel did not sometimes illuminate us."[8]

Teresa signals that supernatural explanations had a questionable status in at least two ways. First, she often alludes to the derision that the contemplative faces from those who do not understand or do not believe that God communes with some of those who love him. In her autobiography she more than once refers to her fear of ridicule by the uncomprehending. Whereas the Inquisition resulted from doubt about the divine origin of supernatural experiences, Teresa indicates that ridicule results when others believe the contemplative "invents" her experiences. The pervasiveness of this latter doubt based on naturalistic scruples calls my claim most seriously into question. The second way in which Teresa demonstrates the extent of dissent about her explanations derives from the first. In the *Interior Castle* Teresa mentions at least twice that those who do not believe that God directly reaches out to communicate with humans will not experience his favors. She writes, "At any rate, my own opinion is that anyone who does not believe that God can do much more than this, and that He has been pleased, and is sometimes still pleased, to grant His creatures such favours, has closed the door fast against receiving them."[9] Here she implicitly acknowledges the extent to which the sort of explanation of experience she employs did not carry decisive cultural weight. She also confirms the analysis of experience that I have advanced. In the inference to the best explanation that comprises experience, if one does not begin with the belief that God

[8] Translated by Carole Slade, *St. Teresa of Avila, Author of a Heroic Life* (Berkeley: University of California Press, 1995), p. 145.

[9] *Interior Castle*, E. Allison Peers, tr. and ed. (New York: Image Books, 1961), p. 101.

can communicate with the human soul, one will not conclude that contact with the divine best explains one's experience.

Despite the obvious presence of these dissenting views, however, the response of the religious authorities to Teresa's testimonies, the approbation directed at supernatural explanations in the larger, public culture, and the prestige accorded to Teresa's writings and life demonstrate, I think, the broad sanction accorded supernatural explanations of experience in sixteenth-century Spain. The sort of inferences to the best explanation that characterize her experiences conformed to the values, embraced by her era and locale, characterizing epistemic goodness. The case proves far different today.

EXPLANATION AND MODERN EPISTEMIC VALUES

I propose in this section to demonstrate why I think that supernatural explanations in experience do not exemplify modern values concerning the goodness of explanations of events within the natural world. The explanatory commitments entailed by mystical perception as Alston construes it seem better suited to Teresa's era than our own. Consequently, these experiences do not justify the beliefs based on them. Supernatural explanations, in short, do not make good reasons. It should also become clear why mystical experiences do not add any heft to cumulative case arguments for the existence of God. Other non-experiential arguments would have to render supernatural explanations respectable before religious experiences, which depend on those suspect explanations, could contribute anything to an argument for the existence of God.

In concert with the major emphasis I place on explanation in my account of experience and in my account of justification, I similarly grant explanation a central role in my historicism, in characterizing the epistemic ideals of an era. The range of explanations that humans acceptably and uncontroversially employ (both tacitly in their experience and explicitly in accounting for their experience) reflect the epistemic ideals of a culture. The rules for the evaluation of explanations also indicate a culture's epistemic values.[10] In this section I wish to portray the contemporary standards for the assessment of explanations in such a light as to cast extreme suspicion on supernatural explanations.

Many intellectual historians, following the interpretation suggested by key historical figures themselves, consider the radical rejection of tradition the hallmark of modernity. The Modern Age's self-definition as the era in which the dictates of reason completely repudiate all inherited prejudice has close historical and conceptual links with philosophy's classical foundationalism, the attempt to justify knowledge claims by basing them on indubitably justified beliefs. Both Hans Blumenberg and Jeffrey Stout,[11] however, consider the foundationalist project in its many guises somewhat incidental to the central engines powering the modern era. What Blumenberg calls self-foundation, the pursuit of knowledge *de novo*, does not represent the most defining feature of modernity, he claims. In fact, it obscures the rationale for what he takes to be constitutive of modernity. Similarly, Stout believes the mitigated skeptics (especially Pascal and the Port-Royal Jansenists) responsible for the development of central modern intellectual traits and cultural institutions. Descartes's failed foundationalism, although representing another response to the epistemological crisis initiating the modern era, merely instigated a philosophical agenda. Without entering into lengthy exposition, a glimpse at their position should shed light on modern explanatory commitments. I will use this brief look as a springboard from which to assess super-

---

[10] In a definition congenial to my thesis, Hans Blumenberg, *The Legitimacy of the Modern Age* (Robert Wallace, tr., Cambridge, MA: M.I.T. Press, 1983, p. 66), defines the crucial, transitional periods between epochs, or "epochal thresholds" as "the phases of more or less rapid change in the basic rules for the procurement of very general explanations." The new epistemic values and ideas consequent upon an epochal threshold profoundly influence the most fundamental judgments about the acceptability of explanations. A new epoch for Blumenberg brings a whole new cast of mind: "In man's understanding of the world, and in the expectations, assessments, and significations that are bound up with that understanding, a fundamental change takes place, which represents not a summation of facts of experience but rather a summary of things taken for granted in advance, which in their turn determine the horizon of possible experiences and their interpretation and embody the 'a priori' of the world's significance for man" (p. 138).

[11] *The Flight from Authority* (Notre Dame: University of Notre Dame Press, 1981).

natural explanations. It will also help explain why the collapse of classical foundationalism as a philosophical project does not necessarily lend any support to religious epistemologies.[12]

Blumenberg avers that what he calls "self-assertion" best characterizes modernity. The rise of human self-assertion following the breakdown of the medieval world-view captures the central features of modern thought and culture. Modernity represents the outcome of a dialectic motivated by contradictions within medieval theology. Self-assertion requires that humans give to themselves the standards of thought and action rather than seeking them from an external source, like God. "It means an existential program, according to which man posits his existence in a historical situation and indicates to himself how he is going to deal with the reality surrounding him and what use he will make of the possibilities that are open to him."[13] Self-assertion entails the assumption of a great creative responsibility. Knowledge claims and moral judgments rely for approbation, not on conformity with the God's-eye view, but on conformity to humanly defined standards. Blumenberg repudiates an absolute conception of the world, a conception of reality describing it as it subsists in itself apart from any human conception of it. Rorty describes this modern movement toward greater degrees of self-reliance, an aspiration common to Nietzsche's denunciation of the ascetic ideal and Dewey's instrumentalism, as the willingness "to drop the idea that human beings are responsible to a non-human power."[14]

[12] If one identifies modernity with foundationalism in one of its many senses, one will naturally feel inclined to describe the current period in which foundationalism has lost its grip on us as "postmodern." If, on the other hand, one describes modernity some other way (as do Blumenberg and Stout), one will feel far less inclined to label the current scene "postmodern." Rorty, significantly, limits the term "postmodernity" to "the gradual encapsulation and forgetting of a certain philosophical tradition" ("Cosmopolitanism without emancipation: A response to Jean-François Lyotard," *Objectivity, Relativism, and Truth* [Cambridge: Cambridge University Press, 1991], p. 222). He identifies modernity with the project of classical, philosophical foundationalism and so feels uncomfortable about labeling *culture* postmodern.

[13] Blumenberg, *Legitimacy*, p. 138.

[14] "Science as Solidarity," *Objectivity, Relativism, and Truth* (Cambridge: Cambridge University Press, 1991), p. 39. He footnotes Blumenberg in "Solidarity or Objectivity?" (same volume, p. 33). Pragmatism for Rorty represents something of a culmination of human self-assertion.

Blumenberg's observations corroborate what many, most recently Alasdair MacIntyre and Charles Taylor, have claimed distinguishes the ancient and medieval view of rationality from the modern.[15] Because, among other reasons, of the impact of skepticism and theological voluntarism, seventeenth-century philosophers espouse a procedural conception of rationality in contrast to a substantive conception of rationality. As "ideas" become psychological entities rather than ontological entities ordering the cosmos, the ideal of rationality undergoes a corresponding shift. Whereas rationality signified for ancient and medieval thinkers the proper alignment of theoretical and moral thought with the Reason informing the cosmic order, modern rationality becomes procedural. Rationality for Descartes and Locke, for instance, is a formal notion involving certain canons or standards by which we construct orders in science and life. "Rationality" becomes a term of approbation applied to the conduct or method of inquiry rather than to its proper result. Taylor argues that "the order of ideas ceases to be something we *find* and becomes something we *build*." [16] This idea that modern thought judges itself by its own standards for the construction of theoretical and moral orders clearly resonates with Blumenberg's researches into modern self-assertion.

The oft-noted exaltation of artistic creativity and the visionary artist in modern culture offers support for Blumenberg's thesis from yet another angle. Taylor, among others, has observed that art has come to occupy many of the cultural roles once fulfilled by religion. Art, and not necessarily what the art "represents," comes to be the source of spiritual or moral insight and value. This development in itself suggests that self-conscious creative assertion is central to the characterization of modernity. The modern aesthetic movement within art away from mimesis, moreover, further indicates that important elements of modernity reject responsibility to something non-human.

[15] Alasdair MacIntyre, *After Virtue*, 2nd edn. (Notre Dame: University of Notre Dame Press, 1984); Charles Taylor, *The Sources of the Self* (Cambridge: Harvard University Press, 1989).

[16] Taylor, *Sources*, p. 144.

Blumenberg contrasts self-assertion to self-foundation. The former is his candidate for the central feature of modernity while the latter is its self-description. Whereas self-assertion simply denotes the human activity of establishing criteria of intelligibility and standards of action, self-foundation involves the rejection of all tradition, starting from nothing and arriving at indubitable conclusions justified without recourse to anything dubitable. Blumenberg describes self-foundation as an incidental by-product of historical change. Self-foundation served to reoccupy the position left open by the theological, absolute conception of reality. He believes that self-assertion legitimately characterizes modernity, but that self-foundation in fact undermines the logic of modernity. The force of the demand for self-assertion does not make sense without the historical reasons that contributed to the advent of modernity.

Stout too views the attempts at philosophical foundationalism as somewhat incidental to the really influential modern developments. Philosophical foundationalism which rejected tradition comprised one response to the epistemological crisis afflicting sixteenth-century Europe. The skepticism enlisted in the Reformation conflict of authorities demanded a means of settling disputes on neutral grounds. Stout cites Ian Hacking's research on the origins of modern statistical probability and argues that this development had decisive and profound cultural implications.[17] Although Daston and others have complicated the story of early modern probability, their work does not imperil Stout's contention.[18] The formation of a conception of internal evidence linked to statistical frequency provided a much needed epistemic tool. It rendered skeptical concerns culturally obsolete. As the complex of problems including skepticism and foundationalism became the philosophical question *par excellence*, it lost its cultural importance. In Burnyeat's description (although he supplies another explanation of the fact), skeptical doubt became insulated from ordinary life. The

---

[17] Ian Hacking, *The Emergence of Probability* (Cambridge: Cambridge University Press, 1975).

[18] Lorraine Daston, *Classical Probability in the Enlightenment* (Princeton: Princeton University Press), 1988.

emergence of probability enabled the criticism of religious authorities and thereby secularized debate about vast areas of culture. It allowed rational criticism based on internal evidence rather than authority. Stout claims this loosening of the relations between religious authority, on the one hand, and morality, evidence, and science, on the other, characterizes modernity.

Blumenberg and Stout both locate the essential aspect of modernity not in its pretension to have rationally founded itself free from any influence of tradition, but rather in its creating means of rational criticism and creativity removed from the domain of religious authority and a religious world-view. Both view the paradigmatically modern epistemic values as having emerged from a crisis within the religious order. They both find the move away from a God's-eye conception of Reality characteristic of modernity. They understand the modern model of knowledge to be one which emphasizes the knower's perspective and not the world as it is in itself apart from any faculty of knowing. Foundationalism represents for them a misguided sideshow with little real cultural impact.

Many contemporary religious philosophers assert, conversely, that the modern critique of theism rests on a classically foundationalist epistemology. They link the modern disdain for religion to the inability to justify religious claims on a classically foundationalist basis. By joining the contemporary chorus of critics assailing classical foundationalism, they seek to make theism philosophically respectable again. To this end they fashion epistemologies more congenial to theism. These epistemologies reject evidentialism (that rationality requires one to have evidence in support of religious belief) and place the burden of proof on the non-theist. The minimal foundationalism shared by Alston and Plantinga in his basic belief apologetic represents but one example. D. Z. Phillips adopts an even stronger stance.[19] Relying on a "Right Wittgensteinian" alternate language-games approach (untenable for the same reasons as Alston's) and a fantastic non-cognitivist account of religious

---

[19] *Faith After Foundationalism* (Boulder, CO: Westview Press, 1995).

language, he concludes that in light of classical foundationalism's failure, philosophy of religion must renounce any prescriptive interests. In his desperately cramped view, the only
acceptable role for philosophy is merely descriptive. In fact,
Phillips's language suggests a subservient or protective role for
philosophy in relation to religion. It must conscientiously "wait
on" religion as the "guardian" of its "grammar."

The notion common to Alston, Plantinga, Phillips and
others, that a refashioned epistemology can rehabilitate theism,
rests on the claim that classically foundationalist epistemology
contributed to theism's downfall. Blumenberg and Stout's historical narratives, however, impugn this reading of the history
of theism's intellectual demise. Stout shows, for instance, that
the demise of theism relates much more directly to the rise of
probability than to the philosophical concern with foundationalism. Indeed, he notes that historically the failure of foundationalism to conquer skepticism placed religious beliefs in the
same situation as any other beliefs.

The revival of ancient skeptical writings in the sixteenth century at
first does as much to reinforce the attractiveness of traditional means
for settling disputes as it does to raise doubts about religion, and
whatever doubts it raises about religion tend to be placed on an equal
par with doubts of other kinds. Only a nuanced notion of nondemon-
strative evidence will make religious doubts seem especially severe.[20]

Although thinkers sometimes couch their religious doubt in
terms of their foundationalism, the energy and severity of
modern religious doubt cannot reside in the philosophical
farrago relating to skepticism and foundationalism. One
leading religious epistemologist practically admits as much.

A striking fact about our Enlightenment mentality is that though
science no more fits the foundationalist canons than religion, we have
religiously clung to the conviction that it does, and so, while saying,
"So much the worse for religion," we have continued to embrace our
science. The religious believer has been challenged to display the
grounding for his beliefs, but few have challenged the scientist to show
that his beliefs are grounded in certitude.[21]

---

[20] Stout, *Authority*, p. 109.
[21] Nicholas Wolterstorff, "The Migration of the Theistic Arguments: From Natural

Because science, considered paradigmatically rational, fails as abjectly as religion to conform to foundationalist epistemology, foundationalism could not have motivated modern religious doubt.

Theism, rather, succumbs to the new standards for explanation and evidence. Theistic claims simply seem highly implausible when viewed strictly in the light of these neutral standards. Evidentialism's fortunes depend neither logically nor historically on classical foundationalism. Stout even goes so far as to assert of his work, "Here I shall try to show that the Enlightenment's criticisms of theism are strengthened rather than weakened when reformulated in a nonfoundationalist idiom. I will argue that it was the secularized discourse of the new probability more than the empirical version of foundationalism that caused trouble for theism."[22] He insists that with the rejection of classical foundationalism, theism gains nothing. I further believe that no reformulated epistemology, foundationalist or not, will bolster claims to religious perception because the explanatory commitments involved in such claims do not conform to modern epistemic values. The trouble with supernatural explanations of discrete events lies deeper than epistemological theories. Our naturalism, in fact, constitutes grounds for rejecting epistemological theories which permit supernatural explanation.

Were I interested in corroborating Blumenberg and Stout's accounts of the origin of modern epistemic values I could explore aspects of late medieval voluntarism and nominalism, Renaissance magic, Calvinism, or Descartes's complex relationship with Christian theology to name a few topics. Because I am more interested in laying bare modern epistemic values, I will not try to provide an historical account better found elsewhere. Instead, I will attempt to summarize the features of modern life shared by theist and non-theist alike which substantiate the claim that the fundamental nature of modernity (in comparison

Theology to Evidentialist Apologetics," *Rationality, Religious Belief, & Moral Commitment*, Robert Audi and William Wainwright, eds. (Ithaca: Cornell University Press, 1986), p. 56.
[22] Stout, *Authority*, p. 9.

with Teresa's era) involves a move away from religious authority and a religious explanatory scheme. The weakness of supernatural explanations does not depend on any specific or favored epistemology.

The centrality of institutions of inquiry completely independent of religious commitment represents one particularly salient feature of modern life. Whole domains of culture previously under the aegis of Christian presuppositions and authority have developed into resoundingly secular phenomena in the modern period. Culture's fragmentation has resulted in autonomous disciplines of law and natural science free from religious sanction or guidance. The success and longevity of these institutions has greatly reduced religion's cultural hegemony. Religion has come to occupy a very circumscribed sphere in modern cultural life. Self-assertion or secular forms of inquiry have pushed religious beliefs to the margins of daily life.

The creation of means of inquiry free from religious presuppositions accounts for another defining feature of modern epistemic values. Without recourse to the supernatural, inquirers must limit their explanations to the natural, observable order. In 1931 Carl Becker put these points colorfully.

Zeus, having been deposed, can no longer serve as a first premise of thought. It is true we may still believe in Zeus; many people do. Even scientists, historians, philosophers still accord him the customary worship. But this is no more than a personal privilege, to be exercised in private, as formerly, in Protestant countries, Papists were sometimes permitted to celebrate mass in private chapels. No serious scholar would now postulate the existence and goodness of God as a point of departure for explaining the quantum theory or the French Revolution.[23]

Becker's observations accurately capture the protocol for the practice of inquiry. The quintessentially modern inquirer maintains a unified picture of his endeavors. He rejects any presupposition to inquiry not based on the natural evidence available to him and assumes everything ultimately explicable in terms of a unified causal structure. He employs one causal

---

[23] Carl L. Becker, *The Heavenly City of the Eighteenth-Century Philosophers* (New Haven: Yale University Press, 1932), pp. 15–16.

order for acceptable explanations, believing the world orga-
nized by a unified web available in principle to human inquiry.
Acknowledging what Dewey called "a democracy of individual
facts equal in rank,"[24] he repudiates the idea of mysteries
deemed irresolvable and believes humanly accessible explanations to be the only acceptable ones.[25]

The modern independence of inquiry from religious presuppositions naturally leads to the ultimate form of self-assertion.
Rather than an alternative source of explanations of discrete
events, the supernatural itself becomes a subject of naturalistic
explanations.[26] The significant medieval question about religious experiences, for instance, was whether they were genuine
(i.e. from God) or not. Teresa's major concern, as a case in
point, when recounting her experiences lies in determining
their provenance: whether from God, natural infirmity or the
Devil. After this period, one can look for an unreligious
explanation of the whole topic (i.e. whether there exists such a
thing as a genuine religious experience). This fact bears on
Forman's attempt to establish the existence of the Pure
Consciousness Event. Even if one grants the existence of
contentless consciousness, this admission has no intrinsically
religious importance. The religious significance must be super-
added to the putative cognitive fact of pure experience. The
PCE could, in fact, even serve in a naturalistic explanation of
religion itself. Religions arise in part, so the argument might
run, to account for this universal, but extraordinary experience.

The moment when religion becomes the subject of naturalistic explanation also reckons the ascendancy of modern self-
assertion. It explains a fact about the modern period brought to
light by Michael Buckley.[27] He notes that atheism achieved an

---

[24] John Dewey, *Reconstruction in Philosophy*, enlarged edn. (Boston: Beacon Press, 1948),
p. 66.

[25] See Sidney Hook, "Naturalism and First Principles," *The Quest for Being* (New York:
Greenwood Press, 1963), p. 181.

[26] J. Samuel Preus, *Explaining Religion* (New Haven: Yale University Press, 1987), traces
the history of this line of analysis.

[27] Michael J. Buckley, *At the Origins of Modern Atheism* (New Haven: Yale University Press,
1987). Buckley's major contention, that atheism flourished because the Church
treated it as a philosophical question rather than a Christological or Pneumatological
one, seems jejune. At times Buckley himself draws attention to the historical reasons

unprecedented following and cultural cachet in modernity, but also astutely observes that the term "atheist" enjoys a new use. Whereas in previous eras individuals used "atheist" as a denunciation or accusation of another, in the modern age individuals ascribe it to themselves. " 'Atheist' had been vituperative and polemic; now it had become a signature and a boast."[28] The advent of truly naturalistic presuppositions with which to deny religious claims enabled individuals to label themselves atheists in good conscience. Denying God makes good sense in this context. In previous eras, while possible, it lacked the same rationality. Most so-called atheists simply disagreed with someone about God's nature.

To understand why many early modern free-thinkers felt drawn to atheism further undermines the mistaken view that classical foundationalism is responsible for the downfall of theism. With the cataclysmic effects of religious warfare recent in Europe's memory, many intellectuals harbored moral objections to religion. Even as amoral a figure as the Marquis de Sade felt morally repulsed by religion. In prison he declared himself an atheist and recorded in his notebooks this vivid statement of a not unprecedented sentiment.

Chimerical and empty being, your name alone has caused more blood to flow on the face of the earth than any political war ever will. Return to the nothingness from which the mad hope and ridiculous fright of men dared call you forth to their misfortune. You only appeared as a torment for the human race. What crimes would have been spared the world, if they had choked the first imbecile who thought of speaking of you.[29]

The Reformation not only led to neutral standards for the assessment of evidence and explanation, as seen here it fostered moral objections to theism. These twin effects of the Reforma-

---

why the Church couldn't employ Christological or Pneumatological arguments, namely because the Reformation had eroded any common ground on which to stake such arguments. The patterns of argumentation employed by the Church are better seen as yet another consequence of religious presuppositions losing their foundational status for inquiry.

[28] Ibid., p. 27.

[29] Quoted in Frank Manuel's classic *The Eighteenth Century Confronts the Gods* (New York: Atheneum, 1967), p. 240.

tion jointly represent the preeminent factors responsible for the intellectual demise of theism. In fact, the moral rejection of theism motivated early modern thinkers to try to find evidential reasons to undermine theism, including attempts to explain religion naturalistically. In addition to the moral stance de Sade takes in this quote, he also supplies a naturalistic explanation of religion ("the mad hope and ridiculous fright of men") to counter the religious explanation of religion.

With our modern ideals of self-assertion, our conceptions of an order discernible in nature, and our predominant secular institutions of inquiry, we never reach the point where we declare a naturalistic explanation of discrete events occurring within the natural order unattainable in principle. The success of modern modes of inquiry reinforces this tendency. The incredibly rapid pace of knowledge growth over the last several centuries confirms a hesitation to declare some phenomenon in principle inexplicable on natural principles. Similarly, the necessary specialization of knowledge consequent to the growth of knowledge undermines the confidence of any individual to declare some phenomenon inexplicable. Repeatedly, classes of unexplained events attributed to divine causation have eventually been explained without recourse to supernatural explanations. This lesson has made us reluctant to resort to supernatural orders of causation in explanation. In searching for the best explanation of discrete phenomena, we never choose the supernatural explanation. We await a more economical naturalistic explanation. "The God whom science recognizes," as William James put it, "must be a God of universal laws exclusively, a God who does a wholesale, not a retail business."[30] Anomalies, rather than indicating divine intervention as they did for Teresa, merely point out gaps or inadequacies in our understanding of nature.

Rather than traffic in the finite supernatural, some theists reserve supernatural explanations for accounts of the entire causal nexus. In other words, they limit supernatural explanations to the question "Why something rather than nothing?,"

---

[30] William James, *The Varieties of Religious Experience* (New York: Collier Books, 1961), pp. 383–384.

the question which so captivated Aquinas, Heidegger, Copleston and Tillich, but left Hume and Russell unimpressed. Although my argument in this book essentially concerns the finite supernatural, it is worth pointing out precisely why this famous question has enthralled so many, but seems to others so suspicious. In short, it fails to fulfill the pragmatic conditions, as described in chapter 2, for an explanation request. The topic of a why-question, the description of the fact or event about which one requests an explanation, is not in itself sufficient to individuate a why-question. To constitute an explanation request a why-question must be defined by a relevance relation and its topic must be specified against contrast classes. A relevance relation determines what facts or events, what elements of the entire causal picture, are relevant to an answer to this particular explanation request. An answer to the why-question, "Why is the truck red?," could, depending on the relevance relation, draw on the chemical properties of paint, fire department policies, or safety studies. The contrast class indicates the range of alternatives in light of which the topic needs explanation. The why-question, "Why is the truck red?," will request different explanations depending on whether the contrast class is "the truck is blue, the truck is green, etc." or "the car is red, the building is red, etc." In ordinary cases the context in which one poses a why-question provides both the contrast class and the relevance relation.

The topic of the philosophical question, "Why does something exist rather than nothing?," does indeed have a contrast class which specifies the why-question. In fact, by posing the question in this form, one overtly indicates the contrast class in the question itself. With regard to a relevance relation, however, this question fails. By requesting an explanation of the entire causal nexus, it eliminates the possibility of a relevance relation, a relevant portion of the entire causal picture with which to define the explanation request. The universal nature of this question subverts any possible relevance relation which one might propose, and the question proves deficient in this respect. It removes the background against which we discern the specific meaning of a why-question. Expressed more technically, the question has the syntactic form and semantic content of a why-question, but it lacks one of the pragmatic conditions necessary for a genuine why-question. The question's universal scope renders it, in fact, a pseudo-question. Not unlike how universal skepticism undermines the beliefs which invest the skeptic's language with meaning and thereby prevents her from articulating her skepticism, a universal explanation request undermines the background necessary to invest the question with a specific meaning. The universal question, therefore, is not simply an explanation request which we reject because on our best background theories it could have no true answer (the way we reject the request to know why a particular plutonium atom disintegrated when it did). The problem with the question is more fundamental than that; the question fails even to satisfy the conditions for a genuine why-question.

Because this question systematically repels any possible relevance relation, furthermore, it assumes a baffling or mysterious mien which abets its theological employment. In a devotional or apologetic context the question can work to arouse awe or reverence. The religious evocation of this question, incidentally, is neither limited to Europe, nor to Western monotheism. Hymn 10.129 of the *Ṛg Veda*, for instance, raises ultimate cosmogonic questions while repeatedly rejecting the possibility of any relevance relation.

1 There was neither non-existence nor existence then; there was neither the realm of space nor the sky which is beyond. What stirred? Where? In whose protection? Was there water, bottomlessly deep? ...

6 Who really knows? Who will here proclaim it? Whence was it produced? Whence is this creation? The gods came afterwards, with the creation of this universe. Who then knows whence it has arisen?

7 Whence this creation has arisen – perhaps it formed itself, or perhaps it did not – the one who looks down on it, in the highest heaven, only he knows – or perhaps he does not know.[31]

---

[31] *The Rig Veda*, Wendy Doniger O'Flaherty, tr. (New York: Penguin Books, 1981), pp. 25–26.

Any causal agent which one can suggest in answer to these questions forms a portion of the total causal nexus which requires explanation. The gods, for instance, cannot explain the origin of the universe because they are part of the universe. Any part of the known universe is irrelevant to these questions. In other words, the questions have no known relevance relation. Given the current state of indology, it may be that we can only conjecture about the precise employment of this hymn and the specific emotions it might have aroused. It is nonetheless structurally quite similar to the European question. It frustrates the inquirer in the same way, and is thereby liable to produce some recognizably religious response.

A sustained endeavor to answer the cosmological pseudo-question, moreover, can only result in some variety of apophatic or negative discourse. The moment a proposed answer takes on a determinate shape, it is immediately disqualified. It becomes a "something" about which the question asks. Any attempt to describe determinately the ultimate ground of the cosmos founders because any determinate something cannot be explanatorily ultimate. Even to name the ultimate ground objectifies it; that is, literally makes it an object (comparable to others). To name it makes it a "something." Reflection on the pseudo-question produces in this manner the familiar dynamic of ineffability. Apophatic discourse aims to provide an answer to the pseudo-question while simultaneously frustrating any attempt to describe or name the answer. It systematically works to maintain this inherently unstable position. The relationship between the cosmological pseudo-question and apophatic discourse appears in many divergent traditions. The Upanishads, for instance, closely link cosmogonic speculation to claims that the world ground, Brahman, exists without qualities (*nirguna*). The *Tao-te-ching*, however, represents perhaps the best example. The *tao*, which cannot be named, is described as the mother and origin of heaven and earth.

To return to the previous topic, we identify both perceptions of God and miracles by their anomaly with respect to naturalistic explanations. To designate an event as miraculous we eliminate the possibility of completely explaining the event naturalistically. The grammar of the term "miracle" necessitates a supernatural explanation. The intransigence of certain well-attested anomalies no longer leads to supernatural explanations, but rather to future insight into natural processes. They instigate research programs. We have come to see supernatural explanations as spinning their wheels, as *ad hoc* placeholders for future naturalistic theories (as, in Nietzsche's phrase, "a fat word replacing a very thin question mark"). We no longer brook supernatural explanations, especially when used evidentially, because we generally view them as admissions of ignorance.

What about, one might ask, the legions of mystical perceivers (Alston even cites a survey offering a percentage of the total Christian population) flourishing quite nicely in the modern world? When I claim that "we" reject supernatural explanations, just who is "we"? More pointedly, what about those prominent philosophers who defend and employ supernatural explanations; do I take these paragons of rationality to be, of all things, irrational? When I invoke a vague "we" and disclaim supernatural explanations, I mean to include these mystical perceivers and famous philosophers. I only argue that when "we" examine, in the fine tradition of philosophy (and theology, for that matter), "our" patterns of inference and assertion, we will find some intolerably inconsistent with others which we share. This "Left Wittgensteinian" inquiry merely pushes the onus of proof back onto those who, in the face of these inconsistencies, continue to use supernatural explanations. It amounts to an evidentialism not tied to classical foundationalism.

In the first section of this chapter, I suggested that the protracted controversy surrounding supernatural explanations is itself sufficient to place the burden of proof on mystical perceivers, but here I want to suggest a stronger reason than mere diversity of opinion. By appealing to the common practices of inquiry which I presume these philosophers and mystical perceivers accept uncontroversially and perhaps unreflectively, I intend to give them a reason which appeals to *their* (as well as my own) epistemic standpoint to reject the supernatural explanations implicit in mystical perception. In other words, I hope to convince them that supernatural explanations are unsatisfactory *by their own lights* (as well as my own). In this context of justification, I intend my use of "we" to be fully inclusive and I don't claim that anyone is irrational in any sense stronger than the irrationality in which we all engage regularly: an unacknowledged inconsistency.

Modern theologians have recognized and grappled with the inconsistency. Most have chosen not to shoulder the burden of proving the legitimacy of supernatural explanations. Schleiermacher, the paradigmatic figure in modern theology, argues, for example, the superfluity of discrete supernatural causation.

On the whole, therefore, as regards the miraculous, the general interests of science, more particularly of natural science, and the interests of religion seem to meet at the same point, *i.e.* that we should abandon the idea of the absolutely supernatural because no single instance of it can be known by us and we are nowhere required to recognize it ... In this way, everything – even the most wonderful thing that happens or has happened – is a problem for scientific research ...[32]

He rejects the attribution of supernatural causes to discrete events because we have no basis for such a judgment and recognizes the ubiquity of scientific inquiry. The cultural centrality of something like Schleiermacher's articulation militates against the supernatural explanations implicitly supposed by mystical perceivers. The growth of the modern ideals and values of human epistemic flourishing no longer license the supernatural explanation of experience. Such explanations no longer comprise good explanations of discrete psychological events. They really amount to admissions of ignorance about the natural factors causing the psychological events. In the modern context, their *ad hoc* nature militates against their acceptance.

Although we have no epistemological or metaphysical guarantee that epistemic values could never evolve to a point where supernatural explanations once again become rationally accept-

---

[32] Friedrich Schleiermacher, *The Christian Faith* (Edinburgh: T. & T. Clark, 1928), pp. 183–184.

able, such a turn of events defies the imagination. The logic of naturalism appears insurmountable; how could one ever hope to demonstrate that some event or anomaly in principle resists naturalistic explanation? The mere protracted inability to explain something naturalistically could never in itself legitimate a supernatural explanation. Once developed, the modern explanatory stance appears permanent. In this respect it resembles myriad other features of culture. Despite nostalgia, the logic of disenchantment, like many economic and social developments, appears for all practical purposes irreversible.

The modern theist should then abjure supernatural explanations of experience or anything else. Theism's cultural relevance relies on the fact that it does not detract from the modern ideal of epistemic flourishing. In making this claim, I do not necessarily insist that theism has nothing important or controversial to say about modern modes of life. It must however not present itself in reactionary and unacceptable forms. This fine distinction between theism's potential importance (for those who wish to defend it) and the unacceptable anti-modern elements accompanying it represents the core, I think, of Bultmann's interest in demythologizing the New Testament. Bultmann wanted to avoid the extremes of a liberalism that completely conforms theism to modern attitudes and a conservatism that risks losing the power of kerygma behind an alien mythological world-view. He highlights the pragmatic inconsistency and danger to Christianity of insisting on divine intervention in the causal order. "It is impossible to use electric light and the wireless and to avail ourselves of modern medical and surgical discoveries, and at the same time to believe in the New Testament world of spirits and miracles. We may think we can manage it in our own lives, but to expect others to do so is to make the Christian faith unintelligible and unacceptable to the modern world."[33] Bultmann attends to the importance of modern epistemic ideals for theist and non-theist alike. Whereas before the great impact of the Reformation and the scientific revolution, Teresa may have been justified in her

[33] Rudolf Bultmann, *Kerygma and Myth* (New York: Harper and Row, 1961), p. 5.

supernatural explanation of certain experiences, the contemporary individual explaining experiences with recourse to God violates modern ideals of epistemic flourishing. Some independent, good reason for accepting supernatural explanations, for a reenchantment of the world, would be necessary, therefore, before mystical perception could appreciably contribute to a cumulative case argument for the existence of God.

Bibliography

Almond, Philip, "Mysticism and Its Contexts," *The Problem of Pure Consciousness*, Robert K. C. Forman, ed. (New York: Oxford University Press, 1990), pp. 211–219.

Alston, William, "The Christian Language-Game," *The Autonomy of Religious Belief*, Frederick Crosson, ed. (Notre Dame: University of Notre Dame Press, 1981), pp. 128–162.

"Religious Experience and Religious Belief," *Nous* 16 (1982), pp. 3–12.

"Christian Experience and Christian Belief," *Faith and Rationality*, Alvin Plantinga and Nicholas Wolterstorff, eds. (Notre Dame: University of Notre Dame Press, 1983), pp. 103–134.

"Perceiving God," *Journal of Philosophy* 83 (1986), pp. 655–665.

"Religious Diversity and Perceptual Knowledge of God," *Faith and Philosophy* 5 (1988), pp. 433–448.

"Concepts of Epistemic Justification," *Epistemic Justification* (Ithaca: Cornell University Press, 1989), pp. 81–114.

"Internalism and Externalism in Epistemology," *Epistemic Justification* (Ithaca: Cornell University Press, 1989), pp. 185–226.

"Two Types of Foundationalism," *Epistemic Justification* (Ithaca: Cornell University Press, 1989), pp. 19–38.

"What's Wrong with Immediate Knowledge?," *Epistemic Justification* (Ithaca: Cornell University Press, 1989), pp. 57–80.

Perceiving God (Ithaca: Cornell University Press, 1991).

Anscombe, G. E. M., "Modern Moral Philosophy," *Ethics, Religion and Politics* (Minneapolis: University of Minnesota Press, 1981).

Aquinas, St. Thomas, *Summa Theologiae*, Fathers of the English Dominican Province, trs. (Chicago: Encyclopaedia Britannica, 1952).

Augustine, St., *The Literal Meaning of Genesis*, 2 vols., John Hammond Taylor, SJ, tr. (New York: Newman Press, 1982).

Becker, Carl, *The Heavenly City of the Eighteenth-Century Philosophers* (New Haven: Yale University Press, 1932).

Bernhardt, Stephen, "Are Pure Consciousness Events Unmediated?," *The Problem of Pure Consciousness*, Robert K. C. Forman, ed. (New York: Oxford University Press, 1990), pp. 220–236.

Bilinkoff, Jodi, *The Avila of Saint Teresa* (Ithaca: Cornell University Press, 1989).

Blumenberg, Hans, *The Legitimacy of the Modern Age*, Robert Wallace, tr. (Cambridge, M.I.T. Press, 1983).

Bonjour, Lawrence, "Externalist Theories of Empirical Knowledge," *Midwest Studies in Philosophy*, 5 (University of Minnesota Press, 1980), pp. 53–74.

Boyd, Richard, "Lex Orandi est Lex Credendi," *Images of Science*, Paul Churchland and Clifford Hooker, eds. (Chicago: University of Chicago Press, 1985).

Buckley, Michael J., *At the Origins of Modern Atheism* (New Haven: Yale University Press, 1987).

Bultmann, Rudolf, *Kerygma and Myth*, Reginald H. Fuller, tr. (New York: Harper and Row, 1961).

Burnyeat, Myles F., "The skeptic in his place and time," *Philosophy in History*, Richard Rorty, J. B. Schneewind, and Quentin Skinner, eds. (Cambridge: Cambridge University Press, 1984), pp. 225–254.

Chisholm, Roderick, "The Problem of the Criterion," *The Foundations of Knowing* (Minneapolis: University of Minnesota Press, 1982), pp. 61–75.

Chorpenning, Joseph F., *The Divine Romance: Teresa of Avila's Narrative Theology* (Chicago: Loyola University Press, 1992).

Christian, William Jr., *Apparitions in Late Medieval and Renaissance Spain* (Princeton: Princeton University Press, 1981).

Local Religion in Sixteenth-Century Spain (Princeton: Princeton University Press, 1981).

Clark, Ralph, "The Evidential Value of Religious Experiences," *International Journal for Philosophy of Religion* 16 (1984), pp. 189–202.

Clayton, Philip, *Explanation from Physics to Theology* (New Haven: Yale University Press, 1989).

Cornman, James, "Foundational versus Nonfoundational Theories of Empirical Justification," *Essays on Knowledge and Justification*, George Pappas and Marshall Swain, eds. (Ithaca: Cornell University Press, 1978), pp. 229–252.

Crashaw, Richard, "Hymn to Sainte Teresa," *The Metaphysical Poets*, Helen Gardner, ed. (Baltimore: Penguin Books, 1957), pp. 206–211.

Darwin, Charles, *The Autobiography of Charles Darwin*, Nora Barlow, ed. (New York: W.W. Norton & Co., 1969).

Daston, Lorraine, *Classical Probability in the Enlightenment* (Princeton: Princeton University Press, 1988).

Davidson, Donald, "A Coherence Theory of Truth and Knowledge," *Truth and Interpretation*, Ernest LePore, ed. (Oxford: Basil Blackwell, 1986).

Davies, Gareth Alban, "Saint Teresa and the Jewish Question," *Teresa de Jesús and Her World*, Margaret A. Rees, ed. (Leeds: Trinity and All Saints' College, 1981), pp. 51–73.

Descartes, René, *The Philosophical Writings of Descartes*, vol. II, John Cottingham, Robert Stoothoff and Dugald Murdoch, trs. (Cambridge: Cambridge University Press, 1984).

Dewey, John, *Reconstruction in Philosophy*, enlarged edn. (Boston: Beacon Press, 1948).

Douglas, Mary, *Purity and Danger* (London: Routledge & Kegan Paul, 1966).

   "Self-evidence," *Implicit Meanings* (London: Routledge & Kegan Paul, 1975), pp. 276–318.

Fingarette, Herbert, *Confucius – The Secular As Sacred* (New York: Harper and Row, 1972).

Firth, Roderick, "Epistemic Merit, Intrinsic and Instrumental," *American Philosophical Association Proceedings and Addresses* 55, pp. 5–23.

Forman, Robert K. C., "Introduction: Mysticism, Constructivism, and Forgetting," *The Problem of Pure Consciousness* (New York: Oxford University Press, 1990), pp. 3–49.

Frankenberry, Nancy, *Religion and Radical Empiricism* (Albany: SUNY Press, 1987).

Franks Davis, Caroline, *The Evidential Force of Religious Experience* (Oxford: Clarendon Press, 1989).

Gale, Richard, *On the Nature and Existence of God* (Cambridge: Cambridge University Press, 1991).

Gellman, Jerome I., *Experience of God and the Rationality of Theistic Belief* (Ithaca: Cornell University Press, 1997).

Gellner, Ernest, "Concepts and Society," *Rationality*, Bryan Wilson, ed. (Oxford: Basil Blackwell, 1970), pp. 18–49.

Goldman, Alvin, "The Internalist Conception of Justification," *Midwest Studies in Philosophy* 5 (University of Minnesota Press, 1980), pp. 27–51.

   "Argumentation and Social Epistemology," *The Journal of Philosophy* 91 (1994), pp. 27–49.

Gombrich, E. H., *Art and Illusion* (Princeton: Princeton University Press, 1960).

Goodman, David, *Power and Penury: Government, technology and science in Philip II's Spain* (Cambridge: Cambridge University Press, 1988).

Goodman, Nelson, *Ways of Worldmaking* (Indianapolis: Hackett, 1978).

Green, Deirdre, *Gold in the Crucible* (Longmeadow: Element Books, 1989).

Gutting, Gary, *Religious Belief and Religious Skepticism* (Notre Dame: University of Notre Dame Press, 1982).

Hacking, Ian, *The Emergence of Probability* (Cambridge: Cambridge University Press, 1975).

Harman, Gilbert, *Thought* (Princeton: Princeton University Press, 1973).

Change in View (Cambridge, MA: M.I.T. Press, 1986).

Hook, Sidney, *The Quest For Being* (New York: Delta, 1963).

James, William, *A Pluralistic Universe* (New York: Longmans, Green, and Co., 1909).

Essays in Radical Empiricism (New York: Longmans, Green, and Co., 1909).

The Principles of Psychology (New York: Dover Publications, Inc., 1950).

The Varieties of Religious Experience (New York: Collier Books, 1961).

Pragmatism, in *The Writings of William James*, John J. McDermott, ed. (Chicago: University of Chicago Press, 1967).

John of the Cross, *Spiritual Canticle*, E. Allison Peers, tr. (New York: Image Books, 1961).

Katz, Steven T., "Language, Epistemology, and Mysticism," *Mysticism and Philosophical Analysis* (New York: Oxford University Press, 1978), pp. 22–74.

Kuhn, Thomas, *The Structure of Scientific Revolutions*, 2nd edn. (Chicago: University of Chicago Press, 1970).

Larmore, Charles, *The Morals of Modernity* (Cambridge: Cambridge University Press, 1996).

Lehrer, Keith, *Knowledge* (Oxford: Oxford University Press, 1974).

Levine, Michael, "Mystical Experience and Non-Basically Justified Belief," *Religious Studies* 25 (1990), pp. 335–345.

Locke, John, *An Essay Concerning Human Understanding*, 2 vols. (New York: Dover Publications, 1959).

Losin, Peter, "Experience of God and the Principle of Credulity: A Reply to Rowe," *Faith and Philosophy* 4 (1987), pp. 59–70.

MacIntyre, Alasdair, "Is Understanding Religion Compatible with Believing?," *Rationality*, Bryan Wilson, ed. (Oxford: Basil Blackwell, 1970).

After Virtue, 2nd edn. (Notre Dame: University of Notre Dame Press, 1984).

Malcolm, Norman, "The Groundlessness of Belief," Stuart C. Brown, ed., *Reason and Religion* (Ithaca: Cornell University Press, 1977), pp. 143–157.

Manuel, Frank, *The Eighteenth Century Confronts the Gods* (New York: Atheneum, 1967).

Martin, Michael, "The Principle of Credulity and Religious Experience," *Religious Studies* 22 (1987), pp. 79–93.

Mather, Cotton, *Cotton Mather on Witchcraft* (New York: Dorset Press, 1991).

Mavrodes, George, *Belief in God* (New York: Random House, 1981).

McDowell, John, *Mind and World* (Cambridge: Harvard University Press, 1994).

McGinn, Bernard, review of *Mystic Union*, in *The Journal of Religion* 74 (1994), pp. 98–99.

Mill, John Stuart, *On Liberty* (Indianapolis: Hackett, 1978).

Mischel, Theodore, "Pragmatic Aspects of Explanation," *Philosophy of Science* 33 (1966), pp. 40–60.

Montaigne, Michel de, *An Apology For Raymond Sebond*, M. A. Screech, tr. (London: Penguin Books, 1987).

Murdoch, Iris, *The Sovereignty of Good* (London: Routledge & Kegan Paul, 1970).

Nietzsche, Friedrich, *On the Genealogy of Morals*, Walter Kaufmann and R. J. Hollingdale, trs. (New York: Vintage Books, 1969).

O'Flaherty, Wendy Doniger, *The Rig Veda* (New York: Penguin Books, 1981).

O'Hear, Anthony, *Experience, Explanation and Faith* (London: Routledge & Kegan Paul, 1984).

Peirce, Charles S., "Letters to Lady Welby," *Charles S. Peirce: Selected Writings*, Philip Wiener, ed. (New York: Dover Publications, 1966), pp. 381–432.

"Questions Concerning Certain Faculties Claimed For Man," *Charles S. Peirce: Selected Writings*, Philip Wiener, ed. (New York: Dover Publications, 1966), pp. 15–38.

"Some Consequences of Four Incapacities," *Charles S. Peirce: Selected Writings*, Philip Wiener, ed. (New York: Dover Publications, 1966), pp. 39–72.

"The Fixation of Belief," *Charles S. Peirce: Selected Writings*, Philip Wiener, ed. (New York: Dover Publications, 1966), pp. 92–112.

Peterson, Michael, Hasker, William, Reichenbach, Bruce, and Basinger, David, *Reason and Religious Belief* (New York: Oxford University Press, 1991).

Phillips, D. Z., *Faith and Philosophical Inquiry* (London: Routledge & Kegan Paul, 1970).

Faith After Foundationalism (Boulder: Westview Press, 1995).

Pike, Nelson, *Mystic Union: An Essay in the Phenomenology of Mysticism* (Ithaca: Cornell University Press, 1992).

Plantinga, Alvin, "Is Belief in God Properly Basic?," *Nous* 15 (1981), pp. 41–51.

"Reason and Belief in God," *Faith and Rationality*, Alvin Plantinga and Nicholas Wolterstorff, eds. (Notre Dame: University of Notre Dame Press, 1983), pp. 16–93.

Warrant: The Current Debate (New York: Oxford University Press, 1993).

Preus, J. Samuel, *Explaining Religion* (New Haven: Yale University Press, 1987).

Proudfoot, Wayne, *Religious Experience* (Berkeley: University of California Press, 1985).

Putnam, Hilary, *Realism with a Human Face* (Cambridge: Harvard University Press, 1990).

Reason, Truth and History (Cambridge: Cambridge University Press, 1991).

Rorty, Richard, *Philosophy and the Mirror of Nature* (Princeton: Princeton University Press, 1979).

"Cosmopolitanism without emancipation: A Response to Jean-François Lyotard," *Objectivity, Relativism, and Truth* (Cambridge: Cambridge University Press, 1991), pp. 211–222.

"Is Natural Science a Natural Kind?," *Objectivity, Relativism, and Truth* (Cambridge: Cambridge University Press, 1991), pp. 46–62.

"Science as Solidarity," *Objectivity, Relativism, and Truth* (Cambridge: Cambridge University Press, 1991), pp. 35–45.

"Solidarity or Objectivity?," *Objectivity, Relativism, and Truth* (Cambridge: Cambridge University Press, 1991), pp. 21–34.

Rothberg, Donald, "Contemporary Epistemology and the Study of Mysticism," *The Problem of Pure Consciousness*, Robert K. C. Forman, ed. (New York: Oxford University Press, 1990), pp. 163–210.

Rowe, William, "Religious Experience and the Principle of Credulity," *International Journal for Philosophy of Religion* 16 (1984), pp. 189–202.

Salmon, Wesley, *Four Decades of Scientific Explanation* (Minneapolis: University of Minnesota Press, 1989).

Schleiermacher, Friedrich D. E., *The Christian Faith*, H. R. Mackintosh and J. S. Stewart, eds. (Edinburgh: T. & T. Clark, 1928).

On the "Glaubenslehre," James Duke and Francis Fiorenza, trs. (Atlanta: Scholars Press, 1981).

On Religion, Richard Crouter, tr. (Cambridge: Cambridge University Press, 1988).

Schoen, Edward L., *Religious Explanations* (Durham: Duke University Press, 1985).

Schutz, Alfred, "On Multiple Realities," *Collected Papers*, vol. 1 (The Hague: Martinus Nijhoff, 1962), pp. 207–259.

Sellars, Wilfrid, "Empiricism and the Philosophy of Mind," *Science, Perception and Reality* (London: Routledge & Kegan Paul, 1963), pp. 127–196.

Sherlock, Thomas, *The Tryal of the Witnesses of the Resurrection of Jesus* (London: 1729).

Sidgwick, Henry, *The Methods of Ethics*, 7th edn. (London: Macmillan, 1907).

Slade, Carole, *St. Teresa of Avila, Author of a Heroic Life* (Berkeley: University of California Press, 1995).

Sosa, Ernest, "The Raft and the Pyramid," *Midwest Studies in Philosophy* 5 (University of Minnesota Press, 1980), pp. 3–26.

Stinson, Charles, "The Finite Supernatural: Theological Perspectives," *Religious Studies* 9 (1973), pp. 325–337.

Stout, Jeffrey, *The Flight from Authority* (Notre Dame: University of Notre Dame Press, 1981).

Swietlicki, Catherine, *Spanish Christian Cabala* (Columbia: University of Missouri Press, 1986).

Swinburne, Richard, *The Existence of God* (Oxford: Oxford University Press, 1979).

The Coherence of Theism (Oxford: Oxford University Press, 1987).

Taylor, Charles, *The Sources of the Self* (Cambridge: Harvard University Press, 1989).

"Comparison, History, Truth," *Myth and Philosophy*, Frank E. Reynolds and David Tracy, eds. (Albany: SUNY Press, 1990), pp. 37–55.

Teresa of Avila, "Conceptions of the Love of God," *Complete Works of St. Teresa*, vol. II, E. Allison Peers, tr. and ed. (New York: Sheed and Ward, 1957).

"Spiritual Relations Addressed By Saint Teresa of Jesus To Her Confessors," *Complete Works of St. Teresa*, vol. I, E. Allison Peers, tr. and ed. (New York: Sheed and Ward, 1957).

The Life of Saint Teresa of Avila, J. M. Cohen, ed. (London: Penguin Books, 1957).

The Life of Teresa of Jesus, E. Allison Peers, tr. and ed. (New York: Image Books, 1960).

Interior Castle, E. Allison Peers, tr. and ed. (New York: Image Books, 1961).

The Way of Perfection, E. Allison Peers, tr. and ed. (New York: Image Books, 1964).

Thagard, Paul, "The Best Explanation: Criteria for Theory Choice," *Journal of Philosophy* 75 (1978), pp. 76–92.

Tillotson, John, "A Discourse Against Transubstantiation," *The Works of Dr. John Tillotson*, vol. II (London: 1820), pp. 407–452.

Timmons, Mark, "Outline of a Contextualist Moral Epistemology," in *Moral Knowledge?*, Walter Sinnott-Armstrong and Mark Timmons, eds. (New York: Oxford University Press, 1996), pp. 293–325.

van Fraassen, Bas, *The Scientific Image* (Oxford: Clarendon Press, 1980).

Wainwright, William, *Mysticism* (Sussex: The Harvester Press, 1981).

Review of *Mystic Union* in *Faith and Philosophy* 11 (1994), pp. 488–495.

Weber, Alison, *Teresa of Avila and the Rhetoric of Femininity* (Princeton: Princeton University Press, 1990).

Williams, Bernard, "Left-Wing Wittgenstein, Right-Wing Marx," *Common Knowledge* 1 (1992), pp. 33–42.

Williams, M. E., "St. Teresa, Doctor of the Church (Orthodoxy and Public Opinion)," *Teresa de Jesús and Her World*, Margaret A. Rees, ed. (Leeds: Trinity and All Saints' College, 1981), pp. 89–103.

Wisdo, David, *The Life of Irony and the Ethics of Belief* (Albany: SUNY Press, 1993).

Wittgenstein, Ludwig, *Philosophical Investigations*, 3rd edn., G. E. M. Anscombe, tr. (New York: Macmillan Publishing Co., 1958).

Wolterstorff, Nicholas, "Can Belief in God Be Rational If It Has No Foundations?," *Faith and Rationality*, Alvin Plantinga and Nicholas Wolterstorff, eds. (Notre Dame: University of Notre Dame Press, 1983), pp. 135–186.

"The Migration of the Theistic Arguments: From Natural Theology to Evidentialist Apologetics," *Rationality, Religious Belief, & Moral Commitment*, Robert Audi and William Wainwright, eds. (Ithaca: Cornell University Press, 1986).

Yandell, Keith, *The Epistemology of Religious Experience* (Cambridge: Cambridge University Press, 1993).

Index

Almond, Philip, 92, 95
Alston, William, 2n, 8–11, 12, 28, 41n,
    63n, 64–65, 71, 72, 109–134, 135,
    197, 199–203, 210, 215, 225
alumbrados, 150–151
Anscombe, G. E. M., 78
Aquinas, Thomas, 143, 156–157, 163n,
    206, 222
Augustine, 17–18, 163n, 167, 168, 189

Bacon, Francis, 76
Becker, Carl, 218
Blumenberg, Hans, 211–215
Bonaventure, 166
Bonjour, Lawrence, 63–64n
Boyd, Richard, 55
Buckley, Michael, 219–220
Bultmann, Rudolf, 227
Burnyeat, M. F., 65, 214

Chisholm, Roderick, 61n, 66–67, 73, 114n
Christian, William, 140, 142–145, 189
Clark, Ralph, 133
Clayton, Philip, 14, 51–52, 57
Cohen, Morris, 15
coherentism, 79–85, 121–123
conversos, 149
Copleston, Frederick, 222
Council of Trent, 151
Crashaw, Richard, 135

Darwin, Charles, 1, 8–9
Daston, Lorraine, 214
Davidson, Donald, 32n, 34, 50n, 79n
de Montaigne, Michel, 109, 112, 120
de Sade, Marquis, 220
Descartes, René, 21n, 31, 60–65, 76, 78,
    81, 211, 213, 217
Dewey, John, 15, 50n, 212, 219

direct realism, 38, 122, 123–132, 199, 202
Douglas, Mary, 39

Emerson, Ralph Waldo, 4
evidentialism, 110, 134, 215, 217, 225

finite Supernatural, 16, 222
Forman, Robert, 7, 9–11, 28, 90–108, 124,
    135, 205, 219
foundationalism, 79, 81–82, 109–134,
    198, 202, 211–217, 225
Frankenberry, Nancy, 118n
Franklin, R. L., 92, 94–95
Franks Davis, Caroline, 2n, 41n, 109–112,
    114, 133–134
Frege, Gottlob, 99–100
Freud, Sigmund, 18

Gale, Richard, 43n, 118n, 120
Gellman, Jerome, 2n, 41n, 109–112, 130,
    133–134
Gellner, Ernest, 87n
Gettier problem, 59–60, 70, 81
Goldman, Alvin, 59–61, 69, 75n
Gombrich, E. H., 34–35
Goodman, Nelson, 32n, 84
Gutting, Gary, 2n, 118, 130n, 133

Hacking, Ian, 214
Harman, Gilbert, 37n, 46, 80–83
Heidegger, Martin, 222
Hook, Sydney, 15–16
Hume, David, 94, 222
humility, 160–164, 178, 189, 193

Inquisition, 141, 147, 149, 150, 151, 208–209

James, William, 5, 10, 18n, 23–50, 56,
    87n, 89n, 90, 98, 101, 128, 138, 221

237